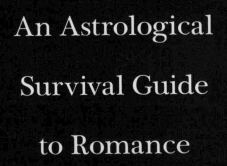

An Astrological

Survival Guide

to Romance

LOVE

on a

ROTTEN DAY

Hazel Dixon-Cooper

A Fireside Book
Published by Simon & Schuster
New York   London   Toronto   Sydney

FIRESIDE
Rockefeller Center
1230 Avenue of the Americas
New York, NY 10020

For information regarding special discounts for bulk purchases,
please contact Simon & Schuster Special Sales at
1-800-456-6798 or business@simonandschuster.com

Designed by Joy O'Meara Battista

Manufactured in the United States of America

10   9

Library of Congress Cataloging-in-Publication Data

Dixon-Cooper, Hazel.
      Love on a rotten day: an astrological survival guide to romance /
Hazel Dixon-Cooper.
           p.   cm.
      "A Fireside book."
      1. Astrology.   2. Love—Miscellanea.   I. Title.

   BF1729.L6D59   2004
   133.5'83067—dc22   2003061783

ISBN-13: 978-0-7432-2563-2
ISBN-10:   0-7432-2563-5

To all the signs I've loved before,
and to Gary, the Pisces, who saved me.

Acknowledgments

Grateful thanks to Marcela Landres, Margret McBride, Peter Bailey, Bonnie Hearn Hill, Larry Paquette, and the Tuesdays . . . the usual suspects who continue to surround me with expertise, friendship, unconditional support, and chocolate. And, to Robin Blakely of Livingston Communications and Trina Rice, associate publicist at Touchstone Fireside, for their extraordinary public relations talent and hard work on my behalf.

Contents

How to Use This Book

The Sun, the Moon, Mars, and Venus make up our basic character and inner emotional personality. The Sun is our character. The Moon rules our emotional nature. Mars and Venus determine what we like under the covers and how we utilize our natural talents to get under the covers with someone we like. *Love on a Rotten Day* takes a quick look at the overall basics in Chapter 1.

At the end of this book is a set of tables in which you can locate the positions of the Moon, Mars, and Venus for yourself or anyone. All you need is the date of birth (month, day, and year). The dates listed are the days the planet moved *into* the respective sign. For the Mars and Venus tables, if no date is listed, the planet was in that sign all month.

For example, Russell Crowe was born on April 7, 1964. To find his Sun sign, simply look at the Contents page. His birthday falls within the Aries Sun sign. Next, turn to the Moon tables and find 1964, then the month and day (April 7, page 203). Crowe's Moon is in Aquarius (moved into AQU on April 6). The Mars table on page 228 and the Venus table on page 233 show that Mars was in Aries for the entire month of April 1964 and that Venus was in Gemini on April 7 (moved into GEM on April 3).

Now that you have his information, Aries Sun, Aquarius Moon, Aries Mars, and Gemini Venus, turn to the respective chapter sections to read all about his love style. To learn about his Aries Sun, read Romancing the Sign (page 5) and 'Til Death Do Us Part (page 7) in the Aries chapter; for his Aquarius Moon, read Moonlight or Gaslight (page 163) in the Aquarius chapter; for his Aries Mars, turn to the Aries chapter again for Mars Is Afflicted (page 14); and for his Gemini Venus, read the Venus Is a Nympho section (page 44) in the Gemini chapter.

For gay and lesbian couples, note that "male" can be interpreted as the more aggressive/outgoing partner and "female" as the more receptive/introspective partner.

Have fun, and remember love may make the world go round, but lust greases the wheels that drive us to the bedroom.

LOVE

on a

ROTTEN

DAY

Chapter One

What's Love Got to Do With It?

It destroys one's nerves to be amiable every day to the same human being.

Benjamin Disraeli (December 21)

A Walk on the Wild Side

That astrology book on your nightstand may describe your Cancer sweetheart as a nurturing homebody, but what it won't tell you is how to disentangle one from around your ankles so you can have an occasional evening out with your friends, or warn you that the only sweet-nothings your Pisces boyfriend is whispering are to the hallucinations resulting from his latest foray into the Ozone, or explain why the passionate nature of your headstrong Aries lover is confined to on-demand sex and nightly temper tantrums.

According to the compatibility chart you bought on the Web, your Suns are trined, your Moons are conjunct, and your respective Mars and Venus are so hot together you could set the sheets on fire. So how come the one you love is a rotten bastard who can't keep his fly zipped or a nasty bitch who gets off on putting you down? Because the rotten truth is that in every romantic relationship, the only constant factor is the continual maneuvering to see who stays on top—in or out of bed.

The word *zodiac* originates from the Greek *Zodiakos*, meaning "circle of animals." The Greeks had another word, *zoon* (zoh-on) that, loosely translated, means "zoo," a perfect description of the celestial soap opera upon which the practice of astrology is based. The real force behind our collective romantic fantasies was a not-so-charming bunch of eternal beings that amused themselves by getting down and dirty up in the celestial firmament. Three thousand years before what's-her-name shot J.R., the heavens were ruled by a cast of characters whose traits of jealousy, deception, sexual license, and revenge made the Ewings look like the Waltons.

Lovers and Other Strangers

Relax and forget soul-mate astrology. Let your own lusty nature out of the closet and use it to win the heart of a wild Fire sign or find the best sin-on-the-side buddy. Learn how to dump a Scorpio, keep a Gemini home, or rid yourself of a clingy Libra. And learn the truth about the hidden motivations that make us want what we can't have and screw up what we do have, chasing all those guilty pleasures.

Each Sun sign has its own chapter and each chapter is divided into the following sections:

♥ Romancing the Sign Whether female, male, gay, straight, or just confused, natives of each Sun sign have similar traits in their respective approach to love and lust. Water signs try to live on love. Earth signs know how much that costs. Air signs talk during sex. And Fire signs eat their young.

♥ 'Til Death Do Us Part
  · Catching One Tips for winning the heart (and body) of the one you desire.

- **Surviving One** Getting out and getting revenge should your boat capsize in the tunnel of love.
- **Keeping One** If you are determined to make it work, you can find anyone lovable, sexy, and irresistible, no matter what anyone else (including me) says.

♥ **Moonlight or Gaslight?** The Moon pulls on our inner, or unconscious, desires like she pulls the tides. Feminine and manipulative, she maneuvers behind the scenes, ruling our basic instincts. In Water, she raises emotional blackmail to a fine art. In Earth, she's cold, critical, and perpetually irritated. In Air, she buries her feelings under a filibuster of irrational chatter. In Fire, she's likely to pick up an axe to prove how much she loves you.
- **The Moon rules everyone's emotional nature.**

♥ **Mars Is Afflicted** Mars is the mucho-macho warrior-god. Anywhere he appears in a chart he brings his aggressive passion and selfishness. In Water, he either boils or evaporates. In Earth, he's excessively stubborn and pathologically possessive. In Air, he's interested only in heated conversations. In Fire, he doubles the lust factor.

♂ *If you are male, Mars through the signs determines your romantic style, i.e., strutting peacock or sulking hulk.*

♀ *If female, he reveals whether you're hooked on romance or spouse abuse.*

♥ **Venus Is a Nympho** Sorry all you Valentine's Day fanatics, but your heroine is the slut of the zodiac. Venus spent her days kissing her mirror and her nights bed hopping around the Universe. In Water, she ups the self-delusion ante. In Earth, she lives to amass possessions, including you. In Air, she loves the sound of her own voice. In Fire, she expands her love of self—if that's possible.

♂ *If you are male, Venus reveals what you desire in a lover, i.e., sensual and mysterious or Mistress/Master of the Whip.*

♀ *If female, it's how you come across to your lovers—saintly or slutty.*

 Fatal Attractions A Sun-sign personal ad compatibility guide for the twisted.

 Scoring
- Best Bets—Hot and good, in and out of bed.
- Just Good Friends—Takes work, but could be very sweet.
- Please Shoot Yourself Now—Definitely difficult.
- The Dark Horse—Worth investigating.

 A List of famous and infamous Lovers Written in the stars is no guarantee of happily ever after.

Chapter Two

ARIES

MARCH 21–APRIL 19

Anything You Can Do, I Can Do Better

Element: Fire. If you can't stand the heat, get out of the backseat.

Quality: Cardinal. Aries is lead horn-dog.

Symbol: The Ram. This animal loves fast, furious, and frequent fornicating.

Ruler: Mars, the god of unbridled passion, unending war, and unrelenting pursuit.

Romantic Idol: The Mask.

Romantic Style: Willing, able, and aggravating.

Favorite Pickup Line: "Your place or mine?"

Dream First Date: Playing naked touch football in the city park at high noon.

Erogenous Zone: Head. Giving it. Getting it. Ramming it against the headboard, dashboard, or scoreboard.

Sexual Quirk: Asks, "Good, huh?" Cheers, coaches, makes animal noises.

Romancing the Sign

All's fair in love and war.
Anon.

Aries-the-Unstoppable loves a challenge. Telling a Ram that he or she can't have the object of his or her heart's desire is a sure way to light the Aries fire of determination. Whether it's a new car, a corner office, or the Heavyweight Boxing title, à la the 50-to-1 odds that Buster Douglas beat to K.O. then-champ (and exceedingly crabby Cancer) Mike Tyson, if Aries wants it, chances are Aries gets it. This includes you.

Once a Ram is smitten, you have nothing to do but grab the roller coaster and hang on. Male or female, a Ram will always take the lead in romance even if you don't want to follow. Aries is the most ardent creature in the Universe, and both sexes are babies at heart. Like a curious toddler, a Ram must explore, touch, taste, smell, and nibble everything that captures its attention. And, be warned, whether animal, vegetable, or mineral, everything captures Aries' attention.

Rams pride themselves on always being prepared for disaster. If only they could realize *they* are the disaster, life in the Universe would be much calmer. When a Ram is angry, the whole neighborhood knows. They endlessly throw down gauntlets, dig up causes to fight for, and make enemies out of hapless friends and relatives. Even the quiet ones occasionally stir the pot. If in a particularly petulant mood, they will goad you until you scream, then feign innocent shock when you order them out of the house. Most are as hotheaded as Leo, except they blow up faster and cool down sooner. Whether that's a blessing or a curse is a toss-up.

Aries is not the best marriage bet in the world. A Ram's ego is bigger than a Macy's Thanksgiving Day balloon, and their incessant self-adulation before, during, and after sex will give you a permanent migraine. Aries never really settles down. You may commit to the long haul, but a Ram's casual attitude toward sex, and talent for forgetting the deed as soon as it's done, enables them to cheat constantly yet genuinely believe they are good mates because they're always home in time for a quickie with you before dinner.

Either sex pursues the object of his or her desire with all

the grace of a steamroller. When Sex Siren Jayne Mansfield was asked for her dinner order at a Hollywood party, she's supposed to have answered, "A steak, and that man on the right," indicating Libra bodybuilder-turned-actor Mickey Hargitay, who would become the second of her three husbands. Mansfield also had a tabloid-hot affair with designer and fellow Aries Oleg Cassini and was involved with her divorce attorney at the time of her death at age thirty-four. She was rumored to have had an off-again-on-again affair with Gemini Jack Kennedy in competition with Gemini Marilyn Monroe for his affections. Rumor has it that Jayne gave Jack a blowjob when she was nine months pregnant. Knowing the Aries and Gemini love of kinky, it's believable.

If you want a mature, considerate, unselfish partner, try an enlightened Virgo if you can find one, or that rare Fish, a sober Pisces, for your Aries lover will be totally oblivious to your needs. Both sexes are demanding, thoughtless, impatient, and prone to temper tantrums until they are too old to throw themselves on the floor. Rams try to win your heart by sheer force of will and are capable of pulling outrageous stunts to prove their love. But, remember this, as soon as they taste the thrill of conquest, your lust appeal will start to wane and he or she is likely to stop calling. In a week, they won't remember meeting you in the first place.

'Til Death Do Us Part

I'd marry again if I found a man who had fifteen million and would sign over half of it to me before the marriage and guarantee he'd be dead within a year.

Bette Davis (April 5)

Catching One

These romantic terrors get off on the adrenaline rush. They are suckers for the I'm-not-sure-I-want-you game. Saying no to an Aries is like pouring gas on a grease fire. They also like to be around people who are successful or on their way up the corporate ladder. Rams don't do modesty and won't notice you if your come-on is understated, shy, or quiet. To intrigue one, you must not be afraid of blowing your own horn, patting yourself on the back, and/or dropping not-so-subtle hints about negotiating big deals. On the other hand, if you need to be rescued, straightened out, sobered up, or have an enemy crushed, the Ram is also your man or woman.

Rams are attracted to the color red like a Capricorn is to money-green. Not the dark maroon of sulky Scorpio, but the bright cherry, candy apple, or fire engine red that can be seen a mile away. Wear a red lace teddy beneath your gray jacket or let your red bikini underwear show through a hole in the back pocket of your too-tight jeans, flirt outrageously one day and offer your cold-but-alluring shoulder the next, and you'll have Aries phoning you every five minutes begging for a date.

Being able to bend your body into unlikely positions, willing to have sex in an elevator or under the table in a crowded restaurant, or engaging in mutual fondling at the family Christmas dinner will keep your Ram drooling with lust. Virtually every Aries is a sports fan, so sex under a blanket at a football game could seal their love, and possibly your fate, forever.

When it is time to hit the sheets, remember Aries is the sign of passionate *action*. So don't say you are ready to screw your brains out unless you are ready at the exact moment you consent. Wearing Velcro-fastened clothing will save your shirt as your Ram leaps from across the room to rip it from your body. However, in bed, Aries are kings and queens of the five-minute fuck. So, if you are someone who thinks foreplay should last longer than getting impaled, or guiding yourself into one of their wet spots, pick any other sign.

The good part is that Rams also recover in about five minutes, so you are in for multiple sessions of hot, albeit quick sex. Of course this can be fun if you use your imagination. Grabbing a quickie in a traffic jam or falling in the bushes on your morning jog will not dampen your Ram's ardor later in the day.

The best time to do it is as soon as your eyes open. Doesn't matter if your Aries partner is still asleep, just roll over and climb on. Faster than you can yell, "Hi-ho, Silver," you'll be screwed, showered, dressed, and on your way to work.

Surviving One

Breaking up with Aries is tricky, because your turnoff is likely to turn him or her on again. They live on *Fantasy Island,* daydreaming about the perfect union and, if one's after you, he or she will keep you up with midnight phone calls full of heavy breathing and frequent threats of self-destruction if you reject his or her advances. Not all are prepared to lop off an ear and send it along, as did Aries Vincent van Gogh. But an Aries in love is dogged in his or her pursuit and simply cannot understand why you don't consider yourself the luckiest person alive to be the object of affection.

All Fire signs were born for battle, and an Aries scorned is also very capable of declaring war. Tossing yours out in the middle of the night one second ahead of his or her clothes and toothbrush could result in smashed windows, slashed tires, and/or jail time for one or both of you. At the least you will suffer random, public shouting matches and searing phone calls from every phone booth outside every bar in town. Fortunately, they are so easily distracted that, just like that three-year-old who throws down the old toy for a new one, your ex will soon find a new victim to torment.

Any astrology book will tell you that Rams are dynamic,

sexy, and generous with their affections. What this really means is that everyone gets a piece, whether wanted or not. Male or female, the Ram's idea of intimacy is how fast you can slap skin. *Eternal love* and *casual sex* are dangerously close to synonymous phrases. Aries has the most-notched headboard and least-used sense of discretion in the Universe.

The best way to dump this egotistical Baby Huey is to feed his or her childish ego with a big, fat lie. Tell yours he or she is too good, too passionate, or too dynamic for you, and that you are setting him or her free to find someone worthy. They will absolutely believe you because that's exactly the way a Ram feels about him- or herself. Or buy yours a cell phone and call every half hour, declaring your undying love. Once yours feels the chains of love snapping firmly around his or her ankles, either gender can disappear faster than Aries Harry Houdini on his best day.

If neither of the above tactics works, say that your doctor forbid you to have sex for six months. That panicked expression will instantly be replaced with a blank look as the Ram just as instantly forgets your name. This sign doesn't do "We'll always be friends." Aries feel if you are stupid enough to let them get away, you are too stupid to hang around with. Also, the word *ex* doesn't exist in a Ram's vocabulary. They are too busy chasing their next ideal romance to regret the past or think about it.

If you get dumped, the best revenge is to act unconcerned, even agree that breaking up is the best thing, especially if you still want him or her. You take a step back, the Ram will bound forward, and soon, your Aries will be hot on your trail once again. If you don't want to make up but do want to twist the knife, buy yourself a red outfit, show up at his or her favorite watering hole with a glamorous Leo or elegant Capricorn on your arm, and totally ignore his or her attempt to win your heart again by lap-dancing on the drunk at the end of the bar.

Can a normal person like you find happiness loving a naval-gazing troublemaker with an erogenous zone attached? Absolutely. Remember, Aries is the baby of the zodiac, and babies love to be cuddled and coddled. Babies also throw tantrums. So, if you intend to stick around longer than a quickie or two, understand that, to a Ram, fighting and screwing are equally arousing.

Aries is not a sign that sits still for very long. Restless Gemini needs mental stimulation, but Aries needs physical action. Dancing, walking, regular workouts, and sports are all ways to keep a close connection. If you are into less strenuous pursuits, sharing a good cause or championing a noble-but-lost one is another way to let your Ram know you understand.

Rams have a lust factor of ten. This is the reason that yours may prefer less sensual foreplay and more hot sex. This doesn't mean you aren't loved or that they are selfish. In fact, to your delight, it most likely will mean that you will begin to walk bowlegged if your relationship is long-term. Your friends will be jealous of that perpetual smile on your face.

Your Ram won't be shy about vocalizing his or her preferences under the covers and will expect you to do the same. Feel free to suggest anything that pops into your head. Few signs will be as eager to try something new. And only Gemini can get kinkier.

Out of bed, Aries loves a good scalp massage. The head, face, and neck areas are all very sensitive (and Aries erogenous zones). Even males will appreciate a facial—in private of course; this *is* macho man.

Whether firebrand or smoldering volcano, Rams thrive on undivided attention, and these boys and girls adore all the blatant trappings of romance. Moonlight and roses, candlelight and wine, or a quiet dinner, just the two of you, will thrill your Aries lover. They love to cry at sad movies nearly as much as the Water signs, and a handwritten card or poem will send yours into a fit of adoring declaration. So will being a good listener. Aries of both sexes are full of ideas, plans, and dreams. Rams are determined to succeed, have no qualms about trying different paths to achieve their desires, and are surprisingly good at just about everything they try. If you listen enthusiastically, be sparing with your criticism, and act appropriately wowed, you'll have little or no trouble keeping your Aries at home.

Either sex will defend their spouse or lover to the death and both have an unbridled zest for life that is nearly impossible to resist. Even if yours has had his or her heart broken a few times, chances are he or she has never lost that optimistic faith in true love. And no other sign can make the rest of us hotter than a firecracker on the Fourth of July.

Moonlight or Gaslight?

In my old bachelorhood, I went out with lots of Virgos and Libras. Now I notice a lot of Leos and Scorpios. What does that mean? People who think a lot of themselves and people who will screw your brains out? I might as well date myself.

Bill Maher (January 20)
ARIES MOON/CAPRICORN SUN

Aries Moons fall in and out of love faster than ten-dollar hookers. Mars' unpredictable behavior acts out within the emotional Moon, resulting in a nervous disposition, quick temper, and sudden impulsive action. The emotional structure of Lunar Rams is focused on self-interest. Both sexes balk at suggestions or direction, won't follow orders, and resent any type of authority. They want all the glory, all the gold, and all the pie, never mind how many pieces.

The Aries Moon also gives an edgy push toward self-destruction as well as self-indulgence. Anywhere bare-knuckles Mars lands in a natal chart he stirs the pot. He loves a battle, and so does the Aries Moon person. The Martian ego merges with the basic emotional structure and what Aries Moons want (just like Sun Aries), they usually get. Trouble is, Lunar Rams have the attention span of a gnat buzzing a bowl of fruit, and an identical attitude toward romance. These are the characters who elope on the first date, make spur-of-the-moment moves across the country, change jobs regularly, and shed spouses quicker than a Gemini. An Aries Moon heats the emotional character of any Sun sign. It bestows a quick mind, roguish charm, and an independent streak wide as the Mississippi and as dangerous as the Amazon. It also increases the chances for serial romancing.

Double-Fire signs, such as Double Aries Marlon Brando, Leo/Aries Antonio Banderas and Whitney Houston, simply ooze danger and sex appeal. The most fun is probably Sagittarius/Aries (Kiefer Sutherland or Katarina Witt), but you'll need track shoes to keep up with this combo, and a large insurance policy because they frequently wear out early from the frantic pace.

The Taurus/Aries blend is more obtuse, less reasonable, and extremely touchy. Comedian Don Rickles may be a quiet steadfast Taurus husband at home, but on stage, his Aries Moon rears its sarcastic head and love of attention. Virgo/Aries is a verbal sleeping tiger you don't want to awaken. They have a flash-fire temperament and take everything personally, but can be very loyal. And, Aries lights Virgo's kinky sexual fire. In Capricorn/Aries, the Goat teams up with the Ram, and nothing less than a nuclear bomb can stop them from doing exactly what they please. This is the warmest temperament of the Goats, who want it all and won't stop until they get it.

Gemini/Aries is wickedly funny, but never faithful, or home. A born con artist who is so detached he or she could forget your name, either sex is great for a lively affair, but you'll need loads of patience, and a steady job, for anything more committed. If you like megavain and purely critical,

Libra/Aries was made for you. These characters have a string of affairs and broken marriages, but are cute, sweet, and born to be wild. Aquarius/Aries is the combo most likely to give you a mercy lay, enjoy group sex, and be able to remain friends before, during, and after the affair.

Even in homebody Cancer the Aries Moon is rarely content, definitely does not like routine, and will demand freedom while demanding you keep the home fires burning. Unless you are into whips and leather, or are an extreme survivalist, run as fast as you can from the Scorpio/Aries combination. These boys and girls have volcanic tempers and are so selfish *nothing* else will come first. Cross Pisces/Aries off your list. These poor devils are so emotionally convoluted they have permanent reservations at the nearest in-patient facility.

Mars Is Afflicted

Winning isn't everything, it's the only thing.

VINCE LOMBARDI (JUNE 11)
ARIES MARS/GEMINI SUN

Mars rules Aries and is at home here, comfortable, powerful, and seething. The Gemini Marquis de Sade had Aries in Mars. Aries Mars must win at everything. Work, play, love, and sex are all competitions and, male or female, this person is an easily aroused, sexually potent force. They are also spontaneous to the point of thoughtlessness, easily bored with routine, and forever searching for the perfect thong. Aries Mars likes to conquer the one they love. Although not all will tie you up and force their will like our demented friend the Marquis, all love risk, challenge, and the occasional trip to the darker side of slap and tickle.

Female Aries Mars

Mars in Aries adds an Amazon warrior, hard-edged, fiery aspect to the most benign character. The average male doesn't stand a chance unless your other planets are in either Water or Earth. Think of classic movie star Aries Simone Signoret, Sagittarius Emily Dickinson. You need a combination Don Juan and King Kong to keep you from self-immolating. Aggressive and combative, you like your sex very physical and very often. Lifetime or overnight, you know what you want and just how to get it.

Male Aries Mars

You have a sexy, dangerous side to your character. You love to play Heathcliffe to your amour's Kathy and sweep her off her feet, carry her to your room, and have your way with her. Think of Aquarius Paul Newman, Cancer Kevin Bacon. After the deed, however, you either want to replay the drama like an old movie or up the ante by thinking up a new game because you are already bored. You are willful, honest, and more interested in getting your own way than being liked. You are hands-on, physical, and demonstrative. And you need to lead.

Venus Is a Nympho

> *There's something about my shaggy-dog eyes that makes people think I'm good.*
>
> Steve McQueen (March 24)
> *ARIES VENUS/ARIES SUN*

Dangerous liaisons, power struggles, envy, drama, and torrid sex. Aries in Venus people love it hot, raunchy, and frequently frightening. Male or female, they are charismatic, arrogant, and very confident in all areas of life. Aries Venus has a force of will and absolute energy that respects nature's raw power. Directed outward, this combination is a born mover and shaker. Directed inward, this coupling produces a character whose interest lies in control and domination of an endless procession of unlucky lovers. The Aries in Venus character runs hot and cold. What turns them on in the morning might just as easily disgust them in the afternoon. These characters are prone to snap judgments, hopping into bed five minutes after you meet them, marrying in haste, and not hanging around long enough to repent.

Female Aries Venus

You're no Snow White and proud of it. You are territorial, possessive, and prone to saying exactly what you think, devil-be-damned. You have an obvious sexual energy that continually smolders, no matter what your Sun sign. Think of Aquarius Lana Turner, Taurus Debra Winger. You want a man who isn't afraid to stir up some conflict now and then, but who is willing to play faithful sidekick versus action hero over the long term. You are perfectly capable of opening your own doors and lighting your own cigar; however, you are also into testing and manipulating the one you love, so on occasion you stamp your feet and howl to see how fast, and how high, your lover will jump.

Male Aries Venus

Your ideal woman is tough, hard to get, and very independent. Whether quiet or bold, you need breathing room and someone who won't mind if you stay out with the boys, or girls, a few nights a week. Think of Pisces Ted Kennedy, Gemini Drew Carey. On the other hand, you might stay out a few months, so she should be a good sport, too. You love arguing and making up, and you don't mind if she forces you to undress and climbs on top. Wishy-washy is something you can't stand. If she's got a past, a dog collar, or a pair of fur-lined handcuffs, you are liable to fall for her in a heartbeat.

Fatal Attractions

Aries/Aries—Crazed but well-meaning egomaniac seeks pushy, competitive partner for wild sex and daily scream fests. Bring own dishes to throw.

Aries/Taurus—Self-serving, rugged individualist who can't cook seeks inert, stodgy gourmand with chocolate fetish for kitchen-table sex. Bring own wok.

Aries/Gemini—Immature, but cute, spendthrift seeks angst-ridden partner with teenage mentality and good credit for merry-go-round lifestyle and frequent fornication.

Aries/Cancer—Overconfident, perpetual babe-in-arms with excessively broken heart seeks egoless smarmy type to blame, whine at, and harass.

Aries/Leo—Hot-to-trot sexual firebrand seeks arrogant party-hound with dramatic flair to barrel through life shouting orders at the ignorant masses. Fabulous sex. Forever love.

Aries/Virgo—Multiple-orgasm champ with giant ego seeks sagacious, reticent complainer for the one-night relationship from hell.

Aries/Libra—Long-suffering hothead, always right, especially when wrong, seeks vain, supercilious underachiever for great sex and shallow-but-meaningful relationship.

Aries/Scorpio—Hopeless romantic loser seeks jealous, obsessive game player for over-the-top sex and underhanded emotional maneuvers. If you quit snarling, I'll try not to yell.

Aries/Sagittarius—Fun-loving hedonistic chatterbox seeks loquacious bore with clown feet for exuberant sex and can-you-top-this game playing.

Aries/Capricorn—Impetuous fly-by-night, used to instant gratification, seeks responsible drudge with cold cash and a heart to match for mutual head butting and brutally honest talks.

Aries/Aquarius—Serious sex machine with own toys seeks perverse-but-harmless space case for a little tomfoolery and lots of insincere flattery.

Aries/Pisces—Fearless Leader type with Savior complex seeks timid, substance-abusing loser to reform, dominate, and stalk.

Scoring

Best Bets—Aquarius, Gemini, Leo, Sagittarius
Just Good Friends—Aries, Capricorn, Taurus
Please Shoot Yourself Now—Cancer, Libra, Virgo
The Dark Horse—Pisces, Scorpio

Adorable and Annoying Aries

Fatty Arbuckle
Warren Beatty
Mariah Carey
Russell Crowe
Doris Day
Hugh Hefner
Lucy Lawless
Pepé Le Pew
Sarah Jessica Parker and Matthew Broderick
Spencer Tracy

Chapter Three

TAURUS

April 20–May 20

My Way

Element: Earth. Mud wrestling is definitely not for sissies.

Quality: Fixed. Taurus never varies either the routine or the position.

Symbol: The Bull. Herd mentality meets human garbage disposal.

Ruler: Venus, the goddess of "I want that . . . and that . . . and that."

Romantic Idol: Archie Bunker.

Romantic Style: Ball and chain.

Favorite Pickup Line: "Can you cook?"

Ideal First Date: Date cleans house, cooks dinner, performs oral sex, and offers profuse thanks for allowing him or her these privileges.

Erogenous Zone: Throat, deep throat.

Sexual Quirk: Get in, get out, get some grub.

Romancing the Sign

A perfect lover is the one who turns into a pizza at 4 A.M.
Anon.

Looking for a whirlwind romance, dancing until dawn, high camp, and/or a laugh-a-minute partner? Then skip this chapter and head straight for Gemini, Leo, or Sagittarius. Taurus is just a hair's breadth less self-absorbed than Aries, and a thousand times more stubborn and boring. Getting a Taurus to rethink a belief is like getting a Pisces to rethink happy hour.

As the second sign of the zodiac, Bulls add love of possessions to love of self. This means not only do they expect you to worship them, but they also expect to own you and everything you bring with you when you move in. If they move in with you, they will stake a claim to the most comfortable side of your bed and the best place on the couch for TV viewing. Like ivy, Bulls take over everything they touch and, if you aren't careful, you'll disappear just like that proverbial little cottage.

Taurus is billed as the sensualist of the zodiac. Marilyn Chambers, the *Ivory Snow* girl, is also known as Insatiable Marilyn, the queen of porn. A review of her performance in the now legendary *Behind the Green Door* said she was bright, good looking, and had the sexual energy of an atom bomb.

Sexually, even average Bulls have as much stamina as a long-haul trucker. Unfortunately, they have the same amount of finesse. Male or female, a Bull's idea of a romantic evening is pizza, chocolate, and sex. Or sex with chocolate followed by a pizza, all eaten and performed in or near the bed. Certainly, your eyes will roll back in ecstasy. You'll also spend the night trying to sleep on bits of pepperoni and picking melted M&Ms out of your hair, or elsewhere.

Taurus is the pack rat of the Universe. Their garages, closets, and bureau drawers are stuffed with prized beer-can tabs, buttons, baseball cards, and jars of pennies. Possessions make Bulls feel secure. This includes you. Taurus loves commitment the way Leo loves to boogie. Orson Welles said of his first wife, Chicago socialite Virginia Nicolson, "We only got married so we could live together." This may have been a sign of the times, but it also demonstrates the Taurus need to formalize his or her relationship. This does not mean that Bulls make good marriage partners. Welles was married and divorced three times.

Declare your undying love to a Bull and be prepared to be figuratively (sometimes literally) chained to the bedpost. They are as jealous as Scorpio, as whiny as Cancer, as infantile as Aries, plus they have that special Bull-only trait of being the most judgmental and least acquiescent sign in the Universe. Taurus is Fixed Earth. Being in love with one is rather like wearing cement shoes. You won't be going anywhere for a long time.

Natural and unpretentious are some other benign traits attributed to the Taurean. If you are expecting a redemptive quality, please note *natural* means infrequent baths and a change of clothing only when the current attire attracts too many flies. Taureans have a hippie's hatred of water, a political opinion just right of fascist, and a don't-clean-until-you-can-smell-the-mold attitude toward housekeeping.

If a Bull wants you, you may not know it unless you make the first move. This deliberate sign takes the slow and methodical approach in love, as in everything else. If a pal you've known since high school "suddenly" asks for a real date, you can bet your Taurus Willie Nelson CDs that he or she is already madly in love and has taken two, five, or ten years to screw up the courage to let you know.

Bulls are king and queen of the double standard. What is OK for a Bull is definitely not OK for you. Although as unfaithful as the rest of us, when Bulls cheat, they pride themselves on long-term liaisons, i.e., five- or ten-year, even life-long affairs. They call it being simultaneously faithful. I call it the herd mentality.

'Til Death Do Us Part

Today, I will rely on the language of love and understanding. If that doesn't work, I'll go back to fear and intimidation.

ACTOR PAT McCORMICK (MAY 12)

Catching One

The fastest way to get a Taurus in bed is to have a sandwich and a cold one waiting on the nightstand. Venus rules Taurus and here she bestows a sensual character, extremely sensitive to sight, taste, smell, and texture. Unfortunately, Taurus had its head in the grain bin when the love goddess dropped this blessing and ever after Bulls have equated food with the source of nearly all sensory pleasure.

Almost anything within the blue spectrum appeals to Taurus, as do shades of brown. Not yellow brown, but rich mahogany, or dark oak. They love velvet and silk, the smells of leather and fresh flowers, and anything with a luxuriant, soft texture. Both sexes equate comfort with safety. This means comfortable furniture, comfort food, and a nonthreatening partner. Wear a blue cashmere sweater, offer a meal of pot roast and mashed potatoes, finished with a sinfully rich dessert, clean up the kitchen while Ms./Mr. Bull catches twenty winks in front of the TV, and you'll have no trouble keeping this beast tethered and docile. If you prefer more excitement, better opt for dinner out followed by half a movie. Half a movie is what Bulls see because of their tendency to fall asleep about an hour, or less, after they sit down and relax. If you want danger, date a Scorpio, or try Libra for an active social life. Taureans are routine addicts who stress out when the family drops by unannounced, or you change the dinner menu at the last minute.

They are just as predictable in the bedroom. So if you like to know a week in advance when your amour is going to be pawing the ground and steaming up your bifocals, yours will be a match made in heaven. But, please don't believe all that steadfast partner stuff. Ever seen a real Bull in springtime? The only difference is that human Bulls have a very brief shelf life of hedonism. By the time they are thirty-something, the perspective changes from *pleasure seeker* to *judgment dispenser*. Of all the signs, Bulls have the shortest memories of their own imperfections, and the quickest finger to point out yours.

When you are ready to do the deed, don't waste your time, or money, buying all sorts of sexy underwear and lingerie. Invite your Bull over for a home-cooked dinner or delivery from a gourmet restaurant. Spread the feast on a blanket between throw pillows on the floor and get naked. Naked turns Taurus on. Naked with chocolate will drive one to multiple-orgasmic nirvana. Naked with chocolate in front of the food channel could damn well kill an older model.

Surviving One

Dumping a Taurus is akin to scraping tar off your ass. You have to do it slowly, methodically, and with care; otherwise, you'll be in a world of hurt. Taurus rarely leaves a relationship of his or her own volition no matter how bad it gets.

Bulls love to bellow and constantly threaten to leave or kick you out. But, after the fiftieth time you witness this rote scene, and notice that no bags get packed, nobody's car squeals out of the driveway, and the next day your Taurus has forgotten he or she called you every vile name ever recorded by mankind, you'll begin to understand. The easiest thing is for you to pack up and move. Preferably, while your soon-to-be-ex is at the office or on a business trip.

However, if you are legally bound, or the house was yours to begin with, getting rid of a Bull will take time and planning. The word *sudden* doesn't exist in the Taurus vocabulary. He and she need weaning, and could easily have a nervous breakdown if you just order him or her out of the house. Leos you don't have to tell twice, they are eager to get out of a bad relationship; and by the time the sun sets, an Aquarius will have found a new home and a new lover. But the Bull doesn't let go. Taureans are geared to regular habits. This means coming home to a pile of clothes on the front porch or getting handed divorce papers at work could send yours into a rage no one wants to behold.

Make a plan. First, quit cooking—that will shake them up even if they, in their infinitely obtuse way, refuse to acknowledge something is wrong. Next let sex dwindle, which should be easy since that's usually the first thing that goes when you want to end a relationship. Work late at the office. Dig out your frequent-flyer coupons and visit your relatives in another state every other weekend. If you have another lover, take extra precautions that Bully doesn't sense this, or you both could end up in the emergency room.

None of the above will make your Taurus more agreeable about admitting it's over, but will let *you* get out of the relationship alive and with most of the family antiques intact. Finally just say, "It's over." Don't mince words, and don't pretend you are a Pisces or a Virgo and take a day to explain. Be as clear, kind, and *quiet* as possible. If you are leaving, walk out the door immediately. If he or she is leaving, make sure the movers pull up on cue, and/or Brutus, your biker neighbor, appears on the doorstep.

Don't worry about getting dumped. You won't. Taurus is notorious for never making the first move, unless it's toward the kitchen. And don't worry about trying to get even, should that rare event happen. Anything you pull will be taken as a sign that you want to make up, or just further proof that you are the nutcase Taurus thought you were in the first place. So, unless you want Mr./Ms. Bovine back on your doorstep at midnight with that pizza and a six-pack, just quietly move on to someone who can at least stay awake through dessert.

Keeping One

Are there any tangible benefits to sticking by this stubborn, sometimes exasperating hardhead? Yes, wonderful ones. That is, if you want a partner who prefers an evening with you alone to making the rounds of the latest *in* spots. And one whose taste runs to understated elegance and definite comfort.

Earth signs are all physical creatures and Taurus is the most physical of all. These natives won't balk at holding hands in public or a little neck nuzzling in the kitchen before dinner. Male or female, Bulls are the hands-down best huggers in the Universe. This is the simplest way to make up after an argument. It's a rare Bull who will purposely turn down a full-body hug. Other full-body pleasures include long, luxurious baths for two, frequent massages, and slow, sensual sex.

Bulls refuse to hurry and, lucky you, this includes under the covers. Forget the nooner or a quickie before your dinner company arrives. Bulls prefer leisurely sex, and the foreplay starts in his or her mind hours before the deed. Your Bull will love a teasing phone call at work or an early-morning hint of what to expect if he or she is on time for dinner. *Subtlety* is your keyword.

Bulls aren't the least bit prudish. However, they are selective about with whom and where they exhibit their earthy nature. Your male may think it's great to tell off-color jokes and let his chauvinistic side shine at his weekly outing with friends. Or your lady Bull may love to serve you dinner wearing nothing but a gold, antique necklace. But, when you are in public, both will observe the proprieties at all times and rarely be anything but charming and reserved. Taurus is one sign that, without exception, totally separates his or her private life from public persona.

Moonlight or Gaslight?

I do unto others what they do unto me, only worse.

JIMMY HOFFA (FEBRUARY 14)
TAURUS MOON/AQUARIUS SUN

In traditional astrology, the Moon is said to be exalted in Taurus. The euphemistic explanation is that the steadfast demeanor of Taurus steadies the emotions, and romantic Venus exerts an artistic and loving influence over the erratic Moon.

Taurus Moon people have fewer emotional problems than any other sign. Instead, they drive the rest of us bonkers because they are the most willful, possessive, and inflexible creatures on Earth. Taurus Moons are do-or-die emotional characters determined to have their own way, no matter the cost.

A Taurus Moon could well be called the Elephant Moon, for these natives never forget a thing. During an argument, they won't necessarily drag up every real or imagined slight you've inflicted upon them throughout the course of your relationship, as will a Water sign. However, be assured, it's all inside his or her mental notebook listed in carefully printed block letters. And one day, if you have been bad enough, you're liable to find yourself on the receiving end of a blunt object. Fortunately, Taurus Moons are so predictable that, once you learn the routine, you can save yourself a trunkload of broken dishes by using paper plates on the days they wake up bellowing. Taurus Moons are slaves to routine—dinner at six, whether you're hungry or not, sex at ten, whether you're horny or not.

These foot draggers also take forever to make up their minds. Don't mistake this for the indecision of Libra. Taurus Moons are on a lifetime search for perfection. And most lose out on many terrific opportunities by either refusing to work through the issues it takes to become successful or having a built-in failure system of being so cautious and deliberate that the world passes them by while they sit at their desks perfecting their plans.

You could easily die while waiting for one to dial 911. Fall off the ladder while washing windows and, first, he or she will ask if you are really hurt. Next they will try to get you to talk, walk, or make some sound that reassures them you are alive. They may try to find a neighbor or call Mom first to see what she recommends while you try to staunch the blood flowing from your head.

Double Taurus Fred Astaire was fanatical when it came to his dance routines. It was not uncommon for him to rehearse a scene a hundred times, until every nuance of motion was to his satisfaction. His Taurus Sun's natural determination to succeed became an obsessive desire for perfection when coupled with his Taurus Moon. Astaire achieved that rare success few people do. So did double Taureans William Shakespeare and Carol Burnett. However, most Taurus Moons can't hack the dedication it takes to satisfy their need to be the best, so they end up ranting and raving about how imperfect *you* are and how that drags them down.

Virgo/Taurus is so inert you'll need a cattle prod to stir yours to action. They're good at commitment though, and usually faithful. Not too kinky, but sweetly romantic. The Capricorn/Taurus combination takes sexual endurance and pleasures of the flesh to an erotic height you won't soon forget. And fattens the checking account to boot.

In Gemini/Taurus, you get Air trapped in Earth. The resulting explosions can either bring up a rich flow of oil or just a lot of sulfurous gas. The good news is this blend stabilizes Gemini's fickleness; bad news is a host of weird friends you must entertain. Venus-ruled Libra/Taurus is in love with love. These creatures spend less time in front of the mirror but more time being duped by a beautiful face attached to a shallow mind. Aquarius/Taurus is like hitching a racehorse to a boxcar. These natives don't know whether to plan dinner or a revolution.

Pisces/Taurus is less likely to drink, but more likely to cause you to. Both sexes are prone to love at first sight and keep score if you don't immediately reciprocate. Pisces wants to dream. Taurus wants to paint the den. In Cancer/Taurus, the cautious Bull helps the cracked Crab hold onto stability at least a couple of weeks out of the month. This duo is homey, faithful, exceedingly loyal, and exceptionally jealous. Opposites attract, and in the Scorpio/Taurus blend you get a partner who's ambitious, determined, loyal, and so sexy you'll feel the vibes a mile away. They are fairly laid back, but be wary of this one's occasional surly mood.

Aries/Taurus is more rational and much less prone to snap decisions. Beware the dark anger. This one could drive a truck through the bedroom wall if you get caught playing footsies. There's absolutely no reasoning with a Leo/Taurus. They always think they are right and will eat anyone who disagrees. Sagittarius/Taurus is one of the Universe's anomalies. This blend produces a public persona and private emotional character. He or she can pull any outrageous stunt at your expense. But setting them up with your own practical joke could get you throttled. Screws around, but with fewer people than your average Sadge.

Mars Is Afflicted

People have tried and they have tried, but sex is not better than sweet corn.

GARRISON KEILLOR (AUGUST 7)
TAURUS MARS/LEO SUN

Hotheaded warrior meets stubborn dictator. In Earth, the fires of Mars burn slowly and sustained. Taurus Mars can be driven in its determination to succeed. Cancer Ginger Rogers had Mars in Taurus. She worked as long and hard as Taurus Fred Astaire at perfecting their partnership in dance, and she is the partner you remember when you think of him. This aspect also adds a need to dominate, even to the most laid-back Sun sign. These natives refuse to quit, either striving for their own success, or riding your ass if he or she thinks you need some critical direction. Both sexes are extremely jealous. When raging Bull and the volatile Ram explode, the temper tantrums can be spectacularly dangerous.

Female Taurus Mars

Romance is fine, but what really turns you on is the sex act. Mars in Taurus adds an earthy seductiveness to the most modest personality. You are one of the Universe's survivors and you are not afraid to pay the price to reach your dreams. Think of Leo Madonna, Cancer Tracy Pollan. Although you desire a partner who's as strong as you are, you have no intention of letting him or her push you around. A powerbroker with a big checkbook could make you bend your rule. But just a bit.

Male Taurus Mars

You hate to waste time, are extremely independent, and usually very goal oriented. You have a tangible sexuality no matter what your Sun sign. Think of Cancer Carlos Santana, Aquarius actor LeVar Burton. When you meet someone whom you want to either bed or wed, you move slowly but deliberately and persistently forward. *Quickie* isn't in your vocabulary. Instead, you love prolonged, sensual sex, and among your lovers your staying power is undoubtedly legendary.

Venus Is a Nympho

Don't make me a role model for anything.

DENNIS QUAID (APRIL 9)
TAURUS VENUS/ARIES SUN

Physical beauty, luxurious surroundings, plush furniture, soft or silky clothing, and long, slow massages with scented oil by candlelight all appeal to the Taurus Venus person. These boys and girls are turned on by the five physical senses. With Taurus in Venus, even the most outgoing sign will have a certain conservative approach to love. What you see on the dance floor, or at the office, is definitely not what you get under the covers. Sexually, both males and females are so slow to arouse that you could get a cramp in your hand during foreplay. But once he or she lets go, they charge like a real Bull and you will soon beg for mercy, and for more.

Female Taurus Venus

Take equal parts understated sexuality, strength of purpose, and quiet self-confidence (Aries Doris Day), add a pinch of gold digger and jealous tyrant (Cancer Imelda Marcos), and you have the basic Taurus Venus personality. You are nearly as vain about your appearance as Libra but much more discriminating in your choice of lovers. You want a lover with looks, intelligence, and money, not necessarily in that order. And the one you'll adore must share your passion for wine, song, and elegant evenings at expensive restaurants.

Male Taurus Venus

You are sexy in a down-to-earth way, loyal, and friendly. Although you love beauty, you prefer lovers with substance versus glitz. Think of Gemini Paul McCartney, Pisces James Taylor. You grudgingly settle for brains, independence, and an earthy good humor. However, predictability and a lifestyle of slavish devotion to your every wish and whim are primary traits of your ideal partner. Few could live up to the combination Nurse Nellie, Suzy Homemaker, and Mysterious Sex Goddess of your fantasies, so consider yourself lucky that the smart ones adore you.

Fatal Attractions

Taurus/Aries—Shy, boring grouch with raging hormonal surplus seeks impetuous, optimistic hedonist to frustrate, fight, and forget. Let's lock horns.

Taurus/Taurus—Stable stick-in-the-mud who loves food, sex, and money seeks same, for long-term relationship full of cannelloni, canoodling, and coin wrapping.

Taurus/Gemini—Judgmental, homeostatic pessimist seeks reform-school dropout with attitude to whip into shape. Bring own whip.

Taurus/Cancer—Stubborn-but-well-meaning parental figure seeks unstable, reclusive disaster magnet to mother, smother, and scold.

Taurus/Leo—Jealous tyrant with short fuse and long memory seeks arrogant tyrant with shorter fuse and no memory at all for physical grappling and verbal duel to the death.

Taurus/Virgo—Quiet-but-determined routine-loving hypochondriac seeks quiet-but-constant critic to clean house and help judge the lesser folk. Conservative, but sensual, sex included.

Taurus/Libra—Resolute, sober stay-at-home seeks flippant, irresponsible liar to share the Venusian love of excess. Short-term titillation, long-term suffering.

Taurus/Scorpio—Church deacon with mirrored ceiling and unholy sexual appetite seeks depraved, willing cheater for secret, long-term affair. No talk. Park in back. Leave before sunrise.

Taurus/Sagittarius—Sermonizing, lazy stay-at-home who prefers TV to real life seeks philosophizing gadabout with wandering eye for mutual mental anguish, terminal misunderstanding.

Taurus/Capricorn—Self-indulgent bore with well-stocked pantry and lots of dough seeks extravagant social climber with Swiss bank account for romantic evenings by the checkbook, mind-bending sexual marathons, and everlasting love.

Taurus/Aquarius—Earthy, seductive animal with barnyard manners and possessive nature seeks militant airhead who would rather talk than screw for fleeting, yet memorably repugnant, affair.

Taurus/Pisces—Sensual pleasure lover with both feet planted firmly on the couch seeks guileless dreamer with sweet tooth for safe sex, safe life, and cozy, albeit predictable, love.

Scoring

Best Bets—Cancer, Virgo, Capricorn, Pisces
Just Good Friends—Taurus, Aquarius
Please Shoot Yourself Now—Aries, Gemini, Leo, Sagittarius, Scorpio
The Dark Horse—Libra

Tantalizing and Terrible Taurus

Pierce Brosnan
Cher
Carmen Electra
Katharine Hepburn
Janet Jackson
Traci Lords
Jack Nicholson
Dennis Rodman
Roberto Rossellini
Randy Travis

Chapter Four

GEMINI

MAY 21–JUNE 20

Love the One You're With

Element: Air. Gemini's silver tongue is renowned for more than just phone sex.

Quality: Mutable. Juggling five or six lovers, a spouse, and two committed relationships takes real talent.

Symbol: The Twins. Double your pleasure—and your pain.

Ruler: Mercury, fastest mouth and shortest attention span in the Universe.

Romantic Idol: James Bond.

Romantic Style: Multiple personality.

Favorite Pickup Line: "Read any good books lately?"

Ideal First Date: Three best friends who adore him or her and congratulate one another all night on their astounding luck.

Erogenous Zone: Hands. Hand job. Hand jive. Handcuffs.

Sexual Quirk: You are making love. Gemini is thinking about a career move, new love, or old flame.

Romancing the Sign

Just because you like my stuff doesn't mean I owe you anything.
Bob Dylan (May 24)

Make the above quote your mantra if you've set your heart on a Gemini. Twins never owe anyone anything. They are rarely guilty. Should the emotion flicker across their souls, he or she will just as quickly shrug it off.

Gemini has no time to waste. Bring your Rollerblades, cell phone, and laptop. You're going to need all three, plus the patience of a saint and the morals of a sinner to get one to date you twice, let alone commit to a long-term relationship. Especially since Twins regularly confuse *long-term relationship* with *long weekend.*

Twins are king and queen of the one-night stand, and even marriage won't necessarily slow them down. Amoral versus immoral, Twins think it's perfectly acceptable (for them) to say he or she loves you madly, then dash off to their next rendezvous and repeat the whole scenario with someone else. The difference between this and a Leo who's carving notches on the headboard, or any Water sign who refuses to let go, is that a Gemini says the words because he or she thinks you need to hear them. Not because he or she means them.

All Gemini have multiple personalities. During the course of one day you may be conversing with many different persons all speaking in the same voice. This can be extremely eerie at night. Some astrologers consider the Twins sexually ambiguous. All agree Gemini will usually try anything once. Androgynous Gemini Boy George is supposed to have said, "My view is we're all made up of equal parts Rambo and Lucille Ball."

In his mid-forties, Gemini artist Paul Gauguin left his wife and five children to pursue his art career, first as the cohort (and possible bisexual lover) of Vincent van Gogh, then on to Tahiti where he is rumored to have taken a thirteen-year-old wife. Historian Nancy Mathews has said in her research of the artist, "Gauguin was a bully and an abusive husband. I began seeing how unpopular he was during his lifetime. How his habits were so in-your-face in a sexual way."

The only rule you need to remember when it comes to wooing a Twin is that there are no rules. Gemini rush headlong into the unknown, like Libra Evil Knievel jumping sixteen boxcars. They also crash as frequently, but manage to survive quite nicely. Traditional astrology says that Gemini's animal is a bird, or butterfly, because they seem to be in constant motion. I think they are more like house cats. More curious than wise, full of mischief, prone to run-and-slash fits and darting out the door and down the street for adventures we humans will never know the truth about. And just like feline *domesticus,* when they get beaten up in an alley, or tossed in a Dumpster, Twins hightail it home to lick their wounds and sleep.

Twins are all razzle-dazzle and sleight of hand. Remember, liquid Mercury is called quicksilver. And the Twin you are trying to pin to the mattress is just as hard to contain. You have to be fast to jump a Gemini's bones. They barely hold still long enough to sleep a few hours, let alone submit to languorous foreplay. Jump on, get it on, get it over with, and jump off. Gemini is one of the few signs that are perked up by sex. You are satisfied, drowsy, and want to sleep. He or she is rejuvenated, revved up, and wants to talk. If you want a rematch, start talking.

Geminis fall fast and hard, but rarely permanently. If you don't respond just as instantly during GWOO (the Gemini Window of Opportunity), the object of your affection is highly likely to just as instantly move on to someone else. GWOO can last anywhere from thirty seconds to a couple of hours—but no longer. When your Twin begins to pant and nibble your neck on the couch, or in the back row of the movie theater, move as fast as possible into the nearest reclining position. Don't mistakenly think that you are rushing these guys and dolls, or that you will offend yours if you restrain yourself. *Restraint* is a foreign word to Twins. And don't prolong the act itself; otherwise that quick Gemini mind will begin counting the pores on your nose and you'll soon find yourself grappling with thin air.

'Til Death Do Us Part

It's easy for me to live in denial. I can get the worst news in the world and not even think about it.

COURTNEY COX (June 15)

Catching One

The way to a Gemini's bed is through his or her mind. To catch one, you absolutely must be up on all the latest trends, fads, and buzz words and have read at least one book by an emerging author. If you work in a media-related field, give yourself extra points. You must be willing to listen and *never* interrupt, although a Twin will interrupt you constantly trying to second-guess what you are about to say, then claim the insight or information as his or her own. It's that Mercurial need to gather, process, sort, and spit out information at the speed of sound.

Most Twins are, at the least, street smart, but even if yours is a less-than-intelligent font of useless minutia, he or she will think that the information he or she spouts is valuable. And if you can impress yours by beating him or her to the draw on occasion, or having a faster wit now and then, chances are you'll have a decent relationship—for a while. Don't make a habit out of being smarter. Geminis admire this trait in friends, business colleagues, and acquaintances at the local nightclub, but when it comes to love, they want a respectful partner who mentally walks two paces behind.

They love to be entertained. If you can juggle limes with one hand and unbutton his or her shirt with the other while you are humming a Gemini Paul McCartney tune, you're practically guaranteed a good time. That time. Subsequent good times demand more tricks. And Gemini loves tricks, especially sexual ones. This sign will literally try anything once. Lucky you. Role-playing is a Gemini specialty. So is overlooking your sordid past. In fact, if you have a few skeletons stashed here and there, or a couple of insane relatives, a Twin will probably think you're extremely interesting—for awhile.

All Gemini have multiple personalities. Don't confuse this with the moodiness of Cancer, the duality of Pisces, or the temperamental displays of Leo. A Gemini can declare mad, passionate love to you one moment and become a cold stranger the next. If you want beer, Mama, and the Friday-night fights, find an Earth sign. All Air signs love freedom. Gemini demands it.

Don't make emotional demands on this sign, like asking what time he or she will be home for dinner. Or expect him or her to manage the checkbook, children, or financial planning. Occasionally, your Twin may look at you as if you were a stranger. Usually, this is when he or she ignores you while dashing out the door with a Leo in a Harley jacket. That's when you need to remind Mr./Ms. Gemini that *you* are his or her spouse, partner, or lover. This behavior doesn't mean they don't love you anymore. He or she's just had a bout of temporary amnesia of the Gemini kind. If you expect to live with one, get used to it.

Surviving One

Getting over a Gemini is similar to walking away from an emergency airplane landing. The initial adrenaline rush from the hair-raising excitement is soon replaced with gratitude that you survived the fall.

Twins are fairly easy to dump. After you tire of the screaming fights, slammed doors, and endless insults, condemnation, threats, and sarcasm, just toss up your hands and say, "You win." Since Twins can't stand to think anyone actually dislikes them, he or she will probably act very distraught. They have feelings. Terribly hurt ones. How could you *do* this?

He's destroyed. She's crushed. It's pitiful to see a Gemini wallowing in emotional excess. Thank God it lasts only about five minutes.

It takes serious and consistent mental and/or physical abuse for a Gemini to really hate you. And if a Gemini *really* hates you, sooner or later you're going to get blindsided with a swift kick out the door, which you no doubt deserve.

If you get dumped and actually want that capricious slave to instant gratification back, wait a week, then appear at his or her favorite spot. Make sure you are wearing the latest fashion look, that your state-of-the-art cell phone rings constantly, and that you *ignore* Gem as he or she follows you through the bookstore or bar. Laugh a lot. Nothing irks a Twin more than to see a former lover having fun. Being the cat-curious creatures they are, he or she will not be able to resist *accidentally* placing him- or herself in your path. Make sure your teeth are commercial white. Smile, act rushed, and say, "I'd love to chat but I'm late." Plant a quick kiss on his or her cheek as you fly out the door. By the time you get home, Gemini will have left six messages on your machine.

Getting even is fun. Cut all ties. Refuse to talk, look, meet, e-mail, wave if you see yours on the street. It drives Gems nuts. Even if yours initiated the breakup, he or she will soon be off on the I'm-so-distraught routine to think you dare disregard his or her larger-than-life presence. Laugh hysterically as you watch your ex mumbling to him- or herself while fumbling for the car keys. As soon as the smell of burning rubber fades, drop to your knees and thank Heaven that you escaped with your mind intact.

Keeping One

Is it possible to find happiness with a domestically challenged lover? Absolutely. Gemini is certainly troublesome. He or she is also irresistible. The first word in Gemini is *fun*. A Gemini lover will make you laugh every day. Twins are natural entertainers who have a wicked observational wit, a mynah bird's talent for mimicry, and a psychic ability to tell just when you need some humor.

Geminis are lively, spontaneous, and happiest when they have both a wide circle of friends to visit and a private place to recharge at home. They like bright colors and uncluttered space (unless the clutter is his or hers). Gemini is the sign of the information gatherer and communicator. You should, at the very least, read the newspaper every day and have the ability to make halfway-decent dinner conversation. Taurus collects antiques, and Scorpio dwells on the past, but Twins are strictly current events.

In bed, they love it when you talk dirty during the deed and keep up the pillow talk afterward. This is one sign that won't mind a TV in the bedroom. Gems think it's delicious fun to get cozy while watching a favorite movie, or surf the sex channels, all the while kibitzing (and barbing) the action on the tube.

Twins love surprises and thoughtful gifts that show you are paying attention to his or her likes and dislikes. Techno gadgets in metallic colors will delight them. Both sexes usually love shoes and silky, airy clothing that doesn't restrict movement. Electric purple, aquamarine, and yellow look great on most Twins.

All Air signs have nervous dispositions, but Gemini is the busiest, and most frantic, of the group. This high-voltage personality is easily overloaded. Help yours relax with a yoga or meditation class, or use calming fragrances, such as lavender, throughout your home. Everyone loves a massage. However, Gemini needs human touch to ground and release the excess energy that floods his or her psyche. Don't forget those flying fingers or fleet feet. Massaging your Twin's hands and feet will soothe his or her whole body.

Make sure the kitchen is stocked with fresh fruits and veggies, lots of quick-fix meals, and energy-boosting snacks.

Twins frequently suffer temporary burnout, and highly nutritious foods they can grab on the run will keep yours operating at peak efficiency.

Love from the Gemini perspective is 50 percent friendship, 20 percent spiritual, 20 percent physical, and 10 percent emotional. You'll never make a Gemini a joined-at-the-hip lover. But if you want pizzazz, variety, and a life outside the routine, you can't find a better companion.

MoonLight or GasLight?

I can always be distracted by love but, eventually, I get horny for my creativity.

GILDA RADNER (JUNE 28)
GEMINI MOON/CANCER SUN

Gemini Moons change direction more often than a weather vane during a tornado. In Gemini, the focus of the Moon's emotional structure is on the next whim, adventure, or thrill. The Moon in Gemini is not a good spot because the emotions become superficial, shallow, and frivolous.

This placement could well be called the Traveling Salesman Moon, for these folks usually have lovers stashed in various towns across the continent. They are restless, dispassionate, and think they have all the answers, when they haven't slowed down their information processors long enough to gather half the facts. Gemini Moons can hold down several jobs, or may have dual careers, such as superstar Aries Omar Sharif, who was as famous for playing bridge as acting. However, you'll rarely see one stuck behind a desk.

Both sexes rely on intellect over emotion and bring all sorts of troubles upon themselves by thinking instead of feeling. Gemini Moons will react the way they *think* they should, or the way they think you want them to, instead of getting in touch with how they really feel. Most shove aside the feeling process in favor of instant logic, which is more often than not faulty. Eventually they blow and go wild.

Gemini Moons are also extremely prone to instant character change. Gemini Sun has a multifaceted character, but the Gemini Moon can be like living with a paranoid schizophrenic. You'd think this nutso would self-destruct. Instead, Moon Twins double-team *you* into tearing out your hair. They are like a TV wrestling tag team. Harold the Hurricane softens you up with relentless verbal hammering, then Mazie the Mortifier moves in for the romantic kill by telling you it's been fun, but she's moving to Bolivia with the Sagittarius she just met in the women's locker room. This is one dynamic duo you have little chance of surviving unless you have lots of Air in your natal chart or are a rich Aries with a hearing loss.

Through the signs, the Gemini Moon adds a definite sparkle, one that can either hone the dullest personality or outwit itself so that it defeats its own purpose. Gemini Moons also have more luck than a pair of loaded dice and more personalities than Double Gemini Mel Blanc (Bugs Bunny) had cartoon voices. Libra/Gemini make great prosecutors—rapid-fire questioning and no visible breathing. They are so charming they're compelled to spread the wealth around, committed or not. Lots of flash, little substance. The high-camp, highly attractive, and high-on-life Aquarius/Gemini can wear a lampshade to a party and start a new fashion wave.

Unless you are a mega–head trip player, stay away from Cancer/Gemini. These guys and dolls turn emotional manipulation into an extreme sport and are more career than home minded. If you like it down and dirty, grab a Scorpio/Gemini. This duo is drawn to the forbidden like a personal injury lawyer to a bus wreck. Pisces/Gemini is funny, interesting, less likely to overdose, and more likely to leave you laughing when he or she inevitably splits.

The Aries/Gemini mind spins faster than a pinwheel in a

windstorm and changes career direction just as quickly can leave you standing at the altar with no regrets. Gemini is glib, glamorous, has a hundred friends, and is wonderfully lighthearted. But you will seldom find a less domestic creature. Sagittarius/Gemini spouts enough hot air to fill the blimp with some left over to pop corn. A compulsive player with a great sense of humor.

A Taurus/Gemini is intelligent and appears reasonable. Not so. The Gemini Moon gives Taurus the ability to talk (versus beat) their victims into submission. Virgo/Gemini raises promise breaking to a fine art and has the irritating habit of disappearing just when you need them most. Capricorn/Gemini has potential. The flighty Moon makes the steady Sun irritable. These folks need a long leash, but one that's securely anchored at home. Lots of superficial interests.

Mars Is Afflicted

I sing to the realists; people who accept it like it is.
Aretha Franklin (March 25)
GEMINI MARS/ARIES SUN

When the volcanic action of Mars heats up the intellectual communication trait of Mercury, you get an aggressively candid, rash, multitasking autocrat. These natives get off on phone sex, writing passionate letters and talking about sex, talking while having sex, and talking after sex. Diversity is a must for Gemini Martians. Whether this means nightly theme screwing with a permanent partner or turnstile sex with multiple players depends on how versatile his or her lover is. Easily aroused and just as easily turned off, Gemini Martians despise routine and will flit out the door at the first whiff of ordinary. Mars heats up the sexual synergy of Gemini, and both sexes will be extremely good at using their hands on your erotic parts. This placement indicates multiple lovers, marriages, and the scary ability to talk themselves in and out of just about anything.

FemaLe Gemini Mars

You need to discuss, debate, and voice a definite opinion on any subject. Even the shyest personality has no fear of telling it like it is with this placement. Think of Taurus Barbra Streisand, Cancer Meryl Streep. A lover who matches your wit, intelligence, and who can hold a decent conversation has the best chance of capturing your attention. Manual skills are a plus, in or out of bed. You are impressed by craftsmanship, professionalism, and a virtuoso performance. A studious type who can play your body like a Stradivarius could settle you down.

Male Gemini Mars

You are the original silver-tongued devil. Few signs can resist your romantic come-on. Even if you use a well-worn line, you seldom fail to arouse the object of your desire-of-the-moment. You are charming, playful, and very changeable in love, and your ideal lover is one who comes without strings, marriage proposals, and/or any notions of tying you down. Think of Taurus Dennis Hopper, Aries actor Eric Roberts. No matter how impassioned your pleas seem, you are rarely out of control. Your brain is two thoughts ahead of your mouth, and your mouth is a mile ahead of your current quarry.

Venus Is a Nympho

I knew what I had and I worked the fuck out of it.

COURTNEY LOVE (JULY 9)
GEMINI VENUS/CANCER SUN

In Gemini, Venus is a chronic flirt. The need to explore life's endless variety of pleasures pervades even the most settled personality. Gemini Venus avoids heavy emotional scenes and clinging partners like a Virgo avoids self-criticism. Love is just one of the many pursuits of people with Venus in Gemini. These characters can drive the sanest lover to commit mayhem; however, they also have that cat's agility to rescue itself from disaster at the last possible moment. Rarely satisfied, Gemini Venus wants to investigate, tweak, rearrange, and experiment. Applied to relationships, this philosophy often ends in a critical assessment and dumping of a perfectly good romance without giving it a proper chance to develop. As with every Gemini placement, the Gemini Venus is prone to multiples in lovers, marriages, jobs, hobbies, and friendships.

Female Gemini Venus

When you are in the mood, no other woman is as charming, sexy, funny, or sociable. Think of Leo Jacqueline Kennedy Onassis, Cancer actress Katherine Helmond. Few can resist your charms because you are so good at reading a potential lover's mind and instantly role-playing the woman you think he or she wants. Sooner or later, though, the game becomes a giant bore and when you switch to the real you, the one you've wooed is left wondering just who's sharing the pillow. Your ideal mate is one who is smart enough to see through your endless charades and not let you know that he or she knows. Looks are important. So is the ability to put up a good fight.

Male Gemini Venus

You have definite tastes. Looks *and* brains. Not necessarily in that order. Think of Leo Laurence Fishburne, Taurus Emilio Estevez. You want a lover who is up to the many tests you love to subject people to and who looks good on your arm or in your bathtub. King of sparkling repartee, you have a social circle as assorted as a political convention and a taste for quizzing the objects of your affection to test their nerves. A Barbie or Ken with an IQ, wit, and a talent for clever conversation could make you snap your cap.

Fatal Attractions

Gemini/Aries—Quizmaster of unceremonious nonsense with master's in carnal knowledge seeks subtle-as-a-crutch motor mouth with hearty sexual appetite to share unbelievable sex and stimulating pillow talk.

Gemini/Taurus—Promiscuous schizophrenic with death-by-boredom wish seeks possessive plodder with tired blood to screw, confuse, dump, and forget.

Gemini/Gemini—Chat-room junkie who's found Elvis seeks foot-loose dandy with cell phone for witty verbal sparing, brilliant sexual innuendos, and serious, committed one-night stand.

Gemini/Cancer—Superficial-but-darling flirt who lives for friends, fun, and serial romancing seeks emotionally clinging recluse for weekend relationship that will seem like two life-times.

Gemini/Leo—Future Pulitzer prize winner who's not shy about success seeks glamorous slut-about-town for fun, games, serious sex, and lifetime love fest.

Gemini/Virgo—Hyperactive, debate-team captain prone to snap decisions and stretching the truth seeks deliberate, careful planner with dustpan for a Guinness record–breaking Shortest Dinner Date in History.

Gemini/Libra—Footloose rascal with multiple personalities, live-for-today attitude, and expensive tastes seeks luxury-loving shopaholic with an eye for style and a body for sin. We'll hit the sheets, and the white sales, together forever.

Gemini/Scorpio—Dueling tongue champ with penchant for pushing the envelope seeks mysterious stranger with venomous streak for mutual emotional assassination and super-hot sex.

Gemini/Sagittarius—Headstrong, loquacious party-hound who loves dispensing advice seeks bombastic armchair philosopher for marathon talk fest, no sex, and verbal duel-to-the-death.

Gemini/Capricorn—Lovable cheat who burns both the checkbook and the mattress at both ends seeks stuffy conservative who secretly craves adventure and sex games. Could be the start of a beautiful friendship.

Gemini/Aquarius—Jiggly, jumpy, jive-talking escape artist with boundless energy seeks anything-goes wild child with fright-night hair and kinky libido for endless fun, continuous surprises, and death-can't-part-us love.

Gemini/Pisces—Unstable airhead with checkered past and questionable future seeks gullible escapist with no self-esteem for rent money, gas money, and 2 A.M. quickies.

Scoring

Best Bets—Aries, Leo, Libra, Aquarius
Just Good Friends—Gemini, Sagittarius
Please Shoot Yourself Now—Virgo, Scorpio, Pisces, Taurus, Cancer
The Dark Horse—Capricorn

Titillating and Tiresome Twins

Bugs Bunny
Johnny Depp
Rudy Giuliani
Anne Heche
Elizabeth Hurley
Angelina Jolie
Paul McCartney
Marilyn Monroe and John F. Kennedy
Priscilla Presley
Wallis Simpson

Chapter Five

CANCER

June 21–July 22

Cry Me a River

Element: Water. Vinegar and water may be cleansing, but it's awfully hard to swallow.

Quality: Cardinal. Cancer is the *Mother* of all signs.

Symbol: The Crab. Cracked doesn't just apply to the crustacean.

Ruler: The Moon. There's no brass ring on this emotional merry-go-round.

Romantic Idol: Carmen.

Romantic Style: Codependent.

Favorite Pickup Line: "Are you going to eat that?"

Dream First Date: Mom drives the car and orders everyone's dinner. Date hangs on Mom's every word and pays bill.

Erogenous Zone: Breasts. Tit-men and suck-the-life-out-of-you women.

Sexual Quirk: Crying before, during, after sex, in gratitude or discontent, or because you came multiple times, or didn't, or they did, or didn't.

Romancing the Sign

Tragedy is when I cut my finger.
Comedy is when you fall in an open sewer and die.
Mel Brooks (June 28)

If you are after adventure, leaps of faith, playing your hunches, and investing in the hottest stocks, try a Leo, Aquarius, or Sagittarius. Cancers don't do spontaneous. They barely do well-planned. Both sexes are morbidly resistant to change, unless he or she initiates the change. If Cancers were plants, they'd be Venus's-flytraps—alluring on the outside, carnivorous on the inside.

Being ruled by the Moon means that these boys and girls are hypersensitive, have a shadowy nature, and moods that can, and do, change hourly. And he or she does *nothing* without a string attached. So be wary. Crabs are kings and queens of the clinging vines. Borrowing a Cancer's car because yours is in the shop could be construed as a sign you want to marry. Both sexes were born with permanent PMS (pardon my sobbing) syndrome. The easiest way to spot one is by the furrowed brow and pained expression as if he or she is either about to cry or has just stopped. Crabs also look either permanently perplexed or as if they just sniffed a foul odor. Watch President Bush's next press conference for a prime example.

And don't forget Mom. Not yours. Theirs. You may be able to bed a Cancer without this lady rearing her ugly head, but you will *never* be able to marry one unless you accept the fact that first and foremost, all Cancers are tied to Mother forever. Artist J. M. Whistler (*Whistler's Mother*) immortalized his dear old mom in oil. Whether yours adores the woman or harbors disappointment, even hatred, for the old bat, *you* are going to have to worship, suffer, or, at the bare-bones least, pretend to like Mother. Cancers remain tied to the apron strings long after most of us have run screaming from our parental hearth.

Compound this if you love a man-Crab. He will forever compare you to Mom and you'd better hope to God that she was wonderful. Otherwise, he'll punish you for all her misdeeds because he's still afraid to tell her to bug off. I wonder whether author, and Cancer, Bryan Forbes's *Stepford Wives* is a tribute to his vision of the perfect mother or a Freudian wish that all women be subservient robots.

Cancers operate from two perspectives, caretaker and guilt inducer. The endurance of this sign is legendary. Cancers' emotional pinchers are just as tough as their zodiac symbol. They have been known to hang on to food, jobs, bad relationships, and marriages way past the pull date. They are miserable. You are miserable. Both of your families and all of your friends are miserable. But Cancer just smiles wanly and puts on his or her *brave face*.

Brave face is one of their favorites. This consists of a slightly pursed mouth, extremely serious countenance, purposeful demeanor, and brimming eyes—clenched hands and/or teeth optional. Walk in suspiciously late from work and you'll see the *brave face*. Or, you could find the *disappointed Mom* face staring at you from across the kitchen table. Male or female, all Crabs were born with this look. Small sigh, slight shake of the head, averted eyes, knitted brows. You know the one. Other looks include the *helpless victim, exasperated adult,* and *cold survivor*. Beware the *cold survivor*. When Cancer goes into survival mode, you can be sure you are going to be in for anywhere from one day to weeks or even months of punishment.

Whether Geezer, Boomer, or Gen-X, all Cancers thrive on the tortured romance. Read up on Camilla Parker Bowles crisis-laden affair with, and long-suffering wait for, Scorpio Prince Charles. The fact that Princess Diana was also a Cancer proves what type of romance hooks a Crab.

Both sexes walk through life permanently cringing because they expect the worst to happen at any moment. Both can whip themselves into a fit of emotional turmoil over absolute trivia. You can cause one to sulk by moving the furniture without permission, and drive one to the therapist if you suggest a weekend away alone. Real Crabs walk sideways. Human ones have sideways emotions. Crabs continually size you up to see whether you measure up to their ever-changing, fluctuating emotional assessment. These crisis magnets frequently make the worst possible romantic match. However, secretly they thrive on the conflict. It gives them a chance to wear one of their looks daily.

'Til Death Do Us Part

I think you get attracted to people who validate your worst fears about yourself.

RICHARD LEWIS (JUNE 29)

Catching One

Cancer wants what it can't have. This isn't like Aries' love of the chase and thrill of conquest. Crabs scuttle forward, backward, and sideways trying to corner you, smother you, and love you, until you give in, in which case they are just as liable to get permanently lost. To pique one's interest, be friendly but aloof. Be unpredictable. He or she may say they hate unpredictable, but will secretly love that trait in you, because he or she is so predictable. It's that wanting what they can't have again. In astrology, *Cancer* and *moody* are synonymous words. Never forget this. Age doesn't mellow them. Logic doesn't faze them. Therapy may help you deal with one.

If you are falling for a Crab, bring kid gloves, a security blanket, three boxes of chocolate truffles, and a case of Kleenex. You are going to need all of this, plus the fortitude of our forefathers hacking through the wilderness to put up with the most sensitive sign in the universe.

Crabs crave security. To get him to loosen his tie or her to take off her shoes, you need to do the home-lover shuffle. You conversationally step forward and talk about a favorite childhood memory, or your mom's great talent for feeding twenty with a loaf and a fish. Crabcakes will, in turn, put out a feeler in the form of a story about a favorite pet. You gush that you just love kids and animals. Talk about the ocean, the Moon, your favorite chick flick, or food. Cancers are easily horrified, so *never* attempt to discuss the latest serial killings or spreading diseases.

The need to feel safe and secure pervades into the bedroom. Cancers are romance addicts, and, male or female, all prefer the slow arousal to a lustful quickie. Music, candles, locked doors, drawn drapes, and unplugged phones will prove that your Crab has your undivided attention. Both sexes like to cuddle and long foreplay is a must.

This is one sign that rarely does the deed on the first date or without some emotional involvement. If you are hot for one, you will need patience in addition to making yours believe all you want from life is a picket fence, a set of double deadbolts, and an old cat. When your Crab invites you over for a home-cooked meal, rent a classic romantic comedy or love story with a happy ending and cuddle him or her on the couch after dinner. Rave about dinner. Rave about your, or his or her, mother (again). After the movie, be reluctant to leave. If Cancer gives you a signal, like offering coffee, hot chocolate, or a nightcap, ask about any of the myriad pictures he or she will have covering the walls. Keep up the verbal dance. Be patient.

When you finally are bestowed with a beaming smile or gooey, teenaged stare, you'll know Mr./Ms. Crab is ready to be gently steered toward the bedroom. No matter *how* horny you are at that moment, if you want a permanent relationship, don't do anything. Cancers fear being used so, if you come on as a bit shy and hesitant yourself, you might get asked to stay. If you aren't, don't worry. Say good night. Don't forget to rave about the coffee or nightcap on your way out the door.

Move in for the sexual kill on the very next date. Cancer's erogenous zone is the breast. Either let your cleavage, or chest, show or stare at his or hers. When the cuddling starts, move your hand slowly toward your Crab's nipples. This sign takes a bit of work to turn on, but once under that down comforter, you are liable to have your socks blasted off. Crabs are not overtly into sexual escapades. However, they are willing participants if you take the role of teacher and tell him or her you can make all those romantic fantasies come true. Win your Cancer's trust and you'll be in for a lifetime of sensual abandon.

Cancer is a Cardinal sign, and Cardinal means *boss*. Male or female, every Crab, no matter how shy, introverted, or fearful on the outside, has an inner instinct that was born to dominate. If you can get yours to channel that tendency into dominating you in bed more often, you'll have a lot less trouble fending off the Crab's emotional manipulations out of bed.

Crabs like after-play nearly as much as foreplay. He or she will probably be hungry and fix a plate of snacks for the two of you to nibble in bed as you cuddle and talk. And the talk will almost certainly turn to love and plans for the future. If you aren't prepared to play I-bet-we'd-have-cute-kids or go to Sunday dinner at Mom's house, at least pretend interest while you've got this ultraemotional creature between the sheets.

Out of bed, Crabs are the champs of self-delusion. If your Crab has the illusion of *happy home* in his or her head, you can be the biggest louse on the planet and he or she will simply ignore signs, signals, even strange scents on your bikinis as he or she clacks and clucks and snaps little claws over tightly shut eyes. Even if forced to acknowledge trouble in Paradise, they will seldom leave. But understand that Cancers are not forgiving—they may make up but you will wish it had been break up. Cancer will punish you by withholding sex. A cold back in the night is not a pretty sight. And these characters can keep their backs turned a long time. If you think you are strong enough to stand it, gird up your loins for a seriously soap opera relationship.

Surviving One

In addition to being sick of Mother, or the old bat's memory, you'll have little privacy, less independence, and will have to fight for every night out sans your Crab. You also will be held accountable for everything that goes wrong within your relationship, whether it was your fault or not. So if you aren't a lying, dirty cheater before you fall for a Crab, you soon will turn into one from the sheer exhaustion of being spied upon, grilled like an FBI suspect, and subjected to never-ending emotional manipulation.

Whether they dump you, or you dump them, splitting up with a Crab will *always* be your fault. Accepting this truth now will save you lots of grief and guilt later. There's rarely a question of whether you can survive without Crabs, but he or she will try to make you believe they can't survive without you. To keep you, even when they know it's over, they are capable of faking a fatal disease.

The least traumatic way to dump a Cancer, from the Crab's perspective, is for you to wean them as you would a baby. However, this could literally take years because Crabs can't let go any better than Bulls. So if you aren't prepared to get late-night phone calls to rush over and help your ex through an anxiety attack, or early-Sunday-morning calls to baby-sit the dog for the next five or six years, my advice is to end it as quickly but kindly as possible. Otherwise you have little chance of finding a new partner understanding enough to suffer an ex born under the sign of Looney Tunes.

Just quietly state that you are leaving, then be prepared for yours to (in no particular order) faint, try to kill you, smash the dishes, or become catatonic. If you actually get hurt in this tirade, so much the better because Crabby will certainly feel guilty later. In the meantime, before you can hobble out the door, he or she will be on the phone to Mother, then every friend and family member. Next he or she will call *your* mom and tell her what a rotten bitch or bastard you are to break up this happy little home. But, don't break your resolve, because these claw clackers will keep reveling in their martyrdom long after you've moved on to greener pastures.

It is hard to disentangle a clingy Moonchild from around

either your ankles or your psyche, so if you aren't up to a cold-turkey breakup, here are a couple of tactics to help you out the door. Say that you are considering becoming a foreign missionary, that you want him or her to move with you, then produce a list of the twelve worst diseases known to mankind, while reassuring your now-green-faced Crab that you think there are vaccines available for most. Or, demand he or she limit Mother's visits to once a week and no phone calls after 5 P.M. Either maneuver should get the ball rolling.

Cancers don't dump; they torment. Your Crab may have moved on to another lover, but he or she will keep you dangling forever, if possible. This tactic comes in many guises such as the hope-you-are-doing-OK phone call, here-I-brought-you-some-soup unannounced visit, or the I-was-in-the-area-how-about-lunch drop-in at your office. All of these maneuvers are designed to see if you are suffering without him or her, to sniff the air in your apartment for any new scents, and to demonstrate to anyone who happens to witness these pseudo-acts of kindness that Crabs are such caring folks. If you fall for this routine, you'll be dangling like a puppet while Ms./Mr. Crabcakes jerks those infernal strings forever.

Keeping One

If you really have your heart set on a Crab, you'll be relieved to know you do not need formal psychiatric training to have a happy relationship. You *do* need an understanding heart, lots of patience, and the faithfulness of a St. Bernard rescuing an avalanche victim.

Your Crab may be a hard-driven executive during the day, but don't let that businessman or woman façade fool you. Nothing is more important to Mr./Ms. Cancer than you and his or her home. Crabs are private and, if given a choice, prefer their homes to be off-limits to casual gatherings of loud persons—unless it's family. This doesn't mean you can't have a party. It means don't allow your unemployed Sagittarius friends to make a habit out of sleeping on the living room sofa.

This up-close and personal sign loves to take trips down memory lane. These are the folks whose walls are decorated with pictures and mementos of favorite family, friends, and special occasions. He or she will love a collage of special snapshots of the two of you to add to the collection.

As does Virgo, Cancers have frequent nervous indigestion and other intestinal tract disorders. Food is both a comfort and a frequent necessity to keep yours healthy. Along with Tauruses, Cancers are born cooks and prefer their own home cooking to any restaurant food. To a Crab, a romantic evening consists of fixing your dinner, sharing the cleanup afterward, and snuggling together on the sofa watching the classic movie channel.

All Water signs are fundamentally insecure, and Cancer leads the group. Crabs don't do independence very well. Relationships make them feel safe. Home makes them feel safe. Crabs need the familiar around them, even when they travel. Like Taurus, Cancer will frequently pack his or her pillow, a favorite photo, and/or scented candle when traveling. They also fear ending up alone. This is why he or she may question every move you make and dream up a hundred reasons why you should not go anywhere without him or her. It's not because you aren't trusted; it's because Crabs are the worrywarts of the Universe. Carrying a cell phone will help yours feel connected when you are out at night with your friends, as will frequent calls home if you are on a business trip. A separate vacation for more than a weekend takes some real effort and about ten years' worth of commitment.

Should you happen to slip and betray your Cancer, no matter how remorseful you may be, or how forgiving he or she seems, you will be under suspicion for the rest of your life, and treated accordingly. A Pisces might talk it out; an Aries, fight it out. A Libra would seek couples counseling, and an

Aquarius wouldn't care as long as you eventually came home. Your Crab will continue to go through the motions, but his or her emotions will freeze, and it will take years of living on a choke chain to unfreeze them. Even then your indiscretion will never be forgiven.

But, assuming you are honorable, trustworthy, and loyal, your Crab will love, honor, protect, and nurture you forever.

Moonlight or Gaslight?

I don't want to run around with new people. I feel safer with my friends.

Adam Sandler (September 9)
CANCER MOON/ VIRGO SUN

If you think Cancer Suns are hopeless victims of their emotions, a Cancer Moon kicks any Sun sign's whine factor up several notches. The Moon may be at home in Cancer, but it's more *Psycho House* than *Happy Days.* Cancer's excessive emotionalism and fluctuating moods coupled with the constant waxing and waning of the Moon's cycles create a personality scarily close to manic-depressive. Self-pity is never far removed from a lunar Crab's psyche. They invented the pity party. They are more possessive than Taurus, more controlling than Scorpio; and their nag-meter is set at shrew.

Cancer Moon children's emotional entanglements with dear old Mom usually verge on either worship or rage. All Cancer Moons have extremely intense feelings for their mothers and drag this emotional baggage around most of their lives. Just as they are tied to their mothers' aprons, their favors, sacrifices, and loyalty to you come with so many strings you'll think you're Pinocchio. And you'll learn to lie just as much to get any semblance of independence within a relationship with one. Cancer Moons can be surprisingly stubborn, viciously critical, and unmatched at the art of instilling guilt in others. They seldom operate from an overt position of dominance. Cancer Moons often act like the family doormat, but they never stop maneuvering for control. They have an exceedingly close circle of family and friends that rarely ebbs and flows other than with a birth or death.

Cancer Moons can live in victim mode for weeks or years, then switch overnight to cheerful loony bird. You might think the fun side is easier to take. Not so. It's as in-your-face and frantic as the downside is under-the-bed and sulking. These natives can be on top of the world today and literally under the couch tomorrow.

All Double Cancers (think Harrison Ford, Robin Williams) have an almost tangible vulnerability, or lost-child quality that makes *you* want to mother *them*. This curious mix is, simultaneously, a sucker for a sob story and just as determined not to be taken advantage of. They will give you the shirts off their backs but won't accept a ride to the grocery store. Scorpio/Cancers are doubly moody and triply possessive. They are also catch-your-breath sexy and can be hypnotically good looking—be very careful. These sexual explorers are self-possessed and stalker possessive. Pisces/Cancer is simply dazed and confused. These children of the Xanax god are prone to panic attacks and weird psychological diseases. They cheat regularly but go to their graves without admitting guilt.

The double Cardinal mix of Aries/Cancer produces an exceedingly bossy, overprotective exterior and a whiney, ego-conflicted interior. Like the schoolyard bully, he or she starts a fight, then sobs hysterically when you fight back. Leo/Cancers are in their natural Sun/Moon placement. The result is one tough cookie. The upside is a sweetheart who's uncomplicated, loyal, giving, and just plain wonderful. The downside? Imagine a wounded Lion with PMS. Sagittarius/ Cancers stray less, talk less, and dream of a perfect world. But if you can't make it happen, he or she won't hesitate to leave.

Forget Taurus/Cancer unless you are a masochist looking for a controlling, grudge-holding manipulator. The terminally grouchy Sun and ultrasensitive Moon result in a character that's always pissed off. The granola-eating Virgo/Cancer is obsessed with health and has a surprisingly volatile temper when pushed. And these characters won't care if you are at home or in church when they start screaming. The Capricorn/Cancer blend is definitely not the life of anyone's party. Reliable, but serious, loyal, but so traditional you'll think you've stepped into Smallville. Good provider.

Gemini/Cancers are slick, charming, and champs at blindsiding you. They are very prone to theatrics and feigned illnesses to get their ways. Nasty moods. Libra/Cancers make your protection their life's mission but they never cease to tell you how much they are sacrificing for your benefit. The Aquarius/Cancer is grounded and less prone to making wild promises he or she can't keep. Has a quirky humor and love of kinky sex. This Water Bearer will also hang around the house more often.

Mars Is Afflicted

My mother was the fiercest drag queen I've ever known.
RuPaul (November 17)
CANCER MARS/SCORPIO SUN

Cancer's watery nature weakens the passion of Mars, where it becomes darkly subtle and overly sensitive. Cancer Mars natives have often been at war with, or the victims of, their mother or another nurturing parent figure during childhood. As an adult, he or she is usually protective of the home they've created, which is the only place he or she feels totally secure. Highly intuitive, critical, and possessive, this combination is the most easily turned off of the Mars configurations. If Cancer Mars feels his or her partner is not responding properly, the fires of passion can instantly turn to icebergs of disinterest or volcanoes of anger. As with any other Cancer placement, these natives tend to cling to unhappy relationships. Cancer in Mars often produces a constant, moody irritation and regular temperamental outbursts.

Female Cancer Mars

Mars in Cancer makes you passionate about feeling secure. And without feeling safe, you will never feel like heating up the sheets. Your emotions are shaky and you frequently work yourself into a frenzy over imagined tragic scenarios that never materialize. Your ideal lover is a romance-novel hero—deeply passionate, macho-but-vulnerable, and someone who can simultaneously rescue you and need you. Think of Pisces Liza Minnelli, Virgo Rebecca De Mornay. Your love can be deep, powerful, and forever, providing you live long enough to find a real-life Rhett Butler.

Male Cancer Mars

Unruly, moody, and vulnerable, your passions are never far from the surface and threaten to erupt at the slightest provocation. Think of Virgo Richard Gere, Scorpio Burt Lancaster. You are an emotional catch-22. Are you a macho, assertive caveman or a sensitive, vulnerable peacekeeper? You crave family, home, and hearth, but fear losing your independence in the trade. Your ideal lover is so responsive that he or she can read your mind and sense your moods before they swing. A psychic connection sends you into ecstasy.

Venus Is a Nympho

> Words and music must be so inseparably wedded to each other that they are like one.
>
> COLE PORTER (JUNE 9)
> *CANCER VENUS/GEMINI SUN*

In Cancer, Venus needs to merge completely with a lover and is forever connected to the childhood home and family. However, in typical Cancer style, these natives usually attract the flotsam and jetsam of humanity, and home is often more asylum than refuge. The Cancer Venus person is subjective versus objective and relies on an often-faulty emotional identification with the object of his or her affection. These folks often marry neighbors, a childhood sweetheart, or one of their relatives' friends, or, in some parts of the country, a relative. Neither sex forgets the old neighborhood and often longs for his or her hometown.

Female Cancer Venus

In Cancer, Venus loves tradition, home, and apple pie and won't hesitate to bash anyone who believes differently. Think of Leos Marilyn Quayle and Elizabeth Dole. You have a nurturing side to your character, no matter how hard you may be climbing the ladder of success. Secretly, you want a lover you can smother with affection and boss around. One who will smother and mother you in return while letting you call the shots.

Male Cancer Venus

You love to be babied, attended to, and pacified. And you usually have a lineup of potential lovers who are willing to accommodate your every whim. Think of Gemini Clint Eastwood, Leo Dustin Hoffman. However, all Sun signs with this placement share a difficulty in expressing deep feelings. Your ideal mate is a mommy you can screw. One who will have dinner on the table, an unending interest in your dreams and schemes, and always, but always, put you first. And if she or he doesn't, you know just how to have a megasideways fit, sulk, and withdraw for days, or weeks, until you get your way.

Fatal Attractions

Cancer/Aries—Romance-novel savant with martyr complex seeks kinky serial romancer for unbelievable sex and an unbearable morning after.

Cancer/Taurus—Serious, possessive homebody, who cooks in and out of bed, seeks serious, possessive protector who loves to eat. True love and sensual sex guaranteed.

Cancer/Gemini—Love-starved clinging vine with terminal hangnails seeks self-serving hedonist with a rabbit's idea of foreplay and ability to inflict serious emotional damage upon an already fractured ego.

Cancer/Cancer—Migraine-afflicted shut-in with Oedipus complex seeks whining hypochondriac for shared passive-aggressions and crisis-to-crisis lifestyle. First one to commit suicide wins.

Cancer/Leo—Shy-but-sensual housekeeper with French-maid uniform seeks outlandishly brazen defender to serve, worship, and stroke the right way. Perfect master/slave relationship, but guess who is boss?

Cancer/Virgo—Irritable, moody, and underhanded manipulator seeks irritable, critical, and perpetually pissed-off partner for great sex and true affection. True love might take too much effort.

Cancer/Libra—Woebegone sacrificial lamb with masochistic streak seeks vain, flippant lover with altar and willing attitude.

Cancer/Scorpio—Professional martyr with own sackcloth and ashes seeks sinfully sexy partner whose taste for meaningless vengeance titillates and helps perfect victim act.

Cancer/Sagittarius—Travel-phobic, sidestepping, double-shuffler who mumbles seeks brutally honest loudmouth with lifetime airline miles for interesting but hopeless romance.

Cancer/Capricorn—Emotionally-infantile-but-sweet hypochondriac, who's prone to panic attacks and death fantasies, seeks a no-nonsense parental figure into domination, subjugation, and humiliation. Cool sex. Convenience-store romance.

Cancer/Aquarius—Collector of useless trinkets with seriously impaired relationship judgment seeks mad-scientist type with own lab for terminal misunderstandings and sex that could chill a penguin.

Cancer/Pisces—Smothering caregiver with flair for the mundane, and award-winning chicken soup recipes, seeks deluded ne'er-do-well with big dreams to wet nurse, cover for, support, and love.

Scoring

Best Bets—Taurus, Leo, Scorpio, Pisces
Just Good Friends—Capricorn, Cancer
Please Shoot Yourself Now—Aries, Gemini, Libra, Sagittarius, Aquarius
The Dark Horse—Virgo

Cuddly and Carnal Crabs

Pamela Anderson
Edward, Duke of Windsor
Jessica Hahn
Kimberly (Lil' Kim) Jones
Courtney Love
Princess Diana and Camilla Parker Bowles
Sylvester Stallone
Ringo Starr
Patrick Stewart
Liv Tyler

Chapter Six

LEO

July 23–August 22

Born to Be Wild

Element: Fire. Play with this Fire and you're bound to get heartburn.

Quality: Fixed, on top of your panting, sweating, worn-out body.

Symbol: Lion. These big cats like to nibble their prey, too. Yum!

Ruler: The Sun. Exalted ruler of the Universe, the bed, the couch, and the remote.

Romantic Idol: Johnny Bravo.

Romantic Style: Lord and master.

Favorite Pickup Line: "Try the best and you'll forget the rest."

Dream First Date: Date swoons at first sight, fawns in the restaurant, gushes when introduced to friends, and begs to get laid. Polishes boots before leaving.

Erogenous Zone: Heart. Flattery and a nipple ring will get you everywhere.

Sexual Quirk: Loves to be serviced. Expects profuse thanks afterward.

Romancing the Sign

I have no intention of uttering my last words on stage, darling.
Room service and a couple of depraved young women
will do me quite nicely for an exit.
Peter O'Toole (August 2)

Groupies to the right, hero worshippers to the left. Happily, everyone has a chance for a fling with the king and queen of party-'til-the-cows-come-home. You quiet types can stop reading here. Unless the Lion you are setting a trap for has an Earth-bound Moon, or lots of Water in his or her chart, you are liable to get left with a lick and a promise as your target races out the door and down the street to play with the wild bunch. Leos are ruled by the Sun, the brightest star in our little corner of the universe. And male or female, the Lion expects you to revolve around him or her, just like the planets orbit old Sol. This is a very simple fact and, in fact, the only thing you ever need remember.

Leos thrive upon, demand, and need your undivided attention *at all times.* They don't walk into a room; they make an entrance. This includes flouncing into the kitchen for dinner and slamming the door when he or she gets home from work in order to make sure you notice them.

Leos live for high drama. This differs from the crises-ridden emotionalism of the Water signs. A Lion's sense of self-importance is inflated to the point of idiocy. They consider themselves too important for such menial labors as taking out the garbage or cleaning the bathrooms. And they are lazy to boot. Unless, of course, he or she is trying to impress you with how humble and helpful they are.

Lions can be generous to a fault. In fact, they have a tendency to be the check grabbers, big spenders, and over-tippers of the zodiac. Wonderful news, unless you are the partner of a creature who will happily spend every penny you both earn to impress the second cousin of his boss's nephew's new squeeze.

Leos rarely stay home on Saturday night. If you like to spend the weekend unwinding with a good book, or doing chores and getting prepared for the next work week, in addition to being a Virgo, you will be spending your evenings alone if you're hooked up with a Lion.

Romantically, Leo equates beauty with goodness. However,

even if you are not the one out of a thousand movie-star-beautiful faces, you still have a good chance of snagging a Lion if you are expensively dressed and wearing *real* gold jewelry. Remember I said expensively, not necessarily tastefully. Leo rivals Libra's dubious sense of style, so they won't care whether or not your leopard-skin duster matches your elephant-hide boots, as long as they are genuine.

In the classic movie *Breakfast at Tiffany's*, the character Holly Golightly was described as a phony who didn't know she was a phony, meaning that Holly was all show and no substance, but genuine because she didn't know she was a fake. Your average Leo. Holly was an unemployed runaway from the back woods who earned rent money by dating "rats and superrats," who regularly gave her fifty-dollar bills for the powder room—and passing messages from a mob boss in prison to his lawyer on the outside. However, in her mind, she was living the high life because she partied every night and had breakfast in front of Tiffany's window every morning. Leo to the core, Holly preferred style versus substance and never gave a second thought to when she would eat her next meal. The pseudo-glamorous life she fashioned for herself was all she needed.

Gemini may have a house cat's sense of playfulness and mischief, but Leo is pure wild animal. As are their jungle counterparts, human Lions are born guerrilla fighters. If they want you, or what you have, they will not hesitate to pounce. *Carpe Diem* is the Leo motto. They also seize whatever else happens to catch their fancy. Lions take it to the limit. And he or she will push you to yours.

'Til Death Do Us Part

I am a deeply superficial person.

ANDY WARHOL (AUGUST 6)

Catching One

Attracting Leo is ridiculously easy. Stand upwind and wave a wad of greenbacks. This jungle cat will be hot on your scent in a heartbeat. It's not that Lions are mercenary, it's just that they live for fun, and spending money tops a Leo's list of the ten best things to do. It's most fun when it's other people's money, but they will also ruin their own credit ratings to show the world they are A–No. 1 at keeping ahead of the Joneses.

Leo humans, whether they are the most boorish show-offs in the world or quiet stay-at-homes, are not shy, or retiring, or reticent. So you must be bold. Tell your Leo you want him or her. Be dramatic and romantic. Stand under the window or on the porch and sing. Send daily flowers. Write poetry. Leos thrive on romance and will lap up this attention. Most Leos like to drink a bit. Loosening one up with alcohol is a well-known fast track to the bedroom. Of course, this could turn ugly if your Lion gets stinking drunk and tosses his or her cookies on your new velvet bedspread. Moderation is the key if you take the booze route.

Leo colors are gold, yellow, bright red, and royal purple. They love food as an aphrodisiac. Serve oysters, figs, or other exotic taste treats. Everything should be larger than life and filled with fun and excitement. A Leo appreciates an outgoing partner who can match his or her love for partying, playing, and general dissipation. Call your Leo at work and tell him or her you are wearing gold lamé underwear or a purple thong. Say that you bought tickets to the opening of a new show or a gala charity event, and that you can't wait to show him or her off at the event or for the private limo ride home.

Flattery will certainly lure a Lion into the jaws of your love trap. Praising the Lion's mane, even if it's a scary shock like Leo Don King's, will always get a smile. Leos are suckers for compliments, admiration, even blatant overtures you both know are bullshit. Don't confuse this with Scorpio's susceptibility to flattery. Deep down, Scorpios are suspicious of compliments because they rarely dispense one without an ulterior motive. Your Royal Highness Leo will think you are clever and astute to recognize his or her obvious superiority over mere mortals. A few extravagant-as-you-can-afford dates, praise laid on as thick as Lioness Martha Stewart's pretentious good breeding, and blatant adoration in front of your respective families and friends will seal Leo's fate.

Once you've plied your Lion with praise, fine wine, a lavish night or two on the town, and an appropriately expensive, preferably solid gold, trinket, getting him or her under the covers is easy. Once in the sack, continuously spouting an adoring string of adjectives will keep your Lion happy. It may seem shallow to you, but to the human jungle cat, this is tantamount to purring. When you are lolling in the linens with a sexy Lion, also remember this sign appreciates strength and won't mind if you take control. The first session will be primal, noisy, and athletic. The second time your Lion rolls over, the mating will be slower, more tender, and last longer.

Surviving One

When you've run out of kudos and you're tired of having to fawn over how well Mr./Ms. Leo fills your cereal bowl, the best way to get out of the relationship is to tell the truth, followed by "Let's always be friends." You can remain friends, even sexual ones, after the affair is over, even after you've both found someone else. Along with Scorpio and Libra, Leos make good bed buddies. Scorpio can't resist a clandestine affair, Libra can't resist trying to make you cheat, but Leo will stay to play.

However, if you don't ever want to see that grinning, overinflated ego maniac again, the fastest way to turn him or her off is to (1) use words like *settle down, grow up,* or, *take responsibility;* (2) serve cold sandwiches or fast food on a regular basis; and (3) start buying your clothes at the local secondhand store. You may have to suffer one of the infamous Leo laundry lists of faultfinding he or she saves for occasions such as this one. You'll be reminded of everything you've done that's upset, angered, or hurt your ex since the day you met. Leo is the most theatrical of the signs, so be prepared for the works: arm flapping, finger-pointing, pacing, shouting, tears, recriminations, broken vases. Ah . . . the gaudy glamour of it all.

Leos are notorious for roaming the asphalt jungle and seldom fail to grab the opportunity for a quick, clandestine affair. Plus, the fact that Leo is one of the easiest romantic targets in the zodiac may result in you being unceremoniously replaced with a Pisces he or she picked up in the glow from a neon violet bar marquee.

Should you get dumped and want revenge, public humiliation (if you are tough enough) is the route to go. Unlike Water signs who secretly love public emotional displays, or the other Fire signs who will overlook a nasty remark in front of friends, Leo will not tolerate anything but your reverent deference in public, no matter how you two brawl in private. This doesn't mean you have to show up at the bar screaming. A quiet public put-down, such as "I adore your hair; the dye job looks so natural" or "You walk really well with the lifts in your boots" will do the trick nicely.

Keeping One

Think you need unlimited funds and a permanently bent back from bowing and scraping to keep a Lion happy? Not at all. To be sure, Leo loves the spotlight and all the fun stuff money can buy; however, when the going gets tough, your human Lion can track down a bargain with the best Virgo. And most are the center of attention because they are so much fun to be around.

The term *sunny disposition* fits this happy sign. Lions are trusting, idealistic, humane, and very intelligent. Your Leo's generous nature includes a generosity of spirit and fair play as well as the monetary. A Leo will be the first to loan you gas money or let you crash at his or her house when you've just lost your job.

Although Leos are huge flirts, once they fall in love for real, they rarely stray. Being ruled by the Sun bestows a natural spontaneity and warm-heartedness. No doubt about it, your Leo will appreciate your undivided attention. And will be most happy to give you his or hers. In bed, they like to direct the sexual show, so you can lay back and moan with delight while yours demonstrates that famous Leo creative flair.

Out of bed, a little TLC and regular nights out on the town will keep a Lion purring. Leo appreciates a clean, well-appointed home. Although Lions love luxury, this doesn't mean you have to hire a decorator. They love comfort. Lions are basically lazy and like to come home and fall on an overstuffed couch or favorite chair and put up their feet. For yours, keep thinking *luxury* for food, clothing, etc. Leos love flair. So even if yours is on a diet, pay attention to the way you serve his or her salad and low-fat dessert. Presentation is everything. And packaging. This includes food, decorating, and *you.* Never but *never* make a habit of padding around the house in yesterday's jeans or without your hair and teeth brushed. Remember that jungle cat and how it spends a good part of the day grooming itself. Your human version will do the same and expects you to do likewise.

No matter what your age, think young. Even Leos well past retirement usually look younger than their age. More importantly, they *act* young all their lives. The Sun is ageless, so is your Lion. What better way to spend your life than with someone who loves to laugh, refuses to submit to a rocking chair, and has a zest for living rarely matched by any other sign?

Moonlight or Gaslight?

I was the most popular person in my family. I was like a celebrity.
I was the entertainment. And I was always the boss.

Jennifer Tilly (September 16)
LEO MOON/VIRGO SUN

If you think Aries is egotistical and Gemini is fanatical about its freedom, you ain't seen nuthin' until you've hung out with a Leo Moon. Vain and extravagant Leo brings unwavering Fire to the Moon. In contrast to Aries, which ups the selfish-baby ante, and Sagittarius, which scatters the emotional structure, arrogant Leo makes bad-behaving Sun signs determined to hold onto their irritable, greedy, arrogant, or flamboyant traits. Consider Cancer P.T. Barnum. It's said that P.T. treated his circus performers like family, encouraging their families to travel with them, true to his Cancer nurturing side. However, that old devil Leo Moon was responsible for his extravagant love of the sideshow and his never-ending ability to milk the public for all it was worth. A Leo Moon cannot be dominated. No matter how congenial, generous, and loving other traits may be, even the shiest personality will have a surprisingly strong inner core of independence.

Leo isn't a bad place for the Moon. In fact, most astrologers consider it a beneficial placement. However, it fixes the emotional structure, which can be a dual-edged sword so to speak. On the good side, Leo's Fixed Fire steadies and strengthens the emotional character. On the dark side, Leo Moons can be colossally pompous. So much so that they ruin their own chances for success by refusing to take advice or listen to those who could help them. This is the Glad-Handing Moon.

Double Leos such as Patrick Swayze, Charlize Theron, and Martin Sheen have a presence you can feel before they open the door. Charmers in love with themselves as much as you. Aries/Leo wants it all and this blend can get it. One of the hottest combos in bed, if you can stand the constant need for attention the other twenty-three hours a day. Sagittarius/Leo is delightful. Funny, optimistic, loyal, and honest, this is one of the best of the Sun/Moon combinations.

The mathematical equation for Taurus/Leo is Bull + Lion = Mule. They swing from pompous to absurdly obstinate, but have the potential for wild success. If you cheat, you die. The Virgo/Leo blend is decent, hardworking, and particular. The downside is that the Virgin rarely lets the Lion out to play; the upside is they're loyal, generous, and smart as a whip. Capricorn/Leos are concerned with money, appearance, and position. Females make great wives of power brokers because of an instinct for political correctness. Males are sweet at home, ruthless in the boardroom.

Gemini/Leos are born with an Oscar-caliber flair for drama. One of the most romantic of the Gemini, this duo lives and dies by the double standard. Libra/Leo is the most vanity-driven creature in the Universe. To paraphrase the nursery rhyme, this one's either good or horrid. With the Aquarius/Leo duo, you get a cantankerous fanatic. You never know which way these boys and girls will swing, jump, vote, or change positions, in or out of bed. It's like being in love with a blowtorch.

In Cancer, the Leo Moon balances the Crab's moods a bit. Could be a surprise catch. They need lots of attention, but are more forceful than they appear on the surface. In Scorpio/Leo both sexual sides of the zodiac collide into one hot body resulting in lust, temper tantrums, and treks into the forbidden zone. Either sex can go straight to the top of the career ladder, if you can get them out of bed long enough. Pisces/Leo has the Fish's ability to intuit your desires and the Lion's ability to help you achieve them. They appear more confident and happy than is true and need you more than you'll ever need them.

Mars Is Afflicted

I guess I'm too self-obsessed to think of anything that isn't personal.

QUENTIN TARANTINO (MARCH 27)

LEO MARS/ARIES SUN

When fiery, demanding Mars joins the vanity-driven Leo Sun, the result is a personality that *must* be the center of attention. This aspect manifests as either a dedicated natural leader or performing artist or a self-centered and demanding jerk. Either way, the person with Mars in Leo is someone you can't ignore. He or she won't allow it.

Doubling of any element anywhere in the natal chart compounds the traits of that element. Double Fire equals a hot-tempered, hotly sexual person with a quick mind and a forceful will that can't be denied. Think Fixed Fire Leo and Cardinal Fire Aries. These folks are decidedly bossy and believe they were born to lead. The character is strong, inclined to grandiose schemes and melodramatic displays. On the flip side, they are extremely warm-hearted, enthusiastic, generous, and as friendly as puppies. When they are good, they are like benign dictators. When bad, they can be unbearable tyrants.

Female Leo Mars

Whether you are a happy-go-lucky Sagittarius or a chick-flick–loving Pisces, you are a woman of substance. Think of Virgo Sophia Loren, Libra Sigourney Weaver. Leo Mars is an extremely masculine energy and whether or not you are overtly flamboyant, bossy, or loud, you can call up these traits at will. You do not suffer fools gladly. Your ideal mate is as strong as you, but not strong enough to cast a bigger shadow. You can do domestic, if it's on your terms. You are no one's house mouse. Your standards are high and you invariably choose quality over quantity.

Male Leo Mars

When you aren't in testosterone overdrive, you are planning your next impossible feat of daring. You thrive on ordering around other people, promoting yourself, and taking risks a normal person wouldn't touch. You are also drop-dead sexy. Think of Leo Robert Redford, Aquarius James Dean. Your ideal lover is one who is suitably impressed by the wonder of you, and who is willing to defer to your judgment. You say you want a strong, independent partner, but what you truly desire is a gorgeous sex machine who lives to wait on you hand and foot.

Venus Is a Nympho

Each of us wages a private battle each day between the grand fantasies we have for ourselves and what actually happens.

Cartoonist Cathy Guisewite (September 5)
LEO VENUS/ VIRGO SUN

In Leo, Venus becomes even more playful and sexy. Leo Venus loves to party and frequently entertains at home. These boys and girls are full of animal magnetism and have no trouble attracting admirers. The trouble starts when the admirer realizes the magnitude of the Leo Venus ego and how much stroking it takes to keep this Lion happy. Vanity can be extreme with this aspect. The attitude is that he or she is so special that the only thing he or she need contribute to the relationship is allowing you to grovel and fawn. Leo Venus is also jealous, prideful, and always the star of the show.

Female Leo Venus

You are no pussycat. However, your personality is so outgoing and fun loving that even the string of broken hearts you scatter along the way seldom end up actually hating you. Think of Virgo Greta Garbo, Gemini Nicole Kidman. You are in love with glitz, glamour, and aren't above a bit of deception to get your way. However, you are also a loyal friend and generous with those you care about. You expect your mate to be your match, but when you find someone as selfish as you are, naturally you try to wrestle him to the ground. The man you'll purr for must be part romantic hero, part lion tamer.

Male Leo Venus

You are happy, outgoing, and Mr. Personality. Think of Cancer Tom Cruise, Libra Charlton Heston. However, you also equate goodness with beauty, and vain, self-centered behavior with interesting personality. As a result, you often get what you deserve because of this naïve trait. You want to be half of the Mr. and Ms. Fabulous team, but usually end up with someone who fights you for the spotlight. Your ideal partner is willful, demanding, and questions your royal authority on every issue. When you are just ready to say you've had enough, he or she strips you naked and leaves you in a quivering heap.

Fatal Attractions

Leo/Aries—Sun-and-fun-loving wildcat seeks enthusiastic, adventurous partner for spontaneously combustible sex, serious jostling for command, fantastic fights, and true love.

Leo/Taurus—Good-humored jungle jive cat with no credit and wandering eye seeks humorless couch potato with fat savings account and maniacal jealous streak for the affair from hell.

Leo/Gemini—Party animal with flair for fearless fornicating seeks attractive-but-bad partner with talent for instant sexual gratification. Fun, lust, and a laugh a minute guaranteed.

Leo/Cancer—Born-to-lead and permanently on the make fun-lover seeks born-to-boss, introverted crossbearer for interesting but frustrating one-night stand. Breakfast optional.

Leo/Leo—Too-sexy-for-the-Universe primal being with dream of world domination seeks same for the hottest sex this side of the Sahara. Permanent partnership possible if we take turns being on top.

Leo/Virgo—Selfish spendthrift with supercharged sex life who soaks car parts in the bathtub seeks germ-phobic stay-at-home who lives in head for a few tense weeks and one hellatious breakup.

Leo/Libra—Spoiled brat with teenage lust drive seeks romance junkie with perpetual need to talk things over. Sizzling sex, so who needs conversation?

Leo/Scorpio—Noble beast with no humility and phone book full of friends seeks hot but emotionally oppressive cynic for jungle sex, midnight revenge, and short-but-savage romance.

Leo/Sagittarius—HRH Look-at-Me with flair for exaggeration and wild sense of adventure seeks court jester with endless supply of one-liners and a beastly sexual appetite. All the world's a stage. Let's play!

Leo/Capricorn—Dominant life-of-the-party, who's generally good natured and cooks between the sheets, seeks dominant overachiever with Swiss bank account and hearty appetite. Hot mating. Cold morning after.

Leo/Aquarius—Compliment-crazy cupcake with flair for down-home philosophy seeks sermonizing activist who's paranoid, anti-everything, and can't dance, for interesting but impossible evening. An itch we can't scratch.

Leo/Pisces—In-your-face feline with taste for tuna seeks sucker-fish whose fins are permanently bent out of shape to feed on, fight with, and screw over, and over, and over.

Scoring

Best Bets—Aries, Gemini, Libra, Sagittarius
Just Good Friends—Leo, Pisces
Please Shoot Yourself Now—Taurus, Virgo, Scorpio, Capricorn
The Dark Horse—Aquarius, Cancer

Lusty and Loutish Lions

Bill Clinton
Kathie Lee and Frank Gifford
Melanie Griffith and Antonio Banderas
George Hamilton
Whitney Houston
Mick Jagger
Lawrence of Arabia
Jennifer Lopez and Ben Affleck
Jackie Kennedy Onassis
Billy Bob Thornton

Chapter Seven

VIRGO

August 23–September 22

Do Nothing 'til You Hear from Me

Element: Earth. Sweeping piles of symbolic dirt under a series of emotional rugs takes a really big broom.

Quality: Mutable. England swings and Virgo does, too.

Symbol: The Virgin, on the outside. Kink-meister on the inside. That's no secret. Is it?

Ruler: Mercury, the god of idle conversation and light gossip—in combat boots, carrying a rule book and a riding crop.

Romantic Idol: Mary Poppins.

Romantic Style: Nag.

Favorite Pickup Line: "Pardon me, but there's a bit of lint on your lapel."

Dream First Date: Dinner Dutch treat, then stop by the megamart to peruse the cleaning-products aisle. Date helps try out the latest germicidal on the kitchen floor before shaking hands good night.

Erogenous Zone: Stomach. Tickling, licking, stroking this Virgin's tummy could land you on yours.

Sexual Quirk: Instructs you during, scores you afterward.

Romancing the Sign

*That love at first sight should happen to me was life's
most delicious revenge on a self-opinionated fool.*
Actor Charles Boyer (August 28)

If you are seeking romantic abandon, spur-of-the-moment impulse, or even the occasional "I love you," find yourself a Fire sign, because the Virgin is as precise in amour as he or she is at the office. Virgos tape lovemaking schedules to the bedroom door, right next to the vitamin chart. They color-code their closets and organize their outfits by the days of the week. A Virgo fashion designer most likely invented Monday-through-Sunday prepackaged panties.

Virgo is the only sign represented by a woman. This imparts a feminine quality to both sexes—that of a persnickety old maid. Virgins are the bicker champs of the Universe. No matter what you say, or do, he or she will make a comment, usually either a criticism or a correction. And no matter how you may scream that after months, or years, or a lifetime of *never* being able to voice an opinion without a corresponding opposition from your Virgin, he or she won't change. Never. It's humanly impossible for Virgos, or anyone with Virgo in any prominent place in his or her natal chart, not to criticize. It's a compulsion.

Force a Virgo to stifle an opinion, critique, or reprimand and they'll turn green and shrivel. Mercury rules Virgo, just as he does Gemini. To get an idea of the Virgin's basic character, think of the fastest planet in the Universe, who's used to rushing here and there, gossiping, chatting, communicating through the air of Gemini, and trap him in the solid energy of Virgo. Mercury gets *really* irritable buried up to his knee-caps in Earth. So his motor mouth becomes cranky and his normally funny and pleasant chattering turns into critical nit-picking.

Even the stodgiest of Virgins seem to be surrounded by a humming sensation, as if they are about to explode. That's Mercury's highly charged sexual nature (think Gemini) careening around behind that implacable exterior. If you can help your Virgin unleash this force, you'll be as amazed as if you separated a Capricorn from his piggy bank.

Blues master B.B. King has fifteen children by fifteen

women, none of whom he married. In his autobiography, *Blues All Around Me,* King notes that his love of women is second only to his love of music. He loves to talk, love, and think about women. "I want a soft shoulder, a soft caress," he writes. "I didn't think of the consequences of having children."

Average Virgos don't do rash. These kings and queens plan *everything.* Even when they fall for you, they will think about your collective future or what you'll be like in bed. And once you get him or her in the sack, they will grade the first performance and every performance thereafter whether you have a one-night stand or fifty years of togetherness. Your bonus will be that, after Cancer, Virgins are the biggest martyrs in the Universe.

To get the attention of a Virgo, you have to at least act morally correct. Don't get me wrong, Virgins aren't exactly prudish, but they *are* discriminating. Never embarrass yours by exhibiting anything less than proper behavior in public. Even the leather-clad, whip-snapping, nose-ring types have a rigid code of what is acceptable. Pay attention or you'll have your Bic flicked, heels clicked, and ego nicked quicker than you can say, "Pass me a pool cue."

'Til Death Do Us Part

They say Virgos are not sensual or sexy. I feel sexy inside. I just don't show it.

KRISTY MCNICHOL (SEPTEMBER 11)

Catching One

To get a Virgo to slip between your sheets, first make sure the sheets are new. And that he or she has his or her own (new) towel, toothbrush, favorite body wash, and terrycloth robe in your bathroom. Even Virgos who don't believe in God believe clean is a righteous state. This is one sign that will never be offended at the offer of a presex shower. In fact, this is a great way to get your Virgo to relax. And if you can keep your eyes locked on his or hers instead of scanning their nakedness, you are going to make big points in the thanks-for-realizing-I'm-basically-modest department. If you are a slob who wears a gas mask in the bathroom and kicks aside three feet of dirty laundry to fall, still clothed, into bed, stop reading here and skip ahead to Sagittarius.

As do their fellow Earth signs, Taurus and Capricorn, Virgos as a rule prefer substance and tradition versus fad and flash. This includes food, decorating, and fashion choices. The majority love to read, so an early and neutral gift could be a book. If you invite the one you have your heart set on over for dinner, *do not* serve fast food from a greasy sack. If you don't cook, find a restaurant that has some health-conscious choices on the menu and offer your Virgin a selection. Make sure your home is spotless, the cat box is sanitized, and the only odors wafting through the air are toasted almonds and Pine-Sol.

Even Virgins who don't necessarily follow the classic slim, slight build of their sign are concerned with their health. Virgos have well-stocked medicine cabinets and vie with Cancer for *hypochondriac of the Universe* title. See that yours is equally well stocked and he or she will be more likely to spend the night knowing the antacid and headache powder are only a few steps away.

Virgos love subtle colors—shades of gray and blue, all greens, and especially the warm, fall colors. White is also a Virgo color, not stark hospital white, but cream and beige, ecru and eggshell. To show your affection, give either sex a gift certificate to his or her favorite clothing shop, health food store, or bookstore.

Before you make your sexual move, start by building trust. This means no tongues until the third date. Maybe longer if you are pursuing a particularly repressed Virgin. These were the kids who believed it when Mom and Dad said sex was dirty. And some still think that the whole act is too germ-laden, sweaty, and smelly to deal with. It's up to you to (1) win yours' trust and (2) *never* show up without being neat and clean smelling before making any move remotely connected to sexual.

When you are ready to steer yours to the bedroom, the first time is best at home. If you feel comfortable following their myriad rules of no shoes on the clean floor, no spontaneous ripping off of clothes and leaving them in a heap, and *never* five or six sessions without breaking for a quick shower, or at least a splash of water and some tooth brushing, then Virgo and you will probably make it past a one-night stand. In fact, if you do happily achieve a multiple whoopy session, change the sheets at least once. Your Virgin will adore you for it. No kidding.

After the deed (and another shower), feed your Virgin. Virgo is the sign of the Bountiful Harvest, so make sure you have handy some whole-grain bread, the freshest of fruits and vegetables, and at least a couple of items from the health food store. Then tidy up the kitchen together, get dressed, and go to the park, the bookstore, or the humane society and adopt a kitten.

Surviving One

Honesty is the best policy. So just tell your Virgin that you are tired of having to shave on the weekends, your skin is raw from the lye soap, and your ego is battered from being constantly assessed and found lacking. Say your therapist told you that if you didn't get some positive feedback soon, you would most certainly resort to an affair with a Scorpio to get some sexual heat. Tell him or her that, although you both are nice people (emphasis on *nice*) the spark just isn't there.

This should get you off the hook or out of the house with your personal belongings intact. However, although Virgos are unlikely to cause a scene, they are not above trying to lay a guilt trip of biblical proportions on you. So be prepared for the saint act. Virgos never admit their faults because they rarely believe they have any. You, on the other hand, will instantly assume the role of heartless bitch or ungrateful bastard as your Virgo, not too sadly, assumes the role of martyr. This could take a bizarre twist if he or she is an above-average anal-retentive. This sign is not above stalking you to prove he or she still loves you. Virgo stalkers can be creepy because they *look* so average. The best places to keep a sharp watch are at the laundromat and in the housewares aisle at your favorite department store.

As with the other Earth signs, Taurus and Capricorn, it's rare that Virgo will dump you. Once any Earth sign plants him- or herself, they would rather hang around and make you miserable than move on. In the unlikely event this happens, you will be subjected to a laundry list of your faults, even probably including the way you fold your underwear.

Get even by inviting your ex over for a let-bygones-be-bygones dinner and don't clean house for a week (or two) beforehand. Happily watch as he or she begins to twitch over the sink full of dishes and grease-spattered stove. Offer microwave reheated fast food, lick the tip of the mustard bottle, and laugh like hell as Ms./Mr. Clean bolts for the door.

Keeping One

All Virgos are service oriented. What they lack in overt romance they make up in devotion to keeping your home ordered, the checkbook balanced, and nutritious meals prepared. Virgo is a work-oriented sign, and that includes spending a great deal of time and effort making your relationship work. If you're looking for a blatant romantic, you will be disappointed. If you are looking for a faithful partner who is truly concerned about your health and home life, you couldn't ask for much better. Virgos are programmed to serve. He or she truly wants to be your partner and helpmate and takes that part about *in sickness and in health* seriously. Virgos are the absolute best at nursing you back to health whether you've got the flu or a major illness.

Keeping yours happy doesn't take much. The first thing you need is a deaf ear. Sometimes, you just have to nod and smile and pretend you are listening. Virgos can't help criticizing, because they truly believe they were put on Earth to make everything better. They are just as self-critical, so help keep yours calm with tummy-soothing herbs and peppermint tea. Stimulants are not good for the Virgin's already overworked nervous system. A glass of acid-reduced orange juice and a citrus-based shower gel will perk up their sluggish morning metabolism.

Patience is the keyword when dealing with your Virgo's sexual side. Anxiety may drive a Water sign to the bedroom in search of sexual healing, but stress acts like a cold shower on a Virgin. Your task is to help yours feel like everything's under control, or at least fixable before he or she will even think about a romp under the covers. This is why spontaneous sex on the sofa while the laundry is waiting to be folded is better left to a more uninhibited Gemini or Aquarius.

Your Virgo is as hot as any other sign. He or she has a sense of order about sex just like everything else. Virgos are as hedonistic as the rest of us, but have to work up to any sort of spontaneous sexual combustion. For example, Virgo wants to learn about, talk about, and test a variety of positions first, after building up the trust factor with you, then he or she will discover his or her own libido and lust factor. And hold on to the bedpost when that happens. You are liable to be experimenting for a long, long time.

MoonLight or GasLight?

When I was married I did the wash a lot. I liked folding Sean's underwear. I like mating socks. You know what I love? I love taking the lint out of the lint screen.

MADONNA (AUGUST 16)

VIRGO MOON / LEO SUN

A Virgo Moon could be called the Mother-in-Law Moon. Mercury's nervous irritability turns the Moon into a rationalizing, self-contained, emotionally cold character. Nothing is good enough for the Virgo Moon. They are just as self-critical and usually have low self-esteem. This results in a character that feels either like the world's biggest failure or too good to waste his or her time on the world. You can spot a Virgo Moon by the trail of failed relationships and number of death threats he or she has amassed.

Virgo Moons are *compelled* to offer criticism on every nuance of life. He or she is also compelled to worry about every aspect of life. Even the most happy-go-lucky Leo will have a critical streak a mile wide with this placement. Virgo Moons drive people away faster than a soused Pisces with a karaoke machine.

Virgo Moons are preoccupied with routine, health, and work, not necessarily in that order. His or her idea of conversation is to issue orders, warnings, and a stream of negative consciousness. They are obsessed with the niggling details of life that the rest of us never notice.

Neither sex has much sentiment and both treat relationships like business arrangements. Both are critical, argumentative, and just plain cold-blooded. Virgo Moons are domestic but romantically superficial, melancholy, scheming, and often full of ulterior motives. This Moon can drive a saint to murder and a sane person to divorce court. These people usually like solitude, which is good, for most of them end up alone. He or she can be like a nasty hermit who hates the world.

Author Theodore Dreiser was speaking eloquently from his Virgo Moon when he said, "Life is a goddamned, stinking, treacherous game and nine hundred and ninety-nine men out of a thousand are bastards." He would have known. Dreiser, who was also a Virgo Sun, left his first wife, and had continual affairs throughout his lifetime, including one with a sixteen-year-old girl when he was forty. When his wife died, he married his cousin, with whom he'd been involved for twenty years.

It's not that Double Virgos aren't sexy (think Sean Connery), but you can also freeze ice cream on one's ass (think Robert Blake). Cold, calculating, and ritualistic, these are the characters that, when you say, "What a lovely sunrise," answer, "Well, it's technically not risen until it's completely above the horizon line." And the day goes downhill from there.

The Taurus/Virgo combination results in an intellectual Bull who thinks excitement means more than flipping to the sports channel. They like independent partners who can live without flowers and candlelight. Capricorn/Virgos could mate with Spock and are born complete with slide rule, dictionary, and precise time frame for climbing the ladder of success.

Impulsiveness turns to ice in the Aries/Virgo duo. This results in a relentless disciplinarian, one with nervous tics because wild Mars is caught under the heel of analytical Mercury. Leo/Virgos are conflicted. Leo just wants to have fun, Virgo wants to scrub the toilets. The resulting irritable inner psyche explodes every so often. Buy several sets of cheap glassware. The Sagittarius/Virgo combo produces Mr. Blathering Nonsense meets Ms. I-Hate-That-Necktie. They stay home more, but you'll soon wish he or she would hit the road—or go play *in* the road.

The Gemini/Virgo duo has a mouth that could stop time and a precise talent for ripping your heart out. The life of a

Libra/Virgo is like that of the *The Princess and the Pea* fairytale. Libra loves to party. Virgo finds the one flaw that ruins every relationship, then wonders why nothing ever lasts. The Aquarius/Virgo has a mind like a steel trap and jaws to match. Both sexes are extremely outspoken, so you'd better be able to take the criticism.

Cancer/Virgos are nice and can smell a lie a mile away. These boys and girls have an underdog appearance with a bulldog attitude. In one of the Universe's infinite mysteries, the Scorpio/Virgo combination seems to take the edges off both these signs. Less prone to affairs, and vitriolic comments, more prone to steadfast devotion, this one can make you rich. They are sexy, sweet, and kinky. Beware of Pisces/Virgo; there's a method to this Fish's madness. They need routine, work, home, and a drink. Life is a rut with an occasional trip to the beach. Intellect wins over emotion every time.

Mars Is Afflicted

I hate flowers. I paint them because they're cheaper than models and they don't move.

GEORGIA O'KEEFFE (November 15)
VIRGO MARS/SCORPIO SUN

Anytime Mars lands in Earth, his natural energy is restricted. In Virgo, Mars becomes mean mouthed, touchy, and as thrifty with passion as money. Here is the perfectionist who won't stop analyzing, picking, and suggesting until you are tweaked to his or her satisfaction—which is never. Virgo's self-critical eye becomes more aggressive and depressing in Mars. These natives often strive for a perfection they know they will never reach. Sexually, this aspect is dispassionate and vies with Capricorn for the least romantic Mars configuration. Unemotional doesn't mean celibate. It means you may get hung up on a character who gets off as much on doing calculus as doing you.

Female Virgo Mars

It's not that you aren't sexy. Think of Aquarius Kim Novak, Gemini Brooke Shields. It's that you're exceptionally fussy. You want the perfect job, house, family, kids (if you choose to have them), life, and partner. You'll pick your way across the zodiac to find such a person. Mars in Virgo fuels the fires of your discontent with every aspect of life and drives you to succeed in reordering everything to your little nit-picking heart's desire. The one that can hold your attention longer than that first scan for food spots on his or her shirt will be just as critical and cranky as you. You were born to argue and, for Virgo Mars, that's a quantum leap ahead of boogie.

Male Virgo Mars

Practical, thorough, analytical Virgo meets headstrong, passionate Mars. The result is that you are passionate about getting your facts straight, before *always* having the last word. You love to be right and will go to any amount of preparation to see that you are on any subject or any occasion. Your earthy, perfectionist nature can lead you to become health obsessed, or at least a guy who loves to pump iron. Think of Cancers Sly Stallone and Richard Simmons. Your ideal lover probably doesn't exist. However, one who is as fanatical as you about being perfect, perfectly beautiful, and perfectly correct stands the best chance.

Venus Is a Nympho

I have never done a nude scene. There's not a nude photo of me floating around anywhere.

Loni Anderson (August 5)
VIRGO VENUS/LEO SUN

Venus is no nympho in Virgo. Here, she is the goddess of tidy, the queen of clean, the empress of impeccable. Whether saint or sinner, she outwardly observes the proprieties at all times. Virgo's discriminating eye is turned toward inspecting potential lovers from the outside in and has the uncanny ability to spot a phony a mile away. In Virgo, Venus is a lint-picker lover who subtly grades your grooming habits, choice of wine, and taste in music. This placement also bestows a youthful appearance, and demeanor, well into old age. Venus Virgo is preoccupied with practical beauty that starts with a healthy mind and body—yours. This is the lover or friend who will drag you to the health food store, the gym, and the doctor to ensure you are eating well, exercising properly, and getting regular checkups.

Female Virgo Venus

You believe that beauty comes from within and are more likely to spend your day perusing the latest youth elixirs and vitamin regimes than searching for makeup to cover your freckled nose. One of the zodiac's Earth mothers, you have a "mother hen" side to your nature and constantly dispense health advice to lovers and strangers alike. Your cool exterior hides an earthy sexuality that delights and surprises those whom you consider worthy. Think of Libra Deborah Kerr, Leo Jennifer Lopez. You need a partner who can heal the sick and raise an herbal garden. Too often, you end up playing nursemaid to a hypochondriac with nervous indigestion.

Male Virgo Venus

You are a practical lover who can fix dinner and the sink and balance the checkbook without wrinkling your nattily pressed pants. However, your tendency to try to repair your many unsteady romantic relationships in the same analytical manner often backfires. Although you prefer a relationship, you are quite capable of living alone because you really like yourself better than anyone else you know. You have a boyish charm, laugh lines instead of wrinkles, and a youthful appearance no matter what your age. Think of Leo Kevin Spacey, Libra Johnny Mathis. Your ideal lover is like the character from *Practical Magic,* an earthy, sensible, happy witch who conjures mystical remedies and love potions that keep your little pointed head spinning.

Fatal Attractions

Virgo/Aries—Selfless, discriminating bookworm who's having second thoughts about living for sense and order seeks rash, needy, rake-about-town for one-night stand and reality check.

Virgo/Taurus—Critical perfectionist tightwad with permanent indigestion and compulsion to clean toilets seeks earthy homebody who loves to eat, watch TV in bed, and have safe sex. True love guaranteed.

Virgo/Gemini—Fun-challenged nitpicker who would rather talk about sex than do the deed seeks irrational chatterbox with string of failed affairs to quiz, analyze, and drive bonkers. Actual sex optional.

Virgo/Cancer—Security-craving nervous Nellie with portable pharmacopoeia seeks long-suffering martyr type to serve, spoon-feed, and mother. Possible soul mates.

Virgo/Leo—Perfectly perfect person with neatly typed five-year plan seeks party magnet whose idea of organization means finding the car keys for desperately incompatible, micromini relationship.

Virgo/Virgo—Methodical workaholic with permanent rash and no cuticles seeks same for endless-but-polite criticizing, midnight discussions on the advantages of buying in bulk, and absorbing sexual exploration. Happiness guaranteed if you don't nitpick.

Virgo/Libra—Chronically anxious procrastinator with doctoral in folk medicine who loves sex, home, and regular bedtimes seeks chronically vapid swinger with unequaled talent for dissipation for pre–destined-to-doom affair.

Virgo/Scorpio—Shy, caring, and seriously underestimated sex toy who can balance the books *and* ring your chimes seeks surly-but-sensitive power broker to seduce, surprise, and send to carnal heaven.

Virgo/Sagittarius—Monogamous stay-at-home with talent for small talk seeks long-winded, serial-affair champ to nitpick into the next millennium. Just joking. This won't last through the appetizers.

Virgo/Capricorn—Neat freak with baby face and calculator brain who loves large bank accounts seeks impeccable, coolly reserved pro who's scaling the corporate ladder, for exceptional romance, polite disagreements, and solid gold future.

Virgo/Aquarius—Meticulous caregiver with sensible shoes and attitude to match who's hooked on the niggling details seeks space case with invisible friends, army boots, and cavalier attitude toward sex for short romp in the hay.

Virgo/Pisces—Routine-loving and well-organized coupon clipper with need for security seeks slapdash romance addict with no money, no job, and little future to mold, prod, and push toward success. Glorious sex. Iffy morning after.

Scoring

Best Bets—Cancer, Taurus, Capricorn
Just Good Friends—Virgo, Libra
Please Shoot Yourself Now—Aries, Gemini, Sagittarius,
    Aquarius, Leo
The Dark Horse—Scorpio, Pisces

Valiant and Visceral Virgos

Ingrid Bergman
Billy Ray Cyrus
Hugh Grant
Beyoncé Knowles
Sophia Loren
Pink
Jada Pinkett
Jason Priestly
LeAnn Rimes
Raquel Welch

Chapter Eight

LIBRA

September 23–October 22

You're So Vain

Element: Air. Whispers hot, breathy come-ons in one ear and cold, faultfinding turnoffs in the other.

Quality: Cardinal. Leading home wrecker of the zodiac.

Symbol: The Scales. Balancing three clandestine affairs and several casual-sex partners while planning *the* wedding of the year assures a hands-down victory as duplicitous lover of the century.

Ruler: Venus, the goddess of fickle pleasures.

Romantic Idol: Blanche Deveraux *(Golden Girls)*.

Romantic Style: Convoluted.

Favorite Pickup Line: "Do you think this color looks good on me?"

Dream First Date: Impossibly gorgeous, fabulously wealthy jet-setter appears at local watering hole. Sweeps aside the crowd. Instantly proposes marriage and a life free of all decisions.

Erogenous Zone: Butt. Lays on his or hers while you do all the work.

Sexual Quirk: Any position is fine, as long as they can see a mirror.

Romancing the Sign

I explained to him that I had simple tastes and didn't want anything ostentatious, no matter what it cost me.
Art Buchwald (October 20)

Libra is the glamour puss of the zodiac. Hollywood is the Libra capital of the world where you can find gaggles of them all looking like refugees from an experimental cosmetic surgery lab. Those Venus dimples attract lovers like Gemini attract divorce attorneys. Look closely at that sweet smile, though, and you'll find it's really a smirk. Libra's pouting Venusian lips are permanently pursed in petulant disdain.

Libras believe in romance-by-osmosis. Like octopi, they affix at least one part of themselves to a part of you whenever they are near. He or she will think it's cute to sit on your lap at dinner and eat from the same fork. If you are a clinging Cancer, or insecure Virgo, you will probably love this behavior. If you are a space-sparing Capricorn or don't-touch-me-until-I-tell-you-to Scorpio, Libra's up-close and personal style is likely to send you reeling for the nearest exit.

Sagittarius Christopher Plummer said that working with Libra Julie Andrews was "like being hit over the head with a Valentine." If one's after you, expect that famous Libra charm to be turned on full force. Soon you'll feel like a rabbit being hypnotized by a cobra as these human scales swing up and down, back and forth, bending you to his or her will. Mr./Ms. Libra comes on all fair play and understanding. But, understand this: Libras compromise *only* when it's to their advantage. They sulk if you don't accept them exactly as he or she is, but will endlessly analyze you, finding fault with nearly everything you eat, think, and wear. Plus they expect you to adhere to the list of improvements they carefully create for your benefit. Don't confuse this trait with Virgo's incessant nit-picking. Virgins are motivated by the belief that they are helping you. Libras measure themselves by the social acceptability of their date. Since they hang with anybody who will have them, this is a moot point.

Sexually, Libra is more interested in setting the scene (just like a movie) and how he or she will look in it, than in doing the deed. Hair, makeup, music, and lighting—all must be perfectly arranged or your Libra lover will lose interest faster than a Sagittarius on a trip through the Bible belt. Libra believes in give-and-take, but is so hung up on equality in bed, you could find yourself screwing in four-four time because he or she is counting the in-and-outs to make sure neither of you is short-stroked.

Astrologically, Libra has been called the marriage sign because those born under the sign of the scales feel out of balance without a partner. What it fails to reveal is that it doesn't have to be Libra's marriage. Partners of friends and relatives work just as well. Labeled as eternal romantics, these boys and girls are actually relationship junkies who need to feel another body to feel complete, and anyone will do in a pinch. That's why they are king and queen of the backseat quickie.

They thrive on lovers' quarrels, secret betrayals, open betrayals, family feuds, and general pot stirring to keep every relationship fomenting. Libra's ideal lover is a combination caretaker and puppet who lives to obey, pacify, and capitulate. Libra Brigitte Bardot's real life has been one tempestuous disaster after another: four marriages, one child she left for relatives to raise, three suicide attempts, and a movie career that ended in 1973 with the crude, and embarrassing, *Colinot, the Skirt Puller-Upper.* Bardot spent the next twenty years publicly fighting for animal rights and asserting herself as an activist concerned with human rights. Privately, she haunted the world's trendiest discos where her prey was any willing, handsome, and much younger man. Her two-decade series of one-night stands ended in 1992 with her fourth marriage to a controversial French politician, purported to be a right-wing bigot. In typical Libra fashion, Bardot chose a powerful, rich protector to keep her in style, while conveniently forgetting he stood for everything she supposedly opposes.

As soon as you hop on one side of the scale, Libra will start piling his or her criticisms on the opposite side. The amount of ass kissing, ego stroking, and changing yourself to meet his or her ever-changing criteria that you are prepared to give will be in direct proportion to the length of your happy life with Lovely Libra.

'Til Death Do Us Part

My mother-in-law broke up my marriage. My wife came home one day and found me in bed with her.

LENNY BRUCE (OCTOBER 13)

Catching One

Think "we" when you set your sights on Libra. This is the sign of partnership and whether it's for an hour, or a lifetime, Libra needs to think that *you* are constantly thinking about him or her. Libras obsess about whether or not you are obsessing over them, and frequently sulk if they think you are thinking of anything else—like whether or not you need surgery.

The best way to get one interested is to titillate with lots of flattery that's short on sincerity and long on sexual innuendo. Libra will know that it's bullshit, but will still think you are after his or her body. They can't help it. All Libras were born with their vain-meter stuck on nauseate.

This includes a fetish for their looks. To impress this appearance-wacky sign on the first date, bring along a small tote filled with lotion, cologne, a comb, mirror (a must), tweezers, mouthwash, and a portable hair dryer you can plug into the car's cigarette lighter. Libra will adore that you are prepared to preen as much as he or she does and it won't cross that scattered little brain that you are just trying to get laid. This is one sign that will lie down for the perfunctory "I love you," even if it's for a quickie in the backseat while the band's on break.

Libras like low lighting that flatters the complexion, shades of blue and lavender, and to dance. That's why so many hang out in bars. Venus gave Libra her hand mirror and a taste for luxury. Libra was so engrossed in kissing the mirror that Venus' sense of perception flew right out the window. That's the reason Libra equates flattery with refinement, and expensive with good taste.

This social sign will appreciate dinner at the trendiest restaurant you can afford and dancing afterward at the hottest spot in town. You must take extra care with your personal appearance as well. Torn Levis and a Grateful Dead T-shirt may suit a comatose Pisces or a combat-boot wearing Capricorn, but Libra insists on style. Of course, Libra equates style with substance, so it doesn't matter if you are Freddie the Forger, as long as you are dressed to kill and know the maître d' personally.

When you are ready to bed-boogie, remember Hollywood and set the scene. Wine, candlelight, or a blue nightlight glowing softly will loosen Libra's libido. Play a sexy CD and slow dance around the apartment. When you head for the sheets, make sure you aren't ripping off either his or her clothes, or yours. Take it slow and easy and use a light touch. Even male Libras don't like to be manhandled.

Libras like sexy, not trashy (this isn't Gemini) talk in bed, but don't ask too many questions, especially if it's your first encounter. Libras are great at small talk, but have a rotten time discussing their real feelings. That's because they can't decide if they have any and/or what those might be. This is another reason they so easily blurt out the *L*-word; it's part of the dialogue in the love scene he or she has already rehearsed in front of the bathroom mirror.

Surviving One

Losing a Libra is like losing a boomerang. You send him or her packing and he or she reappears on your doorstep. Libras bond to everyone they have ever screwed. In the Libra mind, this gives him or her the right to invade your privacy, pass judgment on your new lover, and blame you for everything that goes wrong in his or her future relationships, for the rest of your life. Blaming you for everything that went wrong in your relationship is a given, even if you kicked your Libra out for screwing around on you.

Libras are worse than Aries for playing the I-don't-want-you-but-no-one-else-can-have-you game. These selfish, shallow, conceited vacillators will take months, sometimes years to decide whether or not they even like you. It doesn't matter whether you're already married or in a committed partnership.

Libra seldom makes the first move to leave, unless he or she has your replacement waiting in the wings. Even then, both sexes will try to keep each of you dangling as long as possible. He or she will lie to you that the marked decrease in attention is due to a need to think about the relationship, while telling the piece on the side he or she is trying to break it to you gently.

Bearing this in mind, make it easy on yourself and get eloquently even at the same time. When you tire of the constant need for flattery, inability to make a decision as simple as toast or cereal for breakfast, and incessant fascination with his or her appearance, simply introduce Libra to one of your Leo friends and let nature take its course. Then call that weird-but-fascinating Aquarian you met at Chez Trendy last weekend while waiting for Libra to finish flossing after dinner.

Should you actually want a Libra back, refuse him or her access to your life. Don't do *let's be friends.* Don't write, call, or e-mail. Do be seen around town having loads of fun. Do buy some new clothes, get a new hairstyle, and make sure you are seen dancing the night away with a happy-go-lucky Sagittarius or playing footsy with a winsome Cancer. Soon, a shadow will appear in the open doorway of your favorite hangout. At that precise moment, *your* song will fill the air. In another moment, you'll see your ex, in his or her perfectly coordinated outfit, moving slowly through the crowd, blank faced, eyes haunted, a tear glistening on one cheek, and hand outstretched to lead you to the dance floor. Fade to black.

Keeping One

No, you are not doomed to a life of constant frustration with a sign that can't make up its mind to save its soul. Libra's scales represent partnerships of all kinds. When one side is empty, Libra is of little use to anyone, including him- or herself. It's only when the scales are in motion, balancing and counter-balancing everything from minor daily issues to major crisis moments, that Libra can truly function.

Air signs are the communicators of the Universe. Gemini writes. Aquarius lectures. Both can function alone as long as they have either a good circle of friends or an attentive audience. However, Libra needs human interaction. They are good conversationalists, love to hear and tell stories, and believe in talking out problems. They write letters and notes and usually keep journals listing all their unspoken desires and deep, dark secrets. If you are inclined to snoop, do so at your own risk for if you get caught, he or she will never trust you again. Ever.

Libra is a class act. Diplomatic and harmonious, these folks instinctively know how to put other people at ease and just what to say in any situation. Yes, you may have to make the decision to hire a gardener because your Libra isn't absolutely, positively sure you can afford one. But then, Libra is never absolutely, positively sure of anything. Look on the bright side. You'll rarely suffer the fallout from a rash decision as you would with an Aquarius or a Leo.

Keep your Libra happy with lots of thoughtful attention. Your Libra will love anything that includes just the two of you. He or she will never tire of that romantic weekend away, whether you are celebrating your first year together or your fiftieth. This is one sign that will be a true partner to you in every sense of the word. Libra will work as hard as you, share household and child-rearing duties, and will give as much as he or she takes.

In bed, this means that Libra is into pleasing you as much, or more, than being pleased. This gentle sign is tender, acquiescing, and, with the right partner, gives new meaning to the term *sexual healing.*

Libras love to spend money, especially if it's someone else's. But even if you don't have unlimited funds, small gifts such as scented candles or a new shirt you bought on sale will prove that you were thinking of your Libra lover, and that's what counts. Never ask these dimpled darlings what they want for a birthday, an anniversary, or Christmas. First, neither sex will be able to choose between the latest R&B CD and a luxurious cashmere sweater. Second, if you haven't paid enough attention to already know, shame on you.

Balance is the key to a Libra's heart. If yours is a driven, career-type, plan quiet dinners and frequent weekend getaways. If he or she is trapped in a Dilbert cubicle, go dancing or to a favorite sporting event. Or just fill the bathtub with herbal mud and wrestle that stress away.

MoonLight or GasLight?

I cry a lot. My emotions are very close to the surface, a pustule of emotion that explodes into a festering cesspool of depression.

NICOLAS CAGE (JANUARY 7)
LIBRA MOON/CAPRICORN SUN

In Libra, Venus' dark side influences the Moon's emotional structure, and these natives frequently exhibit extreme jealousy, selfishness, and moral turpitude. A Libra Moon enhances every sign's need for social interaction plus Libra's inclination toward double-dealing, search for the perfect party, and poor judgment in the choice of partners. It also adds an inexplicable charm to the most stolid Sun sign and the ability to attract just about anyone. This is the Charming Bastard Moon, but don't let the male reference mislead you. Women with this placement are just as libidinous, unreliable, and prone to the use of head games to obtain the object of their desire.

Remember, doubles of any sign magnify the good, the bad, and the ugly traits. Double Libras will overlook brains, character, and soul for a beautiful face and/or buffed body. These insidious manipulators are so charming you may find yourself signing over your home, car, and savings account, but not caring, even when you are walking to the homeless shelter for a free meal. Rock and roll's wild man and Double Libra Jerry Lee Lewis is a classic example. Self-abuse with liquor and drugs, an appalling personal life, and a career that swings as crazily as he does all attest to the dangers of an out-of-control Libra Moon.

The Gemini/Libra duo is superficial, shallow, and in love with love. Don't scratch too deep looking for substance, or you'll let the air out of this blow-up doll and be left with nothing but a pile of expensive clothing and dazzling white teeth. Aquarius/Libra accepts everything, believes everything, tries everything—and everyone. They like twenty-year engagements. Your life passes by while this one chases every rainbow.

Saccharine on the surface, sulfur underneath, the Cancer/Libra can out-manipulate a Scorpio on a vengeance kick, and won't hesitate to tie you to the bedpost to protect and control you. Scorpio/Libra wants a romance-novel affair, complete with happy ending. If you can be faithful, nurturing, and attentive, you'll hit one of the Universe's jackpots. Pisces/Libras are perpetually absentminded dreamers who are permanently out of touch with reality. But, they can turn any hovel into a den of libidinous excess.

Aries/Libra requires a beautiful, rich caregiver. Don't

bother. After he or she spends your money and calls attention to each crow's-foot as it appears, you'll be left paying off the credit cards while Mr./Ms. I-must-find-true-love sniffs out the next prospect. A Libra Moon softens boisterous Leo's need for attention. These cats are still bossy, but so cute you won't mind. They often end up rich and powerful. Sagittarius/Libra makes a great party-hopping bed-buddy. Long on burning the candle at both ends and short on the desire to settle down results in multiple marriages, plus dual careers to pay the child support and alimony.

The totally Venus-ruled combo of Taurus/Libra produces one of the nicest persons in the Universe. Both sexes are natural-born peacemakers who can charm the wallet off a Capricorn. The Virgo/Libra blend wants to serve, protect, analyze, and criticize. Good cop material except that he or she is phobic about anything dirty, seedy, or untidy. The Capricorn/Libra blend believes in love at first sight. The Goat's determination is turned toward living in the fast lane and the result is a seductive charmer prone to self-destruction.

Mars Is Afflicted

There is nothing to winning, really. That is, if you happen to be blessed with a keen eye, an agile mind, and no scruples whatsoever.

ALFRED HITCHCOCK (AUGUST 13)
LIBRA MARS/LEO SUN

In Libra, Mars becomes captain of the debate team. Whether the conversation is diplomatic argument or aggressive verbal combat depends upon which side of the Scale this person awoke. Like Dr. Jeykll and Mr. Hyde, the Libra Mars personality can change without warning from harmony-seeking charmer to confrontational harpy. Mars' passion becomes intellectual versus physical. Verbal confrontation excites as much as physical contact. These natives are often sexually detached and can be old-fashioned in their sense of morality and sexual encounters, which doesn't mean they aren't sexy, but if you like spontaneity and/or swinging from the chandeliers, better stick to Leo or Gemini.

Female Libra Mars

You desire to be in sync with your lover at all times and are prepared to lecture your loved one until he or she goes deaf to achieve this harmony. Whether you are subtle and soft-spoken, as was Capricorn Marlene Dietrich, or subtle as a crutch like Scorpio Roseanne Barr, you are compelled to discuss, analyze, and chew over every aspect of your many relationships like a cow chomping its cud. You may say you want a socially conscious and sensitive genius to help you right the world's wrongs. But, an artistic type who is willing to share everything and let you call the shots is your ideal.

Male Libra Mars

You may have a wild heart, but you will also have a respectful, gentlemanly persona. Think of Capricorn Elvis Presley, Sagittarius John Malkovich. You believe in sharing your dreams and expect your partner to be willing to talk out problems. Even the most passionate feelings are filtered through your rational perspective, and therein lies the rub. Or lack of it. When bored, you think it's fun to pick apart your loved one. Your ideal lover can keep the verbal sparing at just below the boiling point and the bedtime talk titillating.

Venus Is a Nympho

I have great faith in fools. My friends call it self-confidence.
EDGAR ALLAN POE (JANUARY 19)
LIBRA VENUS/CAPRICORN SUN

Venus is at home in Libra and this aspect is considered a rare astrological gift. The Libra Venus person is usually talented, lucky, and creative. Unfortunately, few succeed in tapping these abilities because they are too self-indulgent and lazy. Whether connected to a shy or an outgoing Sun sign, the Libra Venus person will literally spend hours in front of the mirror checking his or her appearance at every opportunity. These are the guys and dolls that never have a hair out of place, or a piece of lint anywhere. Finding a flake of dandruff will send one into shock. Libra Venus is a shameless flirt, rarely modest, and probably the least likely of the Venus aspects to indulge in that nasty habit of self-criticism. Even if these creatures don't have it, they flaunt it anyway.

Female Libra Venus

For every Scorpio Grace Kelly or Libra Billie Jean King who actually makes something of him- or herself, there are thousands of Libra Venus females who spend their lives in pursuit of the right shade of nail polish. You can be more concerned with how you look than whether you can pay the rent. Image is everything and, although you desire a man who can see through yours, *and* afford your mania for power shopping, you frequently end up with broke dreamers who mistake your wicked excesses for affluence and think you are going to feed their dreams and foot the bills.

Male Libra Venus

You have a sinful sensuality. You brazenly ignore your own faults, think entirely too much of yourself, and are so devilishly charming that neither of those wicked little foibles seem to bother anyone. Think of Leo Patrick Swayze, Virgo Hugh Grant. In public, your partner must be impeccable, beautiful, and elegant. However, what really turns you on are unpredictable changes. Your ideal lover is one who talks like a Ph.D., balls like a bunny, and cooks like a Taurus. A multiple-personality Gemini whose imagination has run amok could settle you down.

Fatal Attractions

Libra/Aries—Mental maniac into head games and one-dimensional romance seeks self-centered head case looking for a good fight. Guaranteed great sex, trite conversation, and fun until the money runs out.

Libra/Taurus—Passive-aggressive-but-diplomatic swinger who's home just often enough to shower, grab a snack, and get a quickie seeks hooked-on-Emeril drudge who is offended by any sexual encounter less than three hours long. Sounds doomed, but if we compromise, this could be love at second sight.

Libra/Gemini—Hypersensitive, selfish player with gift of gab and titanium MasterCard seeks hyperactive, selfish player with motor mouth and line of credit, for life, love, and lust in the fast lane. Happiness guaranteed.

Libra/Cancer—Luxury-loving spendthrift who's hooked on romance and needs a mommy seeks thrifty caretaker with cozy love nest, large savings account, and ability to serve, cling, and protect for a classic movie-style romance, complete with flowers and champagne.

Libra/Leo—Opinionated party-hound who needs to be worshipped and adored seeks same for the romance from a sci-fi horror flick—*Clash of the Giant Human Egos.* We can be happy, if you have enough money.

Libra/Virgo—Petulant, indecisive harpy, blind to any opinion but my own seeks incessant nit-picking neurotic with no conception that varied options exist for baffling, boring, and terminal miscommunication. The only thing hard here will be our feelings.

Libra/Libra—Lunch-bunch groupie with amoral social conscience seeks waffling, wobbly relationship junkie who understands. Must have own mirror.

Libra/Scorpio—Vain, superficial tease with death wish seeks serious-as-a-heart-attack control freak for dangerous liaison behind the tattoo parlor.

Libra/Sagittarius—Scamp-about-town with exquisite taste, impeccable manners, and flare for sophisticated love seeks energetic, cute slob with the manners of Big Foot, Ma and Pa Kettle's sense of style, and a sexual proclivity for how many how fast for amusing one-hour stand.

Libra/Capricorn—Selfish, spoiled brat will preen and dance naked for Daddy Warbucks type who's willing to toss conservative money and dispense liberal spankings.

Libra/Aquarius—Vibrant and witty conversationalist who breathes romance, listens to Barry Manilow, and thinks lovers should be joined at the hip seeks kind but attention-challenged loner who prefers listening to space noise, tinkering in the basement, and separate vacations.

Libra/Pisces—Selfish-but-charming taker who swings both ways and refuses to acknowledge the seamy side of life seeks selfless-but-whiny doormat who continually spouts drunken observations about the human condition for a short-term but excruciating exercise in futility.

Scoring

Best Bets—Gemini, Leo, Aries, Aquarius
Just Good Friends—Libra, Sagittarius
Please Shoot Yourself Now—Taurus, Cancer, Scorpio,
  Capricorn
The Dark Horse—Virgo, Pisces

Lovely and Licentious Libras

Matt Damon
Fran Drescher
Eminem
Charlton Heston
John Lennon
Jessica Rabbit
Tim Robbins and Susan Sarandon
Will Smith
Gwen Stefani
Sting

Chapter Nine

SCORPIO

October 23–November 21

I Put a Spell on You

Element: Water. Steam heat is soothing, healing, and purifying. It can also asphyxiate, scald, and parboil.

Quality: Fixed, on secrets. What you see is seldom what you get.

Symbol: The Scorpion. Even making love is a duel to the death.

Ruler: Mars and Pluto. In this dynamic duo, Mars builds you up with megahot, intense passion, then Pluto-the-Destructor dropkicks your heart into the next county. Just for fun.

Romantic Idol: Michael Corleone.

Romantic Style: Sarcastic head case.

Favorite Pickup Line: "Hi."

Dream First Date: Locks eyes with a beautiful stranger, has ten or twelve hours of nonstop, ultrawicked, steamy, passionate sex. No names or words are exchanged. Stranger is never seen again. Scorpio has another lost love to mourn.

Erogenous Zone: Sex organs. Has terminal sexual heat rash. No cure. Seeks frequent treatment.

Sexual Quirk: Carries an emergency kit of sex toys in the trunk of the car.

Romancing the Sign

I don't play a good victim, so I'm always the nasty little guy.
Danny DeVito (November 17)

You know how you shiver with fear at the idea of doing something extremely dangerous, but feel compelled to proceed? Falling for a Scorpio is just like that shudder of terrified excitement. The legendary magnetism of this sign is real. A Scorpion in love is erotically powerful, amazingly cunning, and totally dangerous.

Scorpios are the stuff of romance-novel characters: strong, silent men who'll crush you against their chests, mesmerize you with those snake-veiled eyes, and sneer just before kissing you so passionately your bikinis melt. Women sexual sorceresses who will settle for nothing less than total control before allowing you to succumb to their ability to make you stare and babble.

Once the Scorpion fixes his or her beady little eyes on you and starts inching across the room, stinger poised, you are in for an all-out assault. It doesn't matter whether or not you are either available or agreeable to his or her advances. Scorpio is prepared to wait as long as it takes. If you are enthralled, entranced, fixated, and/or just plain horny for a Scorpion, you must understand a few crucial facts. Remember the old saying about *love and war*? Well, to a Scorpio love *is* war. The bedroom is their battlefield, and sex is the weapon they wield.

Scorpios don't play; they strategize. They don't flirt; they obsess. They frequently use sex to seduce and control. Don't let the so-called *sunny* ones fool you. Inside every Scorpio is a mass murder waiting to happen. They don't do moderation. A Scorpio can withhold sex longer than a Pisces can watch *Gilligan* reruns, then switch to insatiable mode in an instant. If you question either action, Mr./Ms. Scorpio will take perverse delight in verbally trying to slash your ego to bits.

Scorpions, including the celibate ones, and those do exist, are fascinated by sex. Even if yours wouldn't dream of participating, he or she is curious about all things sexual. Porno, prostitution, videos, books, everything up to and including clinical research and psychology connected with sexual issues. Shere Hite, Larry Flynt, and Robert Mapplethorpe are classic examples of the span of Scorpio's interest. Hite was the researcher who looked at it from the scientific viewpoint; Flynt was the master pornographer who turned it into a multimillion-dollar career; and Mapplethorpe's exquisitely stark photography captured its palpable sensuality and raw emotion. Toss in televangelist Pat Buchanan, who thinks any style but missionary deserves a one-way ticket straight to hell, and you have a well-rounded picture of your average Scorpio's psyche.

Scorpios are also fanatical about trust. A Scorpio will dump you faster than an Aquarius rushing to a UFO sighting if he or she even *thinks* you've discussed any intimate aspect of your relationship with family, friends, or the psychic hotline. However, be prepared to have your name and worst secrets spray painted all over town should you happen to piss off this guy or doll.

Even their e-mail is cryptic. Scorpions send messages like "Hope you are well. I'm better, now that the cops have left." What does *that* mean? A Gemini would write a page, a Sagittarius a missive. Scorpio messages are tests to see whether or not you care enough to inquire further. They are maddeningly hard to understand and nearly impossible to predict.

Scorpios have perfected the blank stare. Yell, cry, accuse, or threaten, and your Scorpion will stare at you as if you were a total stranger speaking a foreign language. Don't confuse this with a blank look from a Taurus, Scorpio's opposite sign. Taurus is obtuse. Scorpio is devious. The evil husband in the classic movie *Gaslight* was a totally Scorpionic character. He deliberately planned to drive his wife insane in order to get his hands on the family fortune. And he carried out the plot with a cold cruelty bordering on sadism.

A Scorpio's inner space is a ten-foot circle. Libras never take their hands off you, but Scorpios can recoil at a surprise hug. The safest way to approach one is slowly, first extending your hand for him or her to sniff. Both sexes are suspicious and calculating and have skewed emotional perspectives. A Scorpion's idca of making up after a fight is to stare you into submission, tie you to the bedpost, and have his or her way with you. Normally, this would be an exciting proposition, until you watch those hypnotic eyes go blank as he or she rolls off you just seconds before you are satisfied. You may have forgotten the argument in the heat of passion. Your Scorpio is just revving up into punish-you mode.

'Til Death Do Us Part

Anything I've ever wanted to do, I've done. Anyone I've wanted to be with, I've had.

Calvin Klein (November 19)

Catching One

With Scorpio, flattery and some black underwear will get you laid. Getting one to fall for you isn't quite as easy. All the rumors about the intensity of Scorpio passion are true. However, it isn't just physical sex he or she is after. A Scorpio wants a magical, mystical merging of the soul-mate kind and is prepared to screw his or her way around the planet to find such a person. The dark side is that neither sex will relinquish this behavior pattern after marriage, should he or she decide you are OK but not *the one.* Even if you are his or her true love, the Scorpio fascination with all things sexual can eventually lead to a string of affairs.

Scorpions love a mystery ("Why aren't you falling at my feet?") and a challenge ("I'll show you who's the master/mistress"). Act aloof, but not flip, and be excruciatingly slow to reveal details about yourself, and Scorpio will begin to take the bait. Keep the conversation free of sexual innuendo, but *look* so hot you could melt a Capricorn.

Scorpio colors are purples that pale to lavender, black, shades of gray, and maroon that lightens into pink. Form-fitting silk shirts or dresses, underwear from the adult boutique, or anything made of leather will have the Scorpion you're after churning on the inside. On the outside, you'll still get the blank face or maybe the slightest twitch of interest.

If you are strong enough to hold out until *you* decide when to slap skin the first time, remember that Scorpios love the Madonna/whore routine and danger. Invite your Scorpion to an evening out or over to meet the folks. Then provide a semiprivate place, e.g., a dark alley on your way to the theater or your parents' bathroom just before Sunday dinner. Whisper that you are either wearing a metal g-string from Helga's House of Pain or are sans underwear altogether. This will raise Scorpio's lust-o-meter to fry-the-brain. Don't be shy about unzipping trousers or reaching inside panties as you stare directly into his or her eyes. Scorpio's erogenous zone *is* his or her erogenous zone. Don't dawdle around playing should-I-or-should-I-not-touch-you-there, or you're liable to find yourself sitting on your ass among the garbage cans or shoved into the bathtub as your Scorpio walks off thinking you are trying to pull a power play.

Next time, when you are actually slipping and sliding on those black, satin sheets, sex with a Scorpio is guaranteed to blow both your mind and your body. Role-playing, flavored oils, edible underwear, and sex toys from the harmless to the humongous all will interest a Scorpio. If you want multiple orgasms, this sign can make you come until you depart this mortal plane. If one trusts you, he or she will do anything you ask to give you pleasure. The real secret of Scorpio is that he or she gets off on getting you off. This isn't about selfless love. It's that power thing. But who cares after five or six bouts of endless pleasure?

Sexually, this sign rates a 10. Emotionally, the range swings from 0 upward, and can unexpectedly vacillate, even with a Scorpio who is truly crazy about you. Scorpios become annoyed at too much happiness. This is a combination of fear at having their personal happiness entwined with, or dependent upon, anyone else's, and the understanding, on a soul level, that life is a circle. Most of us experience both abject joy and sorrow during the course of our lifetime. Most of us embrace the joy and forget the sorrow. Not Scorpio. When a Scorpion is too happy, they become suspicious. They wait for the circle to turn and the other shoe to drop. And to ensure they keep the reins of power, he or she is liable to pull some just-plain-mean tricks on you. Verbal abuse, disappearing for a week or longer, and withholding sex even if he or she wants you desperately are just some of the tortuous antics Mr./Ms. Scorpio is capable of putting you and him- or herself through.

So even when you feel you have connected on that soul level, and your Scorpion stays over on the weekends, leaving a toothbrush in your bathroom and a pair of handcuffs in your nightstand, you can't let down your guard. The sex will be intense, passionate, and addicting. The war will go on forever.

Surviving One

Hooking up with a Scorpio is a karmic thing. However, instead of assuming you're being punished, look at it this way: The Universe is doing you a huge favor by making you suffer these emotional extremists, because *any* relationship with a Scorpio is worth one hundred thousand points on the karmic redemption scale. If you manage to spend a lifetime with one, you could jump ahead several reincarnations. Surviving a Scorpion is worth bonus points.

The best way to dump one is with a police escort and a pair of Dobermans. Scorpio will never leave you, even if he or she marries someone else. Don't confuse this with Taurus, who's just too lazy to pack up and move out, or Cancer, who's too afraid. A Scorpion thinks that once he or she has screwed you, you belong to him or her forever. Of course, screwing you over counts, too, because you captured his or her attention that long.

If the police refuse to come to your house and your dog is a dachshund, change the locks and your name and convert as many of your assets to cash as possible. Leave town while your Scorpion is at work. Otherwise, at odd moments for the rest of your life, you're apt to feel the hairs prickle on your neck, as you catch a glimpse of a dark shadow hovering in the nearby bushes. Scorpions are like huge, emotional garbage trucks lumbering along under the weight of every lost love and crises-laden moment of their lives. Both sexes either hate the past or yearn for it.

Cutting off all contact is the only way to totally rid yourself of one. Even one that's dumped you, and is loudly swearing to anyone within earshot about how much he or she hates, reviles, and wishes you every disaster and disease known to mankind, won't stop calling. Or showing up at mutual watering holes. Or *accidentally* appearing anyplace you frequent. You must ignore this. Don't get drawn into a verbal or physical battle. Don't return the occasional phone call. Don't fall for the appearance of friendship. Don't allow your Scorpio ex *any* space in your life whatsoever.

If you do get dumped, he or she will also drag the new lover-victim along as witness to your public humiliation. This is the enigma of Scorpio. Pluto, the planet of destruction, bestows a taste for meaningless cruelty in even the best-hearted Scorpion. They remind me of Beast, in *Beauty and the Beast.* No matter how you scrub them up, they still (emotionally) eat with their hands.

The Scorpio reputation for vengeance is fully justified, and unenlightened ones can wait years for the opportunity to shock and humiliate you or try to ruin your reputation. The enlightened ones will just tell all your mutual friends about your nonexistent boobs and cellulite legs or your tweezers-size penis and nonexistent spine. If you want to get even, you must be prepared to be as nasty. If you need to, take barb lessons from a Gemini or polish up your left-handed compliment repertoire with a Sagittarius. It will be worth ducking a few flying objects to see your ex's eyes narrow and lips purse. If you get that curled lip to twitch a bit, you can take pride in knowing that you've sent a zinger right into his or her shriveled little black heart.

You can also take comfort (while you're taking therapy) in knowing that Scorpios are victims of their own Five-Minute Rule. While you sweated at making the relationship work, Mr./Ms. Scorpio couldn't give five minutes' worth of real effort. Once it's over and you've found yourself a decent Leo, or a faithful Capricorn, the rule instantly reverses, and your ex will think about you *every* five minutes—for the rest of his or her life.

Keeping One

Loving a Scorpio really isn't quite the Herculean task it's alleged to be. It does take a special person with a special knack for understanding. It is a challenge. So is anything worth having, and the love, loyalty, and commitment of a Scorpio is certainly worth having.

Gemini is motivated. Taurus is thrifty. Aries is passionate. Cancer is home loving. Scorpio has all of these traits, plus an inner strength that will see him or her, and you, through any crisis, commotion, or upheaval life hands you. No one is more loyal to a friend or loved one.

The mystery of Scorpio—the intense, penetrating stare, purposeful demeanor, and ability to take charge with a cool competency in any crisis—is an outward reflection of the inner potency of *feeling* connected with Scorpio. Think about Fixed Water. A deep, still well can be cool and lifesaving or stagnant and poisonous. Wells accumulate everything that's tossed in, from wishing coins to murder weapons. Scorpions accumulate emotions in the same manner. And because this is a Fixed sign, the natives virtually never clean out their psyches, forget, truly forgive, or let go.

These boys and girls are wound tighter than Grandma's perm. Scorpios have to *feel* that they have the upper hand.

You can do anything you want to, within reason (this isn't doormat Pisces), as long as your Scorpion feels that he or she is all-powerful, like the *Wizard of Oz*.

Some of your life with Scorpio will seem terribly unfair. He or she can have secrets, locked cabinets, off-limit spaces, and time alone. You must bare your soul and ask permission to go out with your friends. He or she can withdraw, snarl, refuse to eat, or come home with a new car, and you are expected to offer comfort, or stay away, eat alone, and smile despite having no choice about the family vehicle.

Some of your life with Scorpio will be beyond wonderful. He or she will protect you, stand by you, and share every joy and sorrow. Your home will be clean, comfortable, and private. Your love life will be intense, passionate, and frequent. You can rely on the Scorpion's shrewd insight and resourcefulness to see you through the tough times and guide your collective successes during the peak times.

All Scorpions share a love of the unknown and an insatiable curiosity about human behavior. Books, movies, or classes on ancient religions or human behavior will appeal. All love sexy, sensual clothing and silk or satin bedding. Ideally, Scorpio should live near water. Water renews and rejuvenates all of the Water signs, but Scorpio needs to see, smell, and feel fresh, clean, flowing water on a regular basis. It helps them wash away some of the accumulation in that bottomless well of emotion. If you live in a land-bound area, try to get your lover to the nearest river, lake, or ocean several times a year.

It takes a tough, savvy, very special person to love a Scorpion on a permanent basis. If you're up to it, you will be loved with a passion that you read about in novels—one that won't diminish with time.

MoonLight or GasLight?

I bring to my life a certain amount of mess.

FRANCIS FORD COPPOLA (APRIL 7)

SCORPIO MOON/ARIES SUN

Here is the Monster-in-the-Closet Moon. Relentless revenge, obsessions, compulsions, and ulterior motives lay just beneath the surface of a Scorpio Moon native's emotional structure. A sex-is-all attitude pervades every Sun sign, and this placement practically guarantees multiple relationships, divorces, and a generally soap opera–style love life. Whether it's wild abandon with an adored lover or sadistic head games designed to destroy depends on how evolved the Sun sign personality is. A Scorpio Moon's emotions are so secret they frequently hide their own feelings from themselves.

Scorpio's extremism manifests itself here, and this can be a classic study in every adverse trait of Scorpio. All people with this placement can be cunning, cruel, and just plain mean. With a Scorpio Moon desire becomes obsession; anger, revenge; and love, an endless power struggle. There is no subtlety here. Scorpio Moons are on or off, hot or cold. Although they have the ability, rarely will these natives stop to consider the nuances of relationships, opposing viewpoints, etc. They feel you are either for or against them. And when pushed, they can turn into an iceberg even a Leo can't melt.

Even the most benign character will seem to have a force field around him- or herself. There's nothing wishy-washy about a Scorpio Moon native. While most people with this placement are relatively normal, they are all given to plotting and scheming, to get their own way. Most are fairly harmless, but all are capable of turning off their emotions as fast as they turn them on—even if you've been together half a lifetime.

In astrology, the Moon in Scorpio is said to be in its Fall position. Not the season, the descent. Think of the Moon being covered by dark storm clouds so that you are only able to now and then catch glimpses of light. Sex is never far from the mind of a Scorpio Moon native, but his or her passion is often wielded like a double-bladed axe. On the good side, these persons are also capable of gaining the highest spiritual fulfillment, once he or she learns to control the physical passions.

Double Scorpio, Bram Stoker's character, Dracula, embodies the perilous traits of the Scorpio Moon native. The count was strong, forceful, dark, and brooding. Dangerously seductive, he mesmerized his victims, and in the act of loving, destroyed them.

Cancer/Scorpio should give you a chill six miles wide. And that's the berth you should give these folks. Either sex will put the make on you in front of your current lover. Nasty moods. Volatile temperament. Blending Pisces/Scorpio produces an often beautiful, certainly hypnotic, and entirely screwed-up personality. This one can out-party a Libra on a binge. Guaranteed sexy, as well as serial, and unhappy, relationships.

Aries/Scorpios, who are both ruled by Mars, *will* win at all costs. That aside, these folks are usually decent, deep, committed, and mostly faithful. Sexually obsessed and scarily irresistible, the Leo/Scorpio combo will make you run screaming into the night, then stand outside and howl at the Moon. The Sagittarius/Scorpio blend produces a serious player. For the short term, you'll have more fun and more sex than you can handle. Don't even contemplate the long term.

Taurus/Scorpio is charming but self-destructive with a vile temper. Tends to be very lucky regarding money, which is good because he or she is often too lazy to work. With Virgo/Scorpio, nitpicking is raised to an art form and is vicious to boot. But they have an earthy sexuality that's hard to resist, so try earplugs with this one. Capricorn/Scorpio is a force with which you should not trifle. This combo does not forgive and is quite capable of tracking you to the ends of the Earth in order to exact revenge. B-r-r-r.

In Gemini/Scorpio, the Marquis de Sade meets the iron maiden. This one has the ability to verbally destroy a tough-as-nails Capricorn and can leave in an instant and never look back. Libra/Scorpios are wildly out of balance. They pull you close with one arm and shove you away with the other. In the Aquarius/Scorpio blend you get a tetchy maniac. Half-humanitarian, half-cynic, all-agitated bundle of nervous tension. This one's better in midlife, after therapy, soul searching, and the correct dosage of Prozac.

Mars Is Afflicted

Marriage is too interesting an experiment to be tried only once.
EVA GABOR (FEBRUARY 11)
SCORPIO MARS/AQUARIUS SUN

In Scorpio's deep water, passionate Mars simmers, boils, and churns. Even the coolest outward character has intense inner feelings. Whether or not these natives have extreme sex lives (and most do), they are all very sexual beings. As with everything Scorpio touches, Mars becomes even more jealous, obsessive, and vengeful. *Never* trifle with these emotions. Danger lurks impossibly close to the surface. These natives are capable of wasting a lifetime seeking revenge when they could be using the formidable force of this combination to build an excellent future.

Female Scorpio Mars

Even if you are all fluff on the outside, inside you are 100 percent power player. Think of Virgos Angie Dickinson and Olivia Newton-John. You are capable of quietly, almost eerily, willing the object of your desire into your web. And the lured are all too willing to accommodate you. The lover whom you will allow to get under your skin as well as your comforter must be loyal to the death, keep all your dreadful secrets, and be as outwardly obsessive as you are inwardly paranoid.

Male Scorpio Mars

Your easygoing surface temperament hides a seething cauldron of emotional excess and sexual energy. Think of Capricorn Mel Gibson, Sagittarius Jimi Hendrix. You could be the zodiac's classic bad boy or a fiercely protective and loyal lover. Either way, you usually have your way and can be ruthless either when crossed or just for fun. Your list of jilted lovers is longer than an Arctic winter and you are a lifetime member of the frequent-fornicators' club. You need a partner whom you can trust enough to reveal your deeply intense emotions. And who will keep you on a short leash.

Venus Is a Nympho

The words, I was wrong, do not come easily to me.

JIM BAKKER (JANUARY 2)
SCORPIO VENUS/CAPRICORN SUN

In Scorpio, Venus could literally love you to death. Here, the lusty goddess smolders, slinks, preoccupies her mind with sex in all its many forms. Scorpio Venus is intense and serious; emotional manipulation comes naturally. So does sexual excess. These are the boys and girls who think about sex every waking moment and are capable of multiple trysts in the same day. Scorpio Venus natives are not into idle chatter, vapid flattery, or anything that smacks of superficiality. On the outside he or she may be the picture of social grace and amiable personality, and these natives have the strength of will to wait a lifetime for something or someone he or she loves.

Female Scorpio Venus

For you, love, sex, and power are all synonymous. You see no point in wasting time or energy on trivial flirtation when you instinctively know you can reduce any partner to love slave. You may display your sexual persona overtly like Capricorn Ava Gardner or conceal it beneath a cheerful surface character like Sagittarius Bette Midler. Your sexual radar is rarely wrong and you can pick up the slightest nuance of interest across a crowded room. Your ideal partner is one whose mind you can't probe. You long to be with someone whose will is as strong as yours, because if it isn't, you'll mate and kill.

Male Scorpio Venus

You are the emotional power broker of the zodiac. Pleasant on the surface, hotly passionate inside, there's nothing you set your mind, or libido, on that you can't have. Think of Sagittarius Kirk Douglas, Capricorn Val Kilmer. You cover your acute sensitivity and emotional nature with a friendly social demeanor. You crave an all-or-nothing-at-all romance that melds love, sex, obsession, adoration, and just plain lust. In other words, your ideal lover is one who will screw you into anorexia while you beg for more.

Fatal Attractions

Scorpio/Aries—Intolerant crank with sex-is-all attitude seeks horny hedonist with flair for marathon sex and megapower plays, for primitive, passionate, and ultrashort romance.

Scorpio/Taurus—Silent-but-deadly revenge-artist-cum-control-freak seeks judgmental, suspicious critic for a Battle of the Titans relationship.

Scorpio/Gemini—Vitriolic-but-sexy mattress junkie with sultry style seeks acerbic relationship savant for sensational sex and interesting but treacherous affair.

Scorpio/Cancer—Cryptic meany on permanent power trip seeks needy recluse for mutual victimization, head games, and crisis-to-crisis lifestyle. Misery loves company. Willing to share therapy costs.

Scorpio/Leo—Irritable grouch who loves dark places, secret rendezvous, and few people seeks whirling dervish who lives for bright lights and an audience for extreme power struggle. If we live until morning, I'll buy breakfast.

Scorpio/Virgo—Critical, irritable killjoy bent on controlling the world seeks critical, irritable nitpicker for mutual verbal flagellation and surprisingly compatible sex.

Scorpio/Libra—Icy hot sexual criminal with lots of rope, who's wanted in several bedrooms, seeks emotionally hot and cold blame-layer with whom to swing—for about an hour.

Scorpio/Scorpio—Emotional bump-and-grind artist with six ex-lovers and custom whip seeks brooding sheet-savage with lifetime membership to the porno channel for fun and games as only we can understand. Stingers up!

Scorpio/Sagittarius—Suspicious pessimist with perpetual axe to grind and myopic love focus seeks cheerful optimist who believes an open relationship should be a two-way street. Interesting midnight conversations. Sensational-but-short-lived sexual heat.

Scorpio/Capricorn—Sulky, sultry seducer whose sexual thermostat is set at roast seeks serious, thrifty, socially adept moneymakcr for languorous lovemaking and surprisingly long-term love.

Scorpio/Aquarius—Sarcastic bore with gold medal in fearsome posturing seeks mental case too self-absorbed to be alarmed. Kinky sex, surprise friendship, could be sweet.

Scorpio/Pisces—Ruthless-but-misunderstood depressive with desire to enslave and consume seeks vacuous-but-romantic mystic with emotional blind spot and own set of chains. A match made in Heaven.

Scoring

Best Bets—Cancer, Capricorn, Pisces
Just Good Friends—Virgo, Scorpio, Sagittarius
Please Shoot Yourself Now—Aries, Taurus, Gemini, Libra, Leo
The Dark Horse—Aquarius

Sensual and Sulky Scorpions

Charles Bronson
Richard Burton
Prince Charles
Sean "P. Diddy" Combs
Hillary Rodham Clinton
Leonardo DiCaprio
Julia Roberts and Lyle Lovett
Demi Moore
Grace Slick
Henry Winkler (and Fonzie)

Chapter Ten

SAGITTARIUS

November 22–December 21

The Wanderer

Element: Fire. Everyone has a chance to be warmed at this hearth.

Quality: Mutable. Sagittarius never met a body he or she didn't want to screw.

Symbol: The Archer/Centaur. Half hunter. Half animal. All untamed wild thing.

Ruler: Jupiter, the Good-Time Charlie god of excessive joviality.

Romantic Idol: The Invisible Man.

Romantic Style: Nonexistent.

Favorite Pickup Line: "Is this bus headed to Albuquerque?"

Dream First Date: Philosophize over a few cold ones, move to a parking lot for a quickie, then unceremoniously dump first date for the hottie he or she spotted through the windshield while humping.

Erogenous Zone: Hips. Keeps college bump-and-grind championship trophy on the dresser, next to the back brace.

Sexual Quirk: Me Tarzan, you Jane—works for either sex.

Romancing the Sign

I think of myself as an intelligent, sensitive human with the soul of a clown, which always forces me to blow it at the most important moments.
Jim Morrison (December 8)

Exasperatingly gauche, and without a shred of social grace, Sagittarius gallops through life looking for the next adventure. Archers are energetic lovers, but spend so much time declaring their need for freedom that very little is left to declare any undying love for you.

Sagittarius walks a fine line between the sacred and the profane. Archers are usually very spiritual, even if totally against organized religion. However, both sexes also love practical jokes, off-color humor, and frequent, meaningless sex. These serial romancers have a near-phobic fear of commitment. This is because, in love, their Centaur side emerges, the mythological half-human, half-horse creature with the insatiable sexual appetite. Adventuresome and philosophical are two primary character traits ascribed to Sagittarius. What this really means is that a wandering eye is about all you can count on from these armchair gurus.

As with all Fire signs, Sadges are not in the least bit shy. More relaxed and less argumentative than Aries, and less attention needy than Leo, Archers bound through life with a slaphappy grin trying to impress you with brainpower. And both sexes are born with the ability to talk for hours about any subject under the sun, including ones he or she knows nothing about. Sagittarius is the Tower of Babel along the information highway. Archers also travel through life with both feet firmly stuck in their mouths. This is a crucial fact should you decide you really want one of these slaphappy characters. If your ego is the least bit fragile, or should you have a personal secret, like chronic jock itch, or silicone boobs, it's better to prepare yourself that, sooner or later, you'll be subjected to a thoughtless remark made carelessly in front of your friends, family, or coworkers. As soon as it hits the Archer's pea brain, it falls off their flapping lips.

If a Centaur in love sets his or her sights on you, you could get trampled in his or her excitement to jump your bones. These kids' lust-o-meters are permanently stuck in the red zone and neither sex has any qualms about sleeping with you on the first date or getting some in the car before you get to the theater, arena, or restaurant. The downside to having such a willing sex partner is that as soon as the deed is done, Mr./Ms. Centaur is liable to lose interest and flirt with the waiter during dinner or the ticket taker at the football game. Like Aquarius, Sagittarius has no inborn need for a long-term relationship.

Sagittarius is the performer of the zodiac and brings a touch of circus to every facet of his or her jam-packed life. Archer Cal Worthington, the California car dealer, who expanded one used car lot into a $600 million business, and King of the Media, will always be known for his over-the-top "My Dog, Spot," commercials. Through more than forty years of TV spots, Worthington has cheerfully appeared leading, holding, or riding a variety of creatures from frogs to gorillas. As for his Centaur side, Cal is in his early eighties now and married to his third wife, who's in her early forties, and with whom he has a two-year-old child. His oldest child is fifty-six. He still manages his businesses, including dealerships in several states and ten ranches. His wife, Bonnie, said in an *L.A. Times* interview that, despite the age difference, she can barely keep pace. "You have to ride motorcycles, play tennis, and travel at the drop of a hat."

If you are looking for a fun partner who's also a pal, start taking your vitamins and look no further. If you want routine, eternal faithfulness, and a little peace and quiet, go see an Earth sign.

'Til Death Do Us Part

I love Mickey Mouse more than any woman I've ever known.

WALT DISNEY (DECEMBER 5)

Catching One

Being involved with a Sagittarius is like loving your best friend, which is great for sharing escapades, fun, and lots of casual action. Not so hot for serious attention and romance.

Dating an Archer/Centaur is not for the faint of heart. Archers have no shame, or guilt, and very little remorse when it comes to relationships. You mustn't, either. They like straightforward approaches, such as playing grab-ass on the dance floor while whispering, "Hey, baby, let's get it on." And they like straightforward sex, anytime, anywhere. Sagittarius Fire is cheery, warm, and steady. It's hot, but it's nonconsuming and everyone who sits at this campfire is welcome.

An Archer feels that, if you want him or her, or vice versa, why act otherwise? If you are a supershy Cancer, or a come-get-me Scorpio, you're liable to be left sitting alone in the corner while the Sadge you have your eye on bounds off after the Aquarius who's discussing the latest ideas for saving the whales.

To catch one's attention, you *must* be able to converse on a variety of topics. If you actually sound like you understand what you're talking about, you'll make extra points. You also should appear busy, superbusy, or even frantically over-booked with dates, meetings, causes, and classes in philosophy, religion, obscure civilizations, or environmental issues. Beware of outright lies, though, as Archers are notorious for scathing honesty. If yours wants to discuss pygmy mating rituals, you should at least know what a pygmy is. Just make a couple of succinct remarks and then sit back and listen. As does its opposite sign, Gemini, Sagittarius communicates. But where a Twin tries to influence, even control your life with his or her beliefs and opinions, Sagittarius lives to expound and inform. What you do with the plethora of information this bunch spews is up to you. Look attentive, smile a lot, and laugh when he or she does, which is about every five seconds, and you'll capture his or her attention long enough to make the next move.

Be direct. Encounters with strangers turn on Sagittarius and, unlike most of us, who feel we should at least have dinner together a couple of times before ripping off our clothes, Centaurs think sex is the best icebreaker toward a happy relationship. Inviting one out five minutes after you've met is acceptable. So is having sex in the car outside the bar before you've learned each other's names. Spontaneity is key to an Archer's heart. So are laughter, frequent trips, midnight talks, and regular gatherings with friends and family.

Archers love the outdoors and most are as happy roughing it in the back woods, or sleeping on the beach without a tent, as staying in a hotel. Talking about your ability to make a lean-to out of strips of bark and pine boughs or to camp for a week living off the land will capture his or her attention. If you aren't into sand fleas and forest creatures, your Archer will also enjoy day hikes and nightly soaks in the hotel spa.

Most will have to seriously watch their weight at some point in life. Expansive Jupiter enlarges the Sagittarius appetite for everything, including comfort food.

Getting an Archer in bed isn't the challenge. To a Sagittarius, bed is probably the least favorite place to have sex. It's boring and this sign lives for the next adventure or thrill. Sex on the kitchen table, in the stairwell of your apartment, at his or her office, on the front lawn, or under the stars in the forest are just some of the places to titillate your Centaur. Don't worry about scents, candlelight, satin sheets, or sexy underwear. Sagittarius gets off on spontaneous combustion. As long as you can keep thinking up new places, keep up a running conversation about myriad subjects, and just keep running, you'll stand a fair chance that yours will want to keep combusting with you. However, any long-term relationship with either the king or queen of horsing around is also a long shot.

Surviving One

As do all Fire signs, Sagittarians have enormous egos, so summarily dumping one, or worse, saying you've found another lover, will only provoke a screaming match, or result in your Archer throwing the river rocks you collected on your camping trip last summer through your thousand-dollar stained glass window. He or she will not hesitate to tell everyone in town what a dirty bitch or bastard you are for daring to want off this mental and physical merry-go-round.

So when you decide you have had enough of the guffawing, cheating, and brutally insensitive observations about your looks, intelligence, and family, and your head is about to explode from the daily bombardment of useless knowledge and boring trivia, the two best things to do are either act depressed or start whining. If you *are* depressed, so much the better.

Sagittarius has no tolerance for moods or anyone who is remotely needy. To be needed means he or she has to be reliable, and to be reliable means that he or she has to stay home and have serious conversations once in awhile. To an Archer, a serious conversation means deciding whether to go to the football game or to the beach this weekend.

Tell yours that you need peace. And quiet. Draw the drapes and turn down the lights. Sigh frequently. Say you don't know what's wrong, but you are sure that if he or she will accompany you to some short-term therapy, you'll be able to discover the cause of your listlessness and lack of interest in life. If you get to the end of this speech, and your Sagittarius is still listening, add that you've also lost interest in sex, saving the whales, and clean air.

If this combination of Crusader Rabbit and Curious George decides to dump you, it will be as fast and unceremoniously as he or she picked you up. The most you can hope for is a five-minute conversation about the need for freedom. At worst, he or she will describe the new love he or she has been screwing behind your back and expect your understanding, because, after all, you know you were never that great in bed.

You'll be wasting time should you try to get even. Appear at your ex's new watering hole with an attentive Libra or an elegant Capricorn in tow, and Mr./Ms. Big Mouth will most likely ask you to dance and try to arrange an orgy with your respective new lover. After all, there's no harm in trying.

Keeping One

Tactless? Sometimes. Independent? Certainly. However, you don't need track shoes, loose morals, or the hide of an elephant to live with a Sagittarius.

You do need a certain amount of independence, a positive attitude, and the understanding that Archers are one of the least routine-loving signs. Gemini doesn't like routine because the Twins are easily bored. Sagittarius doesn't like routine because every Archer has an unending thirst to learn about life's diversity. And once learned, this Jupiter-ruled sign of the teacher and philosopher needs to share that knowledge with others. This means you.

Whether it's a trip around the world or just playing Tarzan in the living room, your Archer craves adventure. Archers need frequent escapes from their overbooked schedules, so keep an overnight bag packed with toiletries and comfortable clothes for those last-minute weekend trips.

If you are worried about getting your Archer to sit down long enough to snuggle on the couch, try luring him or her with a Discovery Channel program on ancient cultures, obscure religion, or self-made success stories. Don't panic. Archers are not total eggheads. They love action and adventure movies, and regular sitcoms, too. However, a surefire way to get one to sit still for an hour or two is to provide entertainment and education at the same time.

Sagittarians are born with a great deal of physical and sexual stamina and need regular exercise, in and out of bed. Since his or her sense of adventure extends into the bedroom, too, you can count on your Centaur to enjoy acting out your wildest sexual fantasy. Put a note in his or her briefcase or lunch sack in the morning and prepare to be delighted that evening.

This is one sign that rarely goes to bed angry. You c̶
a shouting match over dinner and be bouncing on t̶
springs before the dishes are dry. Sagittarius blood r̶u̶
and, very often, arguments have the same effect as foreplay.

Archers young or old frequently suffer aching backs. Aside from the obvious mattress strain, both sexes rarely stop to consider the consequences of rearranging the furniture or lifting heavy objects without help. Heated massage oil applied by you with lots of TLC will help keep your Archer limber and in motion.

Sagittarians fall in love just as deeply as any other sign. The difference is that they are not clinging vines, nor do they want, or expect, you to be. As independent as they are, they are also fair. Unlike Scorpio, who expects you to sit home while he or she is off doing whatever pleases him or her, or Taurus, who expects you to just sit at home with him or her, Sagittarius has learned the secret that having a life together while still maintaining independence within that framework makes for a never boring, forever fresh relationship.

Moonlight or Gaslight?

Well, I didn't get dressed to go unnoticed.

LIBERACE (May 16)
SAGITTARIUS MOON / TAURUS SUN

Sagittarius Moons are incorrigible nonconformists. These natives may be the least domesticated creatures in the Universe. In Sagittarius, the emotional character expands under Jupiter's rule and leans toward an excessive lifestyle. These natives are charming schemers who can adapt to any circumstance and manipulate any relationship to get their way. Some are the jolly jokers of the Universe with little or no common sense.

This is the Look Out World, Here I Come Moon. Even the

most home-oriented Sun sign will have an urge for irresponsible independence and the tendency to dismiss anything but his or her own viewpoint. Sagittarius Moons are often fickle, restless, and unpredictable. They can be so tactless in conversation that they are frequently on the receiving end of a swift kick in the pants from an angry lover or colleague. This native is also intelligent, blunt, forceful, and prone to instant and sometimes violent changes in temperament. Often like a grinning serial killer, these characters are funny, assertive, and flirty on the surface, driven, single-minded, and dangerous inside.

The Double Sagittarius combination can produce a natural-born entertainer who keeps adapting to the times, such as Dick Clark, who's entertained three generations of teenagers; a spectacular risk taker who fails just as spectacularly, as did General George Armstrong Custer; or a charming serial killer, like Ted Bundy.

Aries/Sagittarius is so easily bored you can't count on this one to come home two nights in a row. Leo/Sagittarius is magnetic, smart, totally irresponsible in love, and has a kid's attitude to life. Excellent for a fling; pass on long-term.

The Taurus/Sagittarius combo expands the Bull's penchant for snide comments and snobbery. These creatures want it all and unless you have it to give, they will pass you by without a second glance. Virgo/Sagittarius is slightly schizophrenic, extremely curious, and hard to settle down until after age thirty. Conflicted. Doesn't know whether to propose or proposition. Capricorn/Sagittarius is dedicated to expanding his or her fortunes. Work side by side, don't criticize those big dreams, and you could end up on *Lifestyles of the Rich and Famous.*

Gemini/Sagittarius acts on every impulse, including putting the make on your best friend. Run, don't walk, from this one. The Libra/Sagittarius duo couldn't be faithful on his or her best day. Think hot air and an inflated sense of self that lives to scatter his or her pearls of useless wisdom over the broadest possible range. The Aquarius/Sagittarius blend is friendly, mellow, and optimistic. That's why they keep getting married again and again and again. Every love is a *true love.*

Cancer/Sagittarius produces one of the nicest personalities in the zodiac. The good side is a less-moody Crab who can talk about more than Mom and his or her latest ailment; the rotten side is that the wandering Sadge Moon frequently causes a midlife crisis of mega-proportions. This one could leave a thirty-year marriage and end up on a beach in Bora Bora. The Scorpio/Sagittarius wants to possess you while he or she has total freedom. The harder you are to catch, the harder this one falls. Not good parent material. Pisces/Sagittarius is outgoing, popular, and unencumbered with the usual Fish emotional nature. Not a homebody and has few lasting ties. Believes in love, but the names and faces continually change.

Mars Is Afflicted

I don't recall the so-called devilish things I do. But there are considerable amounts.

JOHN TRAVOLTA (FEBRUARY 18)
SAGITTARIUS MARS/AQUARIUS SUN

In Sagittarius, Mars' passion is directed toward the masses and his already short attention span becomes micromini. People with this placement can be so easily distracted that they will have found a new lover before you pull up your panties. The words *commitment* and *entrapment* are often synonymous. These natives need to be where the action is at all times and staying home with a permanent lover will chafe even the most devoted Sun sign. Sagittarius Mars has a delightful, albeit wicked, wit. When frustrated or restricted in any way, these natives won't hesitate to blame anyone but themselves in order to have the excuse to escape into a new adventure, or affair.

Female Sagittarius Mars

On the outside, you may be as elegantly cool as was Capricorn Loretta Young or as athletic and free-spirited as Aquarius Rene Russo, but inside, you are one curious babe. You have a masculine attitude toward all things sexual and a keen sense of right and wrong—which you often ignore. Friendly, tough, outgoing, and very physical, you seek a partner who can match your physical and mental stamina. The one that wants to conquer the world, or at least his corner of it, will set you afire.

Male Sagittarius Mars

You may have an obvious mischievous look, like Taurus Jack Nicholson, or be a confirmed bachelor lover as was Virgo Maurice Chevalier. No matter which tack you take, your goal is to charm your way in and out of as many beds as possible. You believe in embracing life and chasing the next challenge regardless of how many times you get burned. Your ideal lover is one who can run faster and talk longer, has an even shorter attention span, and who is so unpredictable that you don't know whether you'll be greeted at the door with a kiss or an axe.

Venus Is a Nympho

I have an appetite for love and romance and sex and lust. It's a part of life.

Jeff Goldblum (October 22)
SAGITTARIUS VENUS/LIBRA SUN

In Sagittarius, bad-girl Venus is in love with excess. Sagittarius Venus rushes headlong into a new affair, lured by the sense of discovery and a wild romanticism. These romantic rebels may walk a precipice between being adored and reviled, but they are never ignored. This native is on a search for the perfect love. However, since that would mean losing a measure of independence in favor of committing to another human, the affair cools just as fast as it flared because Sagittarius Mars is unable to sustain the fires of unselfish passion for very long. Warm-hearted and usually delightfully cheerful, these natives use humor to cover up many deeper emotions. Both sexes make loyal and responsive friends as that emotion is easier to achieve and less demanding.

Female Sagittarius Venus

You are strong, nearly fearless, resilient, and uninhibited. Your determined spirit remains virtually undaunted no matter what life hands you, and that's why you frequently realize your dreams. Think of Libra Angela Lansbury, Aquarius Diane Lane. In love, however, you are so frank sometimes that the object of your desire cringes rather than cuddles. You need and deserve a crusader who can share your adventures and help vindicate the downtrodden. However, you, too, often mistake ego for independence and end up with a condescending jerk who tries to stifle your enthusiasm.

Male Sagittarius Venus

Love is a game and you are a grand champion player. It's not that you are callous with emotion; it's that you are so friendly, outgoing, and direct that you often offend as easily as you attract. Your tendency to exaggerate spills into romance when you fervently declare your undying love one minute and hop the first bus out of town the next. Think of Capricorns Cary Grant and Kevin Costner. The lover that can make your head spin will be your best friend and sex object, yet so independent that you have to run to keep up with him or her. A coast-to-coast romance could be your ideal.

Fatal Attractions

Sagittarius/Aries—Independent dreamer with lifetime air miles and passion for arguments, sex, and rock and roll seeks incurable romantic with hot temper and fetish for airplane sex for a life of nonstop loving, fighting, screwing, and fun.

Sagittarius/Taurus—Chatty, uninhibited sex machine who freewheels through both life and the checking account seeks taciturn grouch that hordes money and has no tolerance for spontaneity for the dullest date this side of a funeral parlor.

Sagittarius/Gemini—Garrulous party-hound whose sense of adventure is limited to screwing under a streetlight seeks willing partner and jabberwocky for eight or nine quickies and a short good-bye. We'll always be friends.

Sagittarius/Cancer—Commitment-phobic travel nut known for a winning smile and brutally honest observations seeks chronically whining shut-in to provoke, prod, and push off that emotional tightrope.

Sagittarius/Leo—Flip, funny, fabulously adventuresome optimist seeks sleek, sparkling, sunny screwball to co-star in real-life love story of blockbuster proportions. We'll have the world on a string.

Sagittarius/Virgo—Impulsive risk taker who believes in Chaos Theory, buying underwear versus washing it, and endless philosophical banter that leads absolutely nowhere seeks serious, conventional neat freak with ulcer for agonizing half-a-night stand. This may be over before you can get your socks off.

Sagittarius/Libra—I-am-curious play pal with insatiable appetite for roaming the sexual planes seeks beautiful dreamer with mirrored ceiling, rich fantasy life, and long leash. This could be the start of something permanent.

Sagittarius/Scorpio—Happy-go-lucky and friendly-as-a-puppy gadabout with usually cheerful countenance seeks gruesome sexual android with bleak outlook and power-is-all attitude for grim but passionate one-night stand. Don't call me, and I won't call you.

Sagittarius/Capricorn—Bed-hopping mattress monkey who disregards convention, propriety, and what the neighbors think seeks conservative workaholic who thinks laughter is a waste of serious conversation and laughter in bed is sacrilegious for grate-on-the-nerves affair. Nasty arguments, huge sigh of relief when it ends.

Sagittarius/Aquarius—Full-time comic and part-time philosopher attracted by brains, variety, and willing attitude seeks fun-loving oddball with a sexual imagination beyond the reaches of outer space for mutual, life-long exploration, love, friendship, and just plain fun.

Sagittarius/Pisces—Cute trickster with frivolous attitude toward monogamy and careless use of the word *forever* seeks perpetual victim of poor romantic choices with take-no-prisoners outlook toward relationships. Hot, fanciful, and great in bed, but doomed from the first hello.

Scoring

Best Bets—Aries, Leo, Sagittarius, Libra, Aquarius
Just Good Friends—Gemini

PLease Shoot YourseLf Now—Cancer, Taurus, Virgo,
   Capricorn, Pisces
The Dark Horse—Scorpio

Sappy and Savvy Sagittarians

Woody Allen
Benjamin Bratt
Don Johnson
Indiana Jones
Lucy Liu
Little Richard
Anna Nicole Smith
Britney Spears
Kiefer Sutherland
Tina Turner

Chapter Eleven

CAPRICORN

December 22–January 19

Big Spender

Element: Earth. Stone-cold emotions and rock-hard determination built a brick-wall psyche that you'll need a hammer and chisel to crack.

Quality: Cardinal. All work and no foreplay makes Cappy a dull goat.

Symbol: The Goat. Love may be a part of life, but climbing to the top of the mountain is this animal's goal.

Ruler: Saturn, the god of first take out the garbage, then you can be spontaneous.

Romantic Idol: Hercule Poirot.

Romantic Style: Boss.

Favorite Pickup Line: "I'd like to lay you if I can fit you in my schedule."

Dream First Date: In a bank vault, screwing on piles of new, crisp, one hundred dollar bills.

Erogenous Zone: Knees, you on yours.

Sexual Quirk: In the office. Keeps one eye on you, the other on the Dow Jones.

Romancing the Sign

*I regret to say that we of the FBI are powerless to act
in cases of oral-genital intimacy, unless it has in some way
obstructed interstate commerce.*
J. Edgar Hoover (January 1)

If you are interested in security, sound investment strategy, and a lover who can micromanage the best Virgo right into the ground, look no further. However, if you are seeking wine, song, and unabashed romance, skip this chapter and read Pisces.

If a Goat decides he or she wants you, he or she will approach you in the same deliberate, organized manner that he or she has mapped out the next twenty years of life and career. And, if serious, will not hesitate to check your social standing, credit rating, and moral character before asking you to dinner. Capricorn is as practical in love as he or she is in pawing through a clearance sale. Goats equate money with emotional security. You don't have to be rich, but if you clip coupons and regularly stash some money in a savings account, you'll impress the Goat. Learning ten different ways to cook leftover turkey will ensure you leap several spots ahead on Cappy's list of credible choices.

The Goat symbol is defined as scaling any height to achieve success, and that's true. What's also true is that this metaphorical mountain is also used to climb up out of emotional excess that often confuses and depresses Capricorn. These creatures can become so emotionally distanced from other humans that they become grim workaholics who are the last to leave the office at night and the first to arrive in the morning. And it won't matter if you are married, or seriously committed, with children and family responsibilities. You'll have material success and a cold-natured partner who pencils your lovemaking in his or her calendar—as long as it doesn't interfere with the next board meeting.

Even if you are a slaphappy Sagittarius, or a tell-all-try-all Gemini, you'll entice the Goat if you let him or her take the conversational lead and dutifully provide answers to the questions Capricorn will ask. The more self-reliant, and self-made, you appear, the better Capricorn will like it. Dress as expensively as you can afford. No flash, like Leo, but in one of the classic, ageless styles.

Don't expect sappy love poems or the romantic antics of Aries, Leo, Pisces, or Cancer. Do expect to be taken to the places power players play. Don't display anything more in public except a calm courtesy you would extend to the chairman of the board should he or she take you to dinner. Don't play footsies under the table; the waiter might see. Don't gush. Don't bat your eyelashes. For God's sake, don't flirt with any of his or her friends.

Capricorn is nearly as emotionally dark as Scorpio, but not as deliberately ruthless. Edgar Allen Poe's horrific tales of lost and demented love illustrate the Goat's fear of emotional excess. And cartoonist Charles Addams's portrait of the weird but devoted family that bears his name is typical of the black humor of this sign, and of your life as the mate of a mountain Goat.

'Til Death Do Us Part

I knew I wanted love, so I just followed my erection.

Kenny Loggins (January 7)

Catching One

If you want the Goat you're falling for to stick around after his erection deflates, or her panties dry, you must forget everything you know about overt flirting. Straightforward come-ons, and hedonistic one-night stands are not the approach to take if you are seriously interested in the serious Goat.

Capricorn believes in separating public and private to such a degree that most people never discover just what sexual powerhouses the boys and girls of this sign can be. Cappy is testimony to the classic duality of perfect public demeanor and private sexual beast. This sign is deep-down terrified of public displays of any kind and if you come on as fast and loose in the beginning, that impression will stick in his or her status-conscious mind forever. You can be the toy on the side, but you'll have a horrific time raising yourself up to the standard of dinner-with-the-boss companion, let alone be considered for a permanent relationship. Your first date may feel more like a job interview, as the Goat not so shrewdly pries into your heritage and financial stability.

Sagittarius takes risks. Scorpio is a risk. Capricorn calculates risks. Even if you are an emotionally unstable Pisces, try to act normal until you get the Goat interested. And to get one interested, you must appear socially acceptable, well mannered, quiet, confident, and like you just stepped out of a fashion magazine.

Once you've passed the public-eye test, Capricorn is likely to test you by sharing a small secret or childhood memory. Don't share this tidbit with either the gang around the water cooler or your best friend because Goats are as paranoid about privacy as Scorpio. Any personal information that the Goat doesn't dispense him- or herself is looked upon as betrayal and you're liable to find that your e-mail address has been summarily deleted from your Capricorn's hard drive. This is one sign that doesn't forgive or forget. A Goat won't necessarily plot revenge like Scorpio or punch you in the nose à la Leo, but once you've belittled, humiliated, or betrayed Cappy, you can kiss your relationship adios forever.

Goats are mistrustful of anything that's handed to them or that comes without hard work. Remember that when yours starts panting and pawing the ground in an eager attempt to herd you into the bedroom. Play it cool. Think it over. Take your time. Ask if he or she is serious. Say you are tired of superficial affairs and are searching for an old-fashioned love. Then plant a sweet, lingering kiss on your Goat's hot lips and say good night at the door. During the next week or two, keep building sexual tension and your appeal by using words such as *serious, five-year plan, security, long-term, friendship,* and *respect.* Soon he or she will be lusting after you and simultaneously thinking of a permanent pairing.

When you are ready to climb the mountain of ecstasy, remember this animal likes to mate in private. Make sure the doors are locked, the window shades are drawn, and the answering machine is working. Privacy and your undivided attention turn on Capricorn. So does sexy lingerie, silky sheets, and slow, silent lovemaking. Leave the whips to Gemini, the bondage to Sagittarius, and the emotional torture to Scorpio. The Goat is into pure sexual blending of your two bodies and forgetting the outside world exists. Once yours relaxes, you will happily discover a wildly passionate and extremely loving partner.

Surviving One

When you are weary of having your brains screwed out whether or not you are a willing participant and of being reminded of how lucky you are to have a partner who puts up with your shit, who takes the time to tell you what to wear, how to act, and treats you like a servant in your own home, it's time to dump that coldhearted, ball-busting career junkie.

The best way to do it is straightforwardly, and with the same emotion you'd use in reading the annual corporate report. Be matter-of-fact, honest, and no nonsense. No emotions, please, just cold, hard facts. "I hate your aloof, dispassionate guts, darling." Smile and offer the bitch some tea. "Screw you and your five-times-a-night, robotic humping, dear," and pour him another drink. Capricorn will appreciate your honesty and your good taste in not throwing the Waterford crystal at his or her thick head.

If you are legally bound, make sure you've visited your lawyer first and know exactly what you can and cannot keep, for Capricorn will certainly try to justify keeping everything and kicking you into the gutter, even if you are the one who picked Mr./Ms. Goat up in a redneck bar on the wrong side of the tracks.

If you have the slightest inclination that you are about to be dumped and don't have a prenuptial or palimony agreement, hide as much cash as possible with a trusted friend or relative. Your Goat will not be generous with the settlement.

Don't create a scene. Especially if you have any inclination that the rift can be mended, or you want to attempt reconciliation. Don't bad-mouth your ex in public or private. Be classy. Stay friends. Act more concerned about your next career move than your lost lover. Let it slip that you won the Lotto or received an inheritance from a long-lost relative, and soon you'll get a phone call and a matter-of-fact statement from your ex that he or she wants to see you, tonight, promptly at 8 P.M.

To get even with this coldhearted money grubber, show up at the country club on the arm of an older, richer, and grumpier Capricorn.

Keeping One

You may think your Capricorn is happier balancing the checkbook than taking a moonlit stroll with you. But with a little patience and some foresight, you can help yours have the best of both worlds.

Most Capricorns come from either emotionally or financially deprived childhoods. This lays the groundwork for both the fact that they equate money with security, and that for most of their lives, they are emotionally aloof. It's also the cause of their proclivity for black or despairing moods.

Despite these rough beginnings, Capricorn is one of the best marriage signs. However, his or her partner-skill development takes lots of time, as Capricorn is the emotional late bloomer of the zodiac. The twenties are usually the *decade of decadence* when Cappy tries to act like any normal young adult and screw everything that walks, flies, crawls, or leaps. Realizing this is untrue to his or her inner nature, the Goat moves into the *decade of dutiful career building* and devotes 24/7 to developing a solid future. All Capricorns have an innate fear of eating dog-food stew in a public housing development and this fact alone ensures that most achieve a quite comfortable retirement. At about forty, Cappy's focus shifts slightly and he or she moves into the *decade of lightening up*. If you've married one at twenty and stuck out endless nights of sleeping alone while your Goat climbed the corporate ladder, you'll be happy to know this is when that famous *reverse-aging* process begins to appear. From here on, your Goat will get more light-hearted, affectionate, even agreeable to holding hands in public—sometimes. And sex will also take on a new dimension of spontaneity and romanticism that will be a tremendous and welcome surprise.

If you hook up with one in either of the other decades, you can help the process along by being willing to work as hard for your collective future as does your Goat. And remember praise, kindness, and tolerance are not lost on this diligent sign. Capricorn craves attention, but is often too stoic or too afraid to ask for praise. Even after years of togetherness, a simple thank-you will make your Goat feel appreciated and loved.

Capricorn appears cool on the surface, but has a hilarious, dry wit that often appears without warning. Goats love rich, earthy colors, such as hunter green or deep chocolate, classic designs, and leather furniture. Think understated elegance when picking a gift and remember he or she will appreciate one thoughtful present versus lots of cheap baubles, and one well-designed piece of furniture to a bargain-basement suite bought just to fill up space. This is one sign that's perfectly willing to wait and save for what he or she truly wants.

Capricorns often suffer aching knees, backs, and general joint discomfort. Warmed massage oil, slowly applied by you, will work wonders to relieve tense muscles, aching joints, and the stresses that lead to those notorious brooding spells. Your Goat's depressive moods will also lighten if you prove that you are dependable, stable, and are not going to leave. Convince yours that you are here for them during the bad times as well as the good ones, that you won't leave if they get ill, or old, or lose their job, and you'll have one of the most devoted and stable lovers in the zodiac.

Capricorns make good long-term partners because they understand the value of building relationships and that a good relationship takes time and work. If you are looking for a steadfast, faithful, hardworking partner who's practical forethought will ensure you a very comfortable lifestyle, with a secure old age, and who is as skilled in the bedroom as the boardroom, you've come to the right sign.

Moonlight or Gaslight?

Sad old blokes, I'm told, now dream of me with a whip in hand.
Anne Robinson, HOST, *The Weakest Link* (September 26)
CAPRICORN MOON/LIBRA SUN

Capricorn Moons can be as cold and emotionless as the real moon. This is the Moon of genius and madness, brooding and selfishness. This placement adds an unsympathetic, antisocial, and power-hungry edge to the most laid-back Sun sign. Romantically these natives are often cruel, nagging, and unforgiving to the point of cutting all emotional ties if a lover doesn't behave exactly as told and/or expected. This is the Power Broker Moon—scheming, ruthless, determined. If this one wants you, he or she will come to you.

The Capricorn Moon is likely to be ambitious at the expense of any personal life. These natives often have serious difficulty relating, trusting, or opening up with a potential partner. They are either formal and distant or emotional cripples who connect so tightly to their partner that the relationship is smothered. They can hold a grudge longer than a Scorpio and take longer to assess, measure, and find a partner than the most anal Virgo. Most astrologers agree that Scorpio and Capricorn are the two most difficult places for the Moon to live. Virgo runs a close third.

Excessive worry, unwillingness to understand or associate with anyone with a differing viewpoint, and suppressed affection to the point of withdrawal can also affect these natives. Capricorn Moons can suffer terrible inner loneliness because they have no idea how to develop truly intimate relationships. Like the Capricorn Sun, these natives often suffer several broken relationships in youth and find happiness after midlife.

Very often, the restricted personal happiness of these natives, paradoxically, brings success through public charities and prestigious, well-esteemed careers. The practical ambition, responsibility, and excellent organizational skill of the Capricorn Moon produce some of the most successful and powerful business and government leaders. Aquarius Thomas Edison, Cancer John Glenn, Scorpio Robert Kennedy, and Aquarius Abraham Lincoln are some examples.

Double Capricorn Marion Davies was the companion of Taurus William Randolph Hearst for thirty years. While Davies's personal life was classic Capricorn, fraught with ill health and the sudden loss of fortunes and subject to vilification by the moral code of the times, her public persona was one of a warmhearted, funny, and very caring person.

On the other hand, Double Capricorn Federico Fellini said, "I live in the doubts of my duty. I think there is dignity in this. Just to go on working."

Taurus/Capricorn melds two moody characters into one wonderful package. They still brood a bit, but are mostly funny, solid, loving, and kind. Good for the long-term if you can weather the maturing stage. Virgo/Capricorn is shy, nervous, and aloof. Also considerate, determined, and with a head for business that could make him or her megarich. They grow on you and are definitely worth a second look.

The Gemini/Capricorn is a born con artist. This moody user knows exactly what he or she wants and uses any means to get it. Both sexes rarely settle down because love is the last thing on this one's mind. Libra/Capricorn has a laundry list of vices and jilted lovers. Difficult youth; snobbish adulthood. Don't remind this one of his or her sordid past, or expect any sympathy for yours. The Aquarius/Capricorn duo has big dreams and the inner strength to realize them. Expect to have your part in his or her plan carefully explained. As long as you adhere to it, you'll be fine.

Cancer/Capricorn blends into an earthy homebody who wants an old-fashioned relationship and a well-mannered, well-bred partner. Emotionally deep and very sexy. As with all prominent Capricorn placements, the older you catch this one, the happier you'll both be. The Scorpio/Capricorn duo is passionate about power and status. Either sex can overcome any obstacle to reach a goal. But is so miserly, overbearing, and ruthless, if this one ever mellows, it will be well beyond the age of forty. Pisces/Capricorn lives life backward. One of the oldest souls, this is the child who assumed too much duty too fast, and spends the rest of life lightening the load. A worrywart who falls, at least once, for the user-abuser.

Marriage or long-term partnership is incidental to the Aries/Capricorn. This one can be had, but you'll need a sense of timing that's as impeccable as his or hers. They are bright and crave respect and success. They use people but in such a friendly way, others don't seem to mind—much. Leo/Capricorn has the subtlety of an army tank and about as much sentiment. Extremely picky and expects you to be as driven, plus elegant, loving, and independent. Sagittarius/Capricorn is cynical and judgmental. They value tradition as long as you keep the home fires burning while they roam free. Extremely bright, but will steamroll over your ego.

Mars Is Afflicted

The trouble with the rat race is that if you win, you're still a rat.

LILY TOMLIN (SEPTEMBER 1)

CAPRICORN MARS / VIRGO SUN

The fires of Mars are restricted within deep, solid rock in Capricorn. The passion here is for being in control, prepared, and never caught off guard. Capricorn Mars natives can be driven overachievers who have no time for romance of either the emotional or the physical sort. The strong, earthy sex drive present with this aspect can be easily contained in favor of directing his or her considerable energy toward making money. Capricorn Mars natives wield a cool sexual power and like to stay on top in the bedroom, just as in the boardroom.

Female Capricorn Mars

There's nothing shy about you. You are happy to wear the pants in the family and often give your significant other no choice in the matter. Strong, disciplined, and usually in control, you rarely get sidetracked from a desired goal or love object. Think of Taurus Katharine Hepburn, Pisces Sharon Stone. Wimpy, oversensitive lovers don't amuse you for long. Neither do cave dwellers who refuse to shave and rattle their ice cubes at you for a refill. Your ideal companion is tough but dependable and appears to have a pedigreed background, whether or not it's true. Since you aren't above embellishing your own family tree, you figure why sweat the small stuff?

Male Capricorn Mars

Your climb to the top of any project, or body, is in a slow, steady, determined ascent. You can be extremely single-minded, no matter what your Sun sign. And have a practical, well-organized ability to overcome nearly any obstacle that life hands you. You tell it like it is and prefer to hear it in the same manner. Think of Gemini John Wayne, Sagittarius Noel Coward. You pick your battles and, like a crafty spy, prefer to win them with your wits versus your fists. In love you are always the boss, whether or not it's to your detriment. A partner who can feign even less interest than you will pique your curiosity.

Venus Is a Nympho

Marriage has been a humbling experience. I don't get to be the boss in the marriage.

Bonnie Raitt (November 8)
CAPRICORN VENUS/SCORPIO SUN

In Capricorn, Venus wears a pinstripe suit and no underwear. She's in love with money, position, and, of course, power. But Venus loves a paradox and has gifted this native with both the ability to push the limits of wild, sexy, and dangerous and the common sense to know how to maintain that Capricorn dignity. In love, however, these boys and girls often fall for the most bizarre characters one can imagine. Age, hairstyle, or kink won't matter to the Capricorn Venus—as long as the money holds out.

Female Capricorn Venus

The challenge you love is to make a *real* man, or woman, out of your lover. Publicly, you are frequently off the wall and over the top and seem to have a raw, earthy sexuality that verges on the brink of peril and scandal. Think of Aquarius Lisa Marie Presley, Aries actress Claudia Cardinale. Privately you are rarely struck by love at first sight. Your charm lays in your loyalty to friends and loved ones, and both your beauty and personal power deepen with time. The partner who can make you want to share a lifetime is the one who either has definite goals and plans or whom you feel has the potential for greatness.

Male Capricorn Venus

You appear calm, reserved, and self-assured. You matriculate through the masses with a kindly grin and warm handshake, but never get your hands dirty in the process. Think of Aquarius Paul Newman, Scorpio actor Alain Delon. Your ideal lover is older, wiser, and certainly richer. If he or she acts like the headmistress of a gothic boarding school, you're liable to forget your normally cool reserve and propose on the first date. You don't exactly want a parental figure, but stern, cold authority types turn you on.

Fatal Attractions

Capricorn/Aries—Big wheel with tons of self-respect and the ego to match seeks arrogant, rambunctious wild thing for hot bestiality, hazardous head butting, and not a cow's chance at McDonald's of long-term love.

Capricorn/Taurus—Stern-but-witty miser who's forgotten where the coffee cans are buried seeks steadfast homebody with *Galloping Gourmet* videos and shovel. We'll cook, in and out of bed, and end up fabulously rich.

Capricorn/Gemini—Calm, cool, and collected straight man with morbid sexual curiosity seeks emotionally erratic swinger for an extremely short lesson in letting it all hang out.

Capricorn/Cancer—Remote-but-loyal realist with excellent parenting skill and large financial security blanket seeks vulnerable, timid recluse to protect from the harsh light of day. Sexual healing guaranteed.

Capricorn/Leo—Brooding introvert who thinks overt emotional displays are too, too disgusting seeks kick-ass romantic with flare for public ass grabbing for the blind date from hell.

Capricorn/Virgo—Natural leader born with a silver calculator between a set of perfectly white teeth seeks neatnik with flair for tidying up and making small talk for bedding, wedding, and happily-ever-aftering.

Capricorn/Libra—Serious individualist into security, status, and pristine social grace seeks tiresome, shallow gold digger with morals of a rabbit and reputation for dry humping on the dance floor to use, abuse, and dump. No apologies needed, the feeling's mutual.

Capricorn/Scorpio—Rational-but-hot-blooded corporate raider with hefty stock portfolio and secret bondage fetish seeks churlish-but-sensitive sex slave for a little perversity and lots of genuine affection.

Capricorn/Sagittarius—Commitment-obsessed and cautiously reserved pessimist who's easily embarrassed seeks bohemian wild child who gets off on serial sex marathons for nerve-racking and ultrashort coupling.

Capricorn/Capricorn—Solitary social climber who's lonely at the top seeks merger with corporate raider with stone-cold heart. Looks compatible, but crashes faster than Nasdaq did after Enron.

Capricorn/Aquarius—Professional superachiever, born with a five-year plan in one hand and a PalmPilot in the other seeks off-the-wall and unpredictable madcap who can't plan dinner and wouldn't be home to cook it anyway. No sex. No fun. No way.

Capricorn/Pisces—Stoic workaholic with take-charge personality and steady income seeks resilient dreamer with empathic soul for trust, love, humor, and cozy life.

Scoring

Best Bets—Pisces, Taurus, Virgo
Just Good Friends—Scorpio, Cancer
Please Shoot Yourself Now—Aries, Gemini, Leo, Libra, Sagittarius, Aquarius
The Dark Horse—Capricorn

Cute and Cranky Capricorns

Sydney Biddle Barrows and Heidi Fleiss
Mary J. Blige
David Bowie
Nicolas Cage
Julia Louis-Dreyfus
Faye Dunaway
Ricky Martin
Elvis Presley
Kid Rock
Denzel Washington

Chapter Twelve

AQUARIUS

January 20–February 18

I'll Never Fall in Love Again

Element: Air. *Blow* and *hard* are two words that usually get you hot, but only if there is a space between.

Quality: Fixed. Trying to stand up during a hurricane is dangerous and tricky. It can be done, but you'll have to anchor your feet in a bucket of cement.

Symbol: The Water Bearer. Pours out advice, solutions, predictions, assumptions—everything but his or her heart.

Ruler: Saturn and Uranus, the gods of missionary style and unpredictable kink.

Romantic Idol: Inspector Gadget.

Romantic Style: Possessed.

Favorite Pickup Line: "Have you heard what *they* are doing to the rain forests now?"

Dream First Date: Being abducted and subjected to sexual experiments by a *real* space alien.

Erogenous Zone: Shins and Ankles wrapped in thin, silver chains attached to a diamond naval stud.

Sexual Quirk: Irritating habit of jumping in and out of bed to adjust the video camera.

Romancing the Sign

I've tried several varieties of sex, darling.
The conventional position makes me claustrophobic.
And the others either give me a stiff-neck, or lockjaw.
Tallulah Bankhead (January 31)

There are physical laws and metaphysical laws, but Aquarius-the-nonconformist is a law unto him- or herself. Catching the attention of an Aquarius is akin to being bitten by some exotic species of love-bug. You get all warm and itchy inside but you can't quite decide whether the feeling is comforting or chafing.

It's no accident that the Age of Aquarius was formally ushered in by the psychedelic sixties. Free love, free sex, free clinics, and the cry for freedom of the great masses of enslaved individuals permeate every Water Bearer's psyche. Aquarius is nearly as commitment-phobic as Sagittarius. However, instead of juggling several romances, Water Bearers are serial monogamists. These pseudo-scientists like to analyze, scrutinize, quiz, and mentally autopsy one target at a time.

Aquarius is the most outspoken sign in the zodiac. Don't confuse this with Sagittarius' proclivity for saying the wrong thing at the worst possible moment. Water Bearers speak up and out for causes they believe in and injustices they long to right. When hearing that she was listed on then-president (and Capricorn) Richard Nixon's hate list, Aquarius Carol Channing said it was "one of my greatest honors." In a similar situation, Aquarian Eartha Kitt was banned from Virgo Lyndon Johnson's White House for speaking against the Vietnam War. I suspect that what really pissed off LBJ was that ever-the-honest Water Bearer Kitt was at a White House luncheon with Lady Bird at the time.

Water Bearer natures are cool, distant, and disconnected. Unlike a Cancer or Pisces, who crave a complete emotional blending, or Scorpio and Taurus, who crave total control, Aquarius remains a separate entity, even in a deeply committed relationship. Most view family responsibilities as a great personal imposition. Should one decide you are worth investigating, you'll soon feel like a bug under a microscope. The Water Bearer's favorite game is Why? Why are you crying? Why are you yelling? Why is there air?

This sign will boink on the first date and still respect you in the morning. Aquarius thinks sex is a great way to break the ice. It's also his or her way of testing you. Are you really after a relationship? Or can we get down tonight and still be pals tomorrow?

As marriage or permanent-relationship partners, they are mostly faithful. Their curious natures are directed toward solving the riddles of the pyramids, Universe, and the workings of a washing machine. Complex emotional entanglements baffle and infuriate them. You will soon discover that your lover is a great innovator in the sack, but has to run errands every time you want to discuss anything deeper than what you are having for dinner.

In an interview in the *Calgary Sun,* Aquarius movie star Leslie Nielsen was described as "the consummate funnyman who slips zinger after zinger into his conversation, but who is also an astute, kind, gracious man." Nielsen had a solid dramatic acting career long before his flawless portrayal of the bumbling, lost-in-his-own-world Lt. Frank Drebin in the *Naked Gun* movie series. But the slapstick Drebin and Nielsen seem to have more in common than a movie script. Nielsen is famous for carrying a hand-buzzer, and reportedly never goes anywhere without his whoopee cushion, which he doesn't hesitate to use, especially at formal gatherings. With regard to love, Nielsen says he likes "mischievous women." But doesn't regard himself as a sex symbol. "Neither did any of my four wives," said the actor.

Aquarians remind me of a human version of phosphorescent plankton, floating along in his or her own world unless agitated by the ripple of a passing emotion, then bursting into a weird greenish glow designed to ward off anything that gets too close. It's not that a Water Bearer intentionally decides to hurt your feelings. He or she just doesn't realize you have any.

'Til Death Do Us Part

It's really hard to maintain a one-on-one relationship if the other person is not going to allow me to see other people.

AXL ROSE (FEBRUARY 6)

Catching One

Snagging an independent, romance-phobic Aquarius takes a little planning, lots of interesting conversation, and a deliberate sneak attack. Aquarius invented the phrase *just good friends* and will use it to describe everyone he or she knows, including you, even if you are married or in a committed relationship.

If one of these bright, funny, definitely off-the-wall, and completely unpredictable people causes your heart to skip a beat or gives you that jumpy feeling in the pit of your stomach, I'd advise a thorough checkup to rule out flu, salmonella, or panic attacks before proceeding to try to snag this elusive butterfly.

Water Bearers love the unusual, exotic, forbidden, and original. The stranger your hairstyle, job, or hobby, the better chance you have of piquing these characters' interest. If you can translate Sanskrit, have pictures of yourself at the gates of Vatican City holding a pro-choice placard, or have a relative that regularly contacts life on another planet, you are guaranteed a date. Every Aquarian is part anarchist and loves the sort of David and Goliath story that pits the wits of the underdog against all odds or anything that remotely smacks of conspiracy theory, intrigue, or strange inventions, and human cloning. Sprinkle your conversation with contemptuous statements about Big Brother, big business, and any of the latest fads. Bash the establishment. Talk about your favorite infomercial, or get-rich-quick scheme. Discuss your favorite cause or charity. The more obscure and off-the-wall this is, the better. Say you are a member of the Coalition Against Pigeon Birth Control, or Vegans for Nuclear Power.

Their colors fall within the aqua, violet, blue, and green spectrum but are neon bright or shimmer with a silver sheen. Think electric. Choose a shirt or blouse that blends two or more of the above colors and sparkles in the sun and rustles when you move. Pair it with either plain, wide-legged pants or an ankle-length skirt, sandals, and tousled hair, and you'll pique Aquarius' interest. Aim for the casually thrown together look. Don't forget to put a button or sticker on your book bag, lapel, or ass that supports or condemns something.

Aquarians have no inhibitions, taboos, or aversions about discussing anything, including his or her favorite sexual position, which is a good way to bring up the subject. However, you must *never* appear personally interested, only intellectually curious. Aquarians are skittish with regard to serious emotions and can bolt if they sense you want to be sweethearts versus bed-buddies. When you've convinced your Water Bearer that you are independent, free-spirited, and unfettered by the need for any sort of relationship, it's time to invite him or her home to bed.

Forget the roses, and discuss the Moon only if you plan on traveling there someday. Leave the mushy movies and elevator music to the Water signs and keep your lusty libido well hidden under a cool, chatty exterior. If you have any artwork, knickknack, or collectible that could be remotely considered exotic, retro, or high camp, set it in a conspicuous place. Keep up a running conversation while necking on the couch. Laugh a lot. Don't let the *L*-word escape your lips. Don't look adoringly into those electric blue or green eyes and don't let anything that remotely sounds like a sigh escape your lips.

When you finally hit the sheets, you'll be ecstatic to discover that, under the covers, or on top of the dresser, Aquarius loves hot, abandoned sex as much as the rest of us. The Water Bearer is curious and willing. Mentally, he or she can instantly access that analytical mind to determine whether or not the position you just suggested is physically possible. Verbally, he or she is as outspoken in bed as out. So be prepared to hear truthful pillow talk versus those sweet little lies other signs whisper. "That was OK, for starters. With some coaching, you should get really good" might make you cringe, but Aquarius believes in the truth. And in education. He or she will be all too happy to teach, and learn from, you. After all, what are friends for?

Surviving One

Aquarius is the easiest sign to dump. If you think about it, you never had a real relationship in the first place. You have different friends, interests, and ideals and anything you've suggested for the last six months, or ten years, has *always* been met with opposition or mental manipulation. Your sex life has been so unpredictable that just when you thought Mr./Ms. Water Bearer had embraced celibacy, he or she decided to screw you twelve times in three days.

So, when you tire of the incessant paranoid tirades and grow weary of separate vacations, having a partner who works in another town, or state, and who is in a constant state of frenzied motion that produces little or nothing of value, and want out, just pretend you *are* an Aquarian.

If you are not living together, call and say you need some time alone. It can be just that simple. If you don't call again, neither will your relationship-challenged Water Bearer. Asking "What's wrong?" would mean dealing with emotions, and any Aquarius worth his or her salt would rather be flung off a cliff at low tide.

If you share the sheets and the rent, say that you are extending your separate vacation time to live with your aunt in Pittsburgh for a few months or ask your Aquarius to do likewise until you "think things over." Should yours be so enlightened as to question your reasons, flatly state that you feel trapped, stifled, smothered, or as if you are in prison.

Don't worry about screaming, crying, smashed furniture,

or any of the other emotional displays of the rest of the zodiac. Chances are, before you can say, "But we'll always be friends," your ex will have skipped out the door and off on a new quest.

Don't worry in any case. You will probably get dumped first because Aquarius is notorious for the short-term affair. If you care enough to remain friends and are cool enough to agree to recreational sex, the Water Bearer, along with Leo, Libra, and Scorpio, makes a great playmate on the side. Chances are, he or she wasn't spending too much time alone on all those separate vacations anyway.

As for getting even, if you are a demented Fire sign, or screwy Water sign, and simply must slash a tire or make a hundred obscene phone calls at the end of the affair, go ahead. But don't think for a minute you are doing anything but *slightly* annoying your ex. He or she hasn't a clue to understanding emotional excess and will only be convinced that you are the nutcase he or she always suspected.

Keeping One

If you are worried that your imaginative, nonconforming, and creative Water Bearer is an aloof Mr. Spock clone who wants an open relationship and shirks all responsibility, don't be. Aquarius is one of the most faithful signs in the zodiac. What the Water Bearer wants is freedom within structure.

Aquarius is the most cerebral of the Air signs. Unlike Gemini, who is occupied with everyday communications, and Libra, who communicates within personal relationships, Aquarius is concerned with humanity at large. Your phone will ring at odd hours. Your partner will spend a great deal of time helping the neighbors plant a garden or volunteering at the local soup kitchen. Your home may look like an animal-rescue shelter, or three out-of-work friends or relatives could be sharing the living room floor.

You also will have a partner who is charming, exciting, and intuitive. And one who will understand your desire to have a weekend away with friends or a weekly night out sans him or her. As a rule, Aquarius is not jealous, possessive, or clinging. Every Water Bearer is born with the capacity to love and understand just about any other human. This includes you. There are few problems, issues, details, or situations that you can't openly discuss, if you are willing to discuss them calmly and truthfully with this tolerant, altruistic, and humane sign.

Aquarius appears detached on the surface but has a broad, sometimes bawdy sense of humor and loves anything out of the ordinary. Surprises delight them. Take a weekend road trip, but instead of planning a destination, let your Aquarian navigate by whim.

Rumors about Aquarius' unromantic nature are so untrue. The mundane bores them and this extends into the bedroom. Send him a Valentine in July or give her violets in January. Issue a challenge. Dream up a far-out fantasy. Then prepare to be amazed.

Aquarians are original, interesting, and some of the nicest humans on the planet. They have a special knack of knowing when help is needed and kindly offer it without any ulterior motives. What you see is what you get with a Water Bearer. And what you get is a partner who is anything but boring, and a love that's free of petulance, petty game playing, and emotional excess.

MoonLight or GasLight?

Sex without love is an empty experience, but as empty experiences go, it's one of the best.

WOODY ALLEN (DECEMBER 1)
AQUARIUS MOON/SAGITTARIUS SUN

Here is the Bohemian Moon. Aquarius Moons are detached, rational, and curious. They love variety and are physical, sensual, and usually happy. That's because he or she is the least emotional and least sentimental person you're ever likely to meet.

Aquarius Moons are concerned with groups of people versus one-on-one situations. He or she will often have several circles of friends as diverse as a religious study group, biker gang, and a tech-head organization. None would suspect that this funny, fearless, friendly person was a member of either of the other two. Nor will these groups ever meet. The Aquarius Moon isn't interested in playing games or shocking anyone. He or she is into exploration, education, and fornication totally for his or her own benefit.

Romantically, this Moon can be detached to the point of forgetting your name. Lunar Aquarians treat their partners like beloved pets—something that waits patiently for the door to open and this moonchild to appear and is content with a friendly nuzzle or scratch behind the ears. Aquarius Moons need partners who are as busy, curious, and as detached as they. Someone who travels for a living would be ideal. A partner who stays home but keeps busy with social, career, or family responsibilities is also acceptable, as long as he or she never tries to involve the Aquarius Moon in any day-to-day emotional turmoil.

Aquarius Moons are determined to be successful and often spend half a lifetime reeling from one project, career, or idea to the next. Success is measured by how far removed from an ordinary career it is possible to get. They have big dreams and often fail spectacularly, but rarely will one quit trying. This is the most determined of the Moon placements, and without having the burden of carrying excessive emotional baggage, the one that often realizes his or her dreams.

The Aquarius Moon adds a touch of excitement, eccentricity, and changeability to each Sun sign. It also shakes, rattles, and rolls the zodiac's emotional structure to create a wide variety of assorted oddballs.

Double Aquarians throw themselves wholeheartedly into

any endeavor whether it's conservative, controversial, or just plain quirky. Country star Clint Black burst onto the country music scene with five number one hits from his debut album, a first in music history. Within six years, his electrically charged creative talent penned six albums of all original songs. His Aquarian energy and original quirkiness can be found in publicity photos showing a wall burned from the electrical force of his singed guitar and the "earthquake bridge" effect he uses on stage.

Revolutionary and controversial Double Aquarian Angela Davis gained fame the hard way. Davis worked on behalf of the Soledad (prison) Brothers and was accused of complicity in their subsequent failed escape from the Marin County Hall of Justice on August 7, 1970. Four people, including the trial judge, were killed and Davis was accused of supplying the guns used in the attempted jailbreak. She landed on the FBI's Ten Most Wanted list, spent eighteen months in prison, and was finally cleared of all charges. With the typical Aquarian ability to drop out of the limelight but still proceed ahead, Davis has spent the last twenty years quietly working for change within the system.

Gemini/Aquarius is everyone's sweetheart and nobody's permanent squeeze. Smart, witty, and the life of the party, this one asks lots of questions, but never takes advice, can't be contained, and doesn't understand the first thing about commitment. Libra/Aquarius enjoys debating and debauchery in equal proportions. This love junkie needs to keep repeating that first thrill. When it's gone, baby, so is he or she.

The Cancer/Aquarius blend is intuitive, witty, and less timid than other Cancers. Still has moods, but closer to waterspouts that whirl and die down instead of days of morose pouting. More fun and less homey. Subject to erratic shifts in career and lifestyle. Scorpio/Aquarius melds two Fixed signs ruled by two planets notorious for life-shattering upheavals. A pressure-cooker psyche trapped in a cement-shoes personality. Swings between passion and indifference. Difficult but fascinating. Pisces/Aquarius sees things before they happen and has a philosophical outlook on every subject. Not as detached as other lunar Aquarians, this one seeks ideal love, but in all the wrong places. Prone to excess in sex, substance abuse, and depression.

Taurus/Aquarius is delightful and sincere and genuinely cares about everyone. Loyal to the core. Has lots of friends and loves to tinker with odd gadgets. No ulterior motives. One of the best catches in the Universe. The Virgo/Aquarius is less solid and much more unpredictable than your average Virgin. They believe in true partnership and have the uncanny ability to instantly size up a person or situation. Quirky, definitely offbeat (for Virgo), but so emotionally detached he or she can forget to come home. Blending Capricorn and Aquarius does odd things to the Goat. These creatures want to experience everything and change careers, lovers, and their minds lightning fast. This Goat chases the rainbow and needs a partner who can keep pace.

Aries/Aquarius blend is unconcerned with the opinions of others. Conventional relationships are OK, but this one's eccentricities can include group sex. But, hey, you don't have to participate. They chase the ideal on feet of clay. In the Leo/Aquarius combo, Fixed Fire meets Fixed Air. Can be romantic and philosophical, but is also changeable in love, and indiscreet. Will write your name on the locker room wall. This one yells a lot. Like living in a blast furnace. Sagittarius/Aquarius' head is so far out in space, he or she may actually discover life on another planet. Easily distracted. This one has exceptional personal magnetism, but wants a totally unconventional lifestyle. Minivans and the PTA will cause a complete breakdown.

Mars Is Afflicted

A deaf, dumb, and blind idiot could have made a better world than this.

Tennessee Williams (March 26)

AQUARIUS MARS/ARIES SUN

In Aquarius, Mars fires the passion of debate. Aquarius Mars natives are strongly opinionated, frequently radical, and attract trouble because of their bellicose presentation. They can be addicted to the telephone and/or e-mail, spending hours each day repeating the same tirade to an extensive circle of casual acquaintances. These creatures are social and belong to either casual or formal groups and organizations where they, often as not, end up alienating their fellow crossbearers by speaking their over-the-top version of the truth. Aquarius Mars makes silent enemies who may wait for years to exact revenge.

Aquarius Mars is romantically erratic, runs sexually hot and cold, with frequent periods of near-or-total celibacy followed by a hedonistic orgy with one or several partners. Sex is a frequent and favorite topic for discussion. Of course Aquarius Mars is the expert who knows it all, has tried it all, and will tell all.

Female Aquarius Mars

You are a champion shit disturber. You love to toss out explosive tidbits of gossip, controversy, or perverted facts, then sit back and watch the reaction. Depending on your mood of the moment, you may or may not later regret your actions. But that doesn't stop you. Neither does an opposing viewpoint. You love a hot debate nearly as much as a hot body and will drop whatever you are doing, including work, in favor of arguing your position. Think of Sagittarius Jane Fonda, Taurus

Ann-Margret. You need a mate who will be a friend first, and who will stand by you no matter how outrageous you get. The more eccentric, detached, and opinionated he or she is, the harder you fall.

Male Aquarius Mars

You can be so detached from reality that you frequently forget to eat. You can be crazy and perverse like Sagittarius Redd Foxx, or friendly and sincere like Sagittarius Phil Donahue. But, whatever your style, you are an original thinker. Your mind is clear, strong, and sharp. Your ideas are often inspired, frequently visionary, and sometimes so unconventional that you amaze yourself. You want a partner who will understand that you are a fast-forward man who's far ahead of his time. And who can put up with your detached attitude toward romance, and hot and cold sexual style. You need a belligerent bitch who can put you in your place.

Venus Is a Nympho

I've given my memoirs far more thought than any of my marriages.

Gloria Swanson (March 27)
AQUARIUS VENUS/ARIES SUN

In Aquarius, Venus is smitten with everything—as long as it is *not* conventional. The Aquarius Venus native's choice in lovers is as much for shock effect as romantic intention. These guys and dolls chase the unavailable, unattainable, or downright weird. This is another Aquarian distancing mechanism designed to prove that love is for suckers. They pursue the impossible dream, whether in romance or career, and are exceedingly stubborn and opinionated when crossed on either plane. Often his or her own worst enemy, both sexes pick at least one mate who is the worst possible match.

Aquarius Venus bestows the ability to predict trends and fads and the desire to shake up the status quo by challenging authority. These characters also have the remarkable ability to sway others to their way of thinking.

Female Venus Aquarius

You have principles, scruples, and moral character—within your peculiar style. The odd, quirky, and offbeat turn you on. You are nobody's fool. However, you love to pretend you are anything from a helpless twit to a hard-nosed businesswoman, and few can see through the charade or figure out what makes you tick. Think of Capricorn Kirstie Alley, Aries Reba McEntire. You need a mate who can see through your actress façade to the real, and passionate-about-life woman inside. What you end up with nine times out of ten is a sexy loser you can hypnotize with your candid (and well-rehearsed) wide-eyed stare.

Male Venus Aquarius

You love surprises. You have a low threshold of boredom in relationships and seek a partner who is different, even a little nutty. You are social, flirty, and have about two hundred "close" friends you casually circulate among. Think of Aries James Caan, Sagittarius Dick Van Dyke. Your ideal partner has the ability to keep you laughing, dangling, and expecting the unexpected. You'll pretend to try to figure out his or her mysterious ways, but, in truth, you get off on *not* being able to predict the future.

Fatal Attractions

Aquarius/Aries—Nonconformist with wild sexual imagination and open mind seeks dominating mental midget for sexual-but-precarious relationship. If you act like an adult, we could be the dynamic duo.

Aquarius/Taurus—Free-roaming sprite with sex-is-fun attitude and friends who call after midnight seeks clinging vine with sex-is-serious attitude and no compassion for mismatch of century. Micromini affair.

Aquarius/Gemini—Human dynamo who loves oddball causes and has an endless sexual imagination seeks chandelier-swinging soul mate with hip mind-set and zero tolerance for boredom. Lifetime fun.

Aquarius/Cancer—Breezy character with analytical approach to romance and pet rock seeks teary eyed calamity expert with pet mom, to confuse, irritate, inflict with permanent headache. Possible one-night stand, if we can stand each other that long.

Aquarius/Leo—Sex education expert with green toenails, fright-night hair, and one pair of jeans seeks lust-loving wild thing with elegant wardrobe and sleek mane for decadent sex and deadly morning after.

Aquarius/Virgo—Fun-loving eccentric, affectionately nicknamed Mad Dog, with opinions on every mystery of the Universe and a freewheeling lifestyle seeks sensible stay-at-home who prefers reading about life to living it for stimulating intellectual conversation, no sex, no love, no romance.

Aquarius/Libra—Kind-hearted but totally mad oddball who needs honesty, breathing room, and nonjealous partner seeks kind-hearted but totally self-absorbed screwball who needs adoring declarations and one-on-one attention for short, superficial romance. We'll always be friends.

Aquarius/Scorpio—Sexy-but-detached dreamer who loves mankind, variety, and freedom seeks paranoid fanatic who thinks love means tapping the phone line for peculiar affair, possible love. You'll smile despite yourself.

Aquarius/Sagittarius—Sexual researcher with master's in bizarre positions and need for freedom within a framework seeks fly-by-night bed gremlin who is packed and ready to head to the laboratory for sex among the Bunson burners. Fun, friendship, and long-term love, but no strings attached.

Aquarius/Capricorn—Free spirit with open-door policy on life, five hundred close friends, and stream-of-consciousness conversational style seeks intellectual dwarf with no friends and no interest in anything but being in charge for date that will end before we can fasten the seat belts.

Aquarius/Aquarius—Expert in conspiracy theories, saving obscure species of insects, and life on other planets seeks scientific type with degree in sexual experimentation and fungi collecting, for a match made on Uranus.

Aquarius/Pisces—Crop circle designer with conscious-raising approach to life and hair-raising sexual style seeks unconscious social dreamer with ability to do the splits upside down for abandoned sexual escapade, long-shot romance.

Scoring

Best Bets—Gemini, Sagittarius, Aquarius
Just Good Friends—Aries, Leo, Libra
Please Shoot Yourself Now—Taurus, Cancer, Virgo, Capricorn
The Dark Horse—Scorpio, Pisces

Affable and Aggravating Aquarians

Bobby Brown
Geena Davis
Ellen DeGeneres
Mia Farrow
Zsa Zsa Gabor
Yoko Ono
Lisa Marie Presley
Shakira
Justin Timberlake
Eddie Van Halen

Chapter Thirteen

PISCES

FEBRUARY 19–MARCH 20

Love Potion Number Nine

Element: Water. A kid could drown in this sea of love.

Quality: Mutable. Here today. Freaked out, whacked out, or moved out tomorrow.

Symbol: The Fishes. Moby-Dick meets Charlene Tuna.

Ruler: Neptune. God of false promises and anything wet.

Romantic Idol: Hot Lips Hoolihan.

Romantic Style: Enabler.

Favorite Pickup Line: "Buy you a drink?"

Dream First Date: In the back of a liquor store on a pallet of Dom Perignon with a full moon reflecting off the jug wines.

Erogenous Zone: Feet. Foot fetishes, toe sucking, ankle chains.

Sexual Quirk: Whispers, "I've never done *this* before." Works for a surprisingly long time.

Romancing the Sign

Women need a reason to have sex. Men just need a place.
BILLY CRYSTAL (MARCH 14)

If you are ready for a magical, mystical tour on a bus that leaks oil, belches smoke, and frequently gets lost in the fog, you are in the right place. Pisces is the Mystery Spot of the zodiac. Ruled by illusion, propelled by romance, and fueled with firewater and metaphysical philosophy, the sign of the Fishes is as loosey-goosey as they come.

Touted as the top romantic of the Universe, the Fish are actually kings and queens of "I can't say no." The Pisces-version of an ideal evening includes a declaration of undying love, the lethal combination of rich food and lots of alcohol, assorted cloying-scented candles, and at least one case of histrionics.

Pisces are ruled by instinct and frequently have visceral first reactions when meeting a prospective lover. Of course, because he or she is also likely to be drugged or drunk at the time, this early-warning system rarely functions properly, hence the Fish's propensity for repeatedly making poor choices. Even the clearheaded ones will swim toward the outcast, loser, abuser, or just plain idiot if he or she thinks this person can be redeemed.

Fish are the reason the excuses such as "It meant nothing to me, honey" and "Your check is in the mail" are still valid today. They believe *everything*. Pisces will forgive you for lying, cheating, and/or bankrupting them, as long as you say you are sorry, love their pets, and contributed some of the money to a worthy cause. This isn't as altruistic as it sounds, for Pisces will treat you exactly the same way.

Astrology often cites the sign of the Fish as being visionary, compassionate, and able to do anything from heal the sick to raise the dead. It's a terrible burden to a person who's used to being known in the neighborhood as *that sleazy drunk who's screwing the mail carrier.*

Screen idol Jean Harlow ran away from home at the tender age of sixteen to get married, in the first of several ill-fated romances. Harlow's professional success was in direct opposition to her disastrous personal life. Her posing nude at seventeen, relationships with gangsters, the rumor that she aborted a child fathered by classic movie star Leo William Powell, and the suicide of her second husband, Paul Bern, provided rich fodder for the gossip columns. Harlow searched for ideal love in the worst possible places, underscoring the classic Pisces attraction to life's seamier scenarios. The fact that she was only twenty-six when she died is a testament to how fast and far down a Fish can swim.

Before considering marriage, or a long-term commitment with a Fish, you should spend one weekend in the catatonic ward of your nearest psychiatric facility and one weekend in a classroom for hyperactive children. Pisces are emotionally either *on* or *off*. They are either totally in love with a person or idea, career, etc., or are totally ambivalent. "I don't care," is one of his or her favorite sayings. Not to be polite, but because Fish really don't care about much.

When lost in inner space, Fish spend a significant amount of time staring at the wall, at the TV, out the window, or at the floor where he or she is lying, face down. Pisces will call this anything from meditating to gathering the strength to mop the kitchen. When in manic mode, Mr./Ms. Fishhead throws him- or herself into a frenzy of cleaning and organizing. He or she will also start new hobbies, enroll in night school, and buy a stack of books to study. All of which will be discarded a few days later when the Fish's energy runs out. Think of how a real fish swims. First it lazily drifts along barely moving its tail. Then it jolts and darts through the water too fast to see.

Troll for one in a coffeehouse-cum–New Age bookstore, or any dark restaurant, theater, or stairwell. Pisces are easy to spot because they wear sunglasses indoors and always look confused. Fish are not the brightest stars in the sky. Pisces' awareness rheostat is set permanently on dim. Both sexes flop through life spouting vague references to distant career goals, *things* that will happen *someday,* and general assorted rhetoric that he or she repeats until you have the urge to shove a frying pan in his or her face.

Should a Fish cast his or net in your direction, you will be lured into a tide of romantic excess. You will be wooed with candlelight, moonlight, and wine; quiet conversation, cozy dinners, and wine; poetry and sexy, midnight phone calls. And wine. Beware of this hard-sell romantic come-on, for just as you are about to take his or her bait, Mr./Ms. Fish is highly likely to turn off just as suddenly for no reason and disappear, leaving you wondering what went wrong.

If you're after a practical, sensible, solid-citizen–type partner who can take charge in a crisis, find yourself a Capricorn. Pisces prefers to take the edge off the harsher aspects of reality with a couple of drinks or a little help from a friendly pharmacist. The harsher aspects include paying the rent on time, holding a regular job, and remembering to buy groceries. Fish meander through life on a road filled with fascinating illusions, impossible dreams, and unreachable destinations. If you think you are up to the trip, grab your transcendental meditation tapes, a jug of wine, and climb on board this big bus to nowhere.

'Til Death Do Us Part

Acting isn't really that difficult. It's really just lying well, and I've been practicing that most of my adult life.

Bruce Willis (March 19)

Catching One

It takes more than a loaf of bread and a jug of wine to get a Pisces moaning beside you in the waterbed. It takes a little fantasy, a couple of lies, and walking a fine boundary between sweetheart and swinger. Don't confuse this with looking hot for Scorpio but acting aloof. Scorpions know it's a game and play along for fun. Pisces needs to believe that you have a good soul; otherwise he or she won't be able to justify all the nasty sex that comes later.

Contrary to popular belief, Pisces, as a rule, does *not* do it on the first date. Fish love romance and the feeling of love building slowly, over drinks, dinner, day trips to the beach, and lots and lots of fantasizing. Fantasizing is nearly as good as sex to a Pisces. Feeding his or her fantasies with romantic or funny greeting cards, love notes, and frequent phone calls will earn you points. Sounding lonely, a bit depressed, or sharing a family crisis is worth extra credit. Owning a swimming pool, spa, or bathtub big enough for two will guarantee a date. So will having a police record, a therapist, or a drug habit.

Fish love the colors of the sea. Aquamarine, seafoam green, or silver, and fabrics that are sheer or shimmer are some favorites. He or she also believes in comfort, so when asking for a date, start with something informal. Invite yours to a Renaissance fair or the antiques mall. Wear a poet's shirt and tight pants or clean jeans and a sweatshirt sans logos, sayings, or swear words.

Act slightly detached or worried. Pisces thinks he or she is Rescue Ranger, although neither sex can do much other than listen and nod earnestly. But, one is more likely to let you screw his or her brains out if you appear to need some TLC. So, when you are wandering among the antiques, pick up a figurine of a dog or cat and reminisce about good old Kitty or faithful Spot of your childhood. If you have a memory to dredge up, great; if not, don't worry. Pisces doesn't care about something as mundane as facts as long as your tale is full of feeling.

A Pisces home is a combination ad for an overstuffed furniture store and a sixties museum. All will have at least one of the following: a set of black lights, some floor pillows, a lava lamp, or a collection of protest posters. Even if twenty, he or she will have a flower child's love of sandalwood and exotic music. If Mr./Ms. Fish *is* a flower child, he or she will have an original bong and incense burners that haven't stopped smoking since 1966. Later, at his or her place, be sure to compliment the way your Fish has managed to preserve the look of a hippy pad.

Say that it's been such a great day you don't want it to end. Your Fish's eyes should glaze slightly. Order takeout and offer to pick it up. Stop at the liquor store on the way back for as good a bottle of wine as you can afford. If your Fish doesn't drink wine, buy imported beer, or a fifth of whiskey.

Start cuddling/hugging in a neutral place such as the kitchen. Pisces are cuddle-crazy and will visibly weaken at the touch of a full-body hug. After dinner, remember illusion and keep the lights low and the music sexy; make frequent comments about living on a tropical island or how neat it would be to drop out and really *live* life. Don't bother with details, Mr./Ms. Fish wouldn't hear them anyway.

Freshen the drinks, or open another cold one, and move to the couch. Between sipping and kissing, mumble something that sounds like the *L*-word. This takes practice (unless you are a Scorpio or Leo), because you want the Fish to be doubtful enough to not ask you to repeat yourself. Don't worry, a Fish won't move in the next morning, as would a Libra. Pisces will respond by unbuttoning your shirt, taking your hand, and leading you to the bedroom. The Fish doesn't care what you said, just what he or she might have heard, because it triggered the romance-movie feeling that Pisces needs to proceed to the deed.

Once you dive beneath the covers, it's all *9½ Weeks.* That's the Universe's way of rewarding you for putting up with that soggy, sentimental crap and ruining your stomach lining with excessive alcohol. Once you come up for air, you'll have to start the process all over again. Fish need constant attention, constant illusion, and a partner who will take all the responsibility for keeping the relationship everything he or she dreams, hopes, and wishes it will be. Otherwise, you'll wake up one morning and this flounder will have darted off to Mexico with a pool shark in a pink Cadillac.

Surviving One

When you are sick of having a partner who fakes a heart attack every time she doesn't want to visit your relatives and who wouldn't know the truth if it was driving the semi that flattened him, it's time to dump that lying, emotional double-dealing phony.

Ridding yourself of a Fish takes some forethought, because the worse you act, the more he or she is liable to play doormat in a sick effort to hold onto the relationship. And the direct approach seldom works because Fish flee from confrontation faster than an Aquarius from a self-help seminar.

Have a migraine for a week. Refuse to share the couch or the remote. Say that you despise anything remotely related to New Age philosophy, whales, the homeless, or free puppies. Refuse to bathe or shave on the weekends. Forget to buy beer. Any of these tactics should alarm and disgust your Fish, who will begin to vacillate between shrieking like a dolphin on alert and curling into the fetal position on the bed. Kick it up a notch by saying you bought beer, but drank it all on the way home and threw the bottles at old ladies in the crosswalks. Say you hate children. By this time, if your Fish hasn't disappeared in the middle of the night, simply tell him or her that you just quit your job and it's his or her turn to support *you* for a change.

Along with Cancer and Taurus, Pisces rarely ends a long-term relationship. If this should happen, it means only one thing. He or she has another lover and intends to move directly from your home to his or hers. This ensures that the Fish will never have to spend a minute alone contemplating his or her insane life and also lays the groundwork for the next failed affair.

If you actually want this lying two-timer back, you must be a Water sign, too. Just pick up the phone and dump a sob story on your ex. Say you can't sleep. You need to talk. You have no intention of getting back together; you just need a friend. And don't forget to ask him or her to pick up a six-pack on the way over.

Get even by being cool and distant. Pisces can't stand neutrality when it's directed at them. Dating a brutally frank Sagittarius who will expound on your ex's infinite stupidity for letting you get away, when you *accidentally* bump into him or her at the lounge of the Holiday Inn would be fun, too.

Keeping One

Is it worth your time to stick by this dreamer who is sometimes so detached he or she forgets to eat? Definitely. And you won't need a course in hypnotherapy or a lifetime membership in a substance-abuse support group.

One of the misconceptions about Pisces is that he or she flees from life. This couldn't be further from the truth. Pisces absorbs life. All Water signs are emotional creatures, but Pisces is the empath who *feels and senses* other people's emotions and motives. Fish hone in on subtle undercurrents at home, the office, and with relatives and friends. And your Pisces is the one with the proverbial shoulder to cry upon. All the signs instinctively seek the Fish's sympathetic ear and nonjudgmental attitude. In turn, Pisces needs to download some of this information to you in order to release the tension it creates within his or her psyche. It's a selective process because the Fish is a storehouse of secrets, confidences, even shocking facts that others have willingly shared, which he or she will never disclose. It's this discrimination in passing along the day's events that causes your Pisces to repeat one story to you several times, in several versions, displaying several emotional states in the telling. Your Fish must release the negative energy, but will rarely break a confidence. Listen to him or her. But understand that Pisces isn't asking for advice or help; he or she is simply releasing an emotional overload, like a teakettle releases steam. Pisces also needs periods of solitude. Help yours rejuvenate by creating a private, quiet space at home where he or she can read, record thoughts in a journal, or simply catch one of his or her frequently needed naps.

No sign is as dedicated to romance as is Pisces. Yours will set the mood in his or her mind long before you lock eyes and lips. Your Fish adores small tokens of love. Brief notes in his or her lunch sack, funny or romantic greeting cards, or a sexy voice mail message all prove that your Pisces is never out of your thoughts. Later, you'll be rewarded for your thoughtfulness in a very delightful way.

All Fish love water, so remember to buy bath salts, bath oil, and bubble bath in a variety of scents and colors. A bath for two is one of Pisces' favorite foreplays.

Most have aching feet and you'll make points by giving yours a foot massage or splurging on a high-quality foot spa. Pisces' health can be fragile and Fish tire easily. Help keep yours in tiptop shape with regular exercise (swimming is ideal) and nutritious meals, prepared together and presented with a flourish.

Pisces' ego is directed outward, toward humanity. This leaves precious little inner reserve, so help yours stay balanced with frequent verbal head pats and lots of emotional support. Your Fish is an idealist at heart. Even the strong, silent ones wish for a perfect world and spend a great deal of time thinking about how to help make that ideal a reality.

The symbol of two Fish swimming in opposite directions symbolizes an inward search for enlightenment, as well as the outer lure of human comfort and pleasure. Yes, this sign seems to have a natural proclivity for falling victim to substance and/or emotional abuse. Usually, this only happens when Pisces feels trapped in a dead-end life. Understand that money, fame, or career success has nothing whatsoever to do with how a Pisces feels about life. The key to his or her inner nature is whether or not your Fish is true to him- or herself. Share your Pisces' dreams, add a few of your own, mix well, and presto—you'll have the secret formula for a magical mating with a sensitive, romantic, kind-hearted lover who will make your home a safe harbor, and your happiness one of his or her missions in life.

MoonLight or GasLight?

In my sex fantasy, nobody ever loves me for my mind.

NORA EPHRON (MAY 19)

PISCES MOON / TAURUS SUN

Fantasy is the key word to remember when dealing with a Pisces Moon. These natives abhor reality, and facts are dismissed with a slight shrug of the shoulders and/or confused look. Pisces Moons have mixed sympathies and often favor daydreaming about the way things *should be* instead of facing the truth. This is the Dangerous Liaison Moon. In the watery environment of Neptune, nothing is quite real. Here, the emotional structure is vague and restless. Through the signs, a Pisces Moon heightens the proclivity for substance abuse to make it through the night or a hard day at the office as well as through involvement in the seamier side of life.

Pisces is the weakest placement for the Moon. These are the fatalists of the Universe, who refuse to play the Lotto because they are convinced if they win, they'll be run over by a bus. These folks are also some of the laziest and most slovenly and absentminded creatures in the Universe.

The Pisces Moon is an extremely psychic placement, and these natives have scary talent for intuiting future events. He or she also believes in signs, portents, omens, and usually one of the esoteric sciences. Troubles with children sometimes plague a Pisces Moon.

You could say Double Pisces Joey Buttafuoco had kid troubles when he was sent to prison for his involvement with then-sixteen-year-old (Leo) Amy Fisher. Double Fish Lou Costello's brainless comic persona perfectly illustrates the other side of this hopeless-but-sweet character.

Cancer/Pisces does exactly what he or she pleases—with a smile, of course, because harsh words are unthinkable. They have brutal mood swings and a near-recluse lifestyle that will make you want to commit mayhem. Pisces lightens the Scorpio tendency to brood. These natives actually smile on occasion, especially when taking advantage of someone. They are also demanding, possessive, complicated, and hard to understand. Don't acknowledge you have money until well into the relationship, then prepare for an instant marriage proposal.

Aries/Pisces is in your face one moment and locked in the bedroom, brooding, the next. Secretive for an Aries, and very appealing, but forget marriage unless you approve the open lifestyle. An affair is out of this world with this wildly romantic sex machine. In the Leo/Pisces duo, the Lion demands the spotlight and the Fish pouts if it's turned on someone else. Can be very sweet and generous natured or can be like Jaws of the Jungle. Sagittarius/Pisces is complex. Lots of creatures run rampant in this one. Definitely interested in the religious experience, but whether that would be joining a monastery or just screwing his or her way to heaven is anyone's guess.

Gemini/Pisces is another multipersonality sign. This sweet, smart, charmer is as fickle as a bee in summer. A chronic date breaker who tries every designer drug on the street. Don't worry about a relationship, he or she probably won't show for the first date. Libra/Pisces wants only the unattainable. They put lovers on a pedestal, then immediately become disillusioned. This ensures the romantic turmoil to which this one is addicted. Aquarius/Pisces is an odd duck. Phobias, fears, and crises seem to be the norm. And the fact that he or she thinks it *is* normal will drive you nuts. This one wants to explore space, but is afraid to come out of the closet.

Taurus/Pisces is stubborn, extravagant, vacuous, and obtuse, and will piss off your friends with a smart-ass remark and laugh. Cheats, too. Other than that, not a bad catch.

Chicken Little must have been a Virgo/Pisces. This opposition creates a nervous worrier who constantly fears the worst about every facet of life. Needs a stable home. Every Capricorn/Pisces will have at least one dark secret you'll never discover. They have periods of sullen withdrawal and even after a lifetime, you won't be sure this one ever loved you.

Mars Is Afflicted

I like troubled people. Not that I don't like squared-away people, but I prefer neurotic people.

Stephen Sondheim (March 22)
PISCES MARS/ARIES SUN

Mars is all wet in Pisces. Impressionable and lazy, sensitive and empathetic, Pisces Mars is conflicted. Periods of withdrawal into daydreams and timidity are followed by bursts of maniacal energy and self-assurance. The Pisces Mars native's life and career often reflects this stop-start pattern. This person's anger manifests in the same manner. This is the classic Dolphin/Shark who wants peace at any cost, even mayhem.

Sexually, these boys and girls are pleasure seekers and champions at manipulation by seduction. The seductive art of the Pisces Mars is legendary, and anything goes as long as the mystique is complete, from traditional candlelight and soft music to exotic foods to dangerous drugs and/or alcohol. Casanova had Mars in Pisces and spent a good deal of his time perfecting his techniques. This bunch is prone to secret affairs, multiple partners, random sexual liaisons, and fantasizing about the perfect romance instead of working on the one they have.

Female Pisces Mars

Outside you may be Betty Boardroom, a tough-as-nails professional who can leap corporate ladders in a single bound
(think Libra Martina Navratilova). Inside you are Cinderella,
waiting for Prince Charming to come to your rescue (think
Gemini Marilyn Monroe). You seek a soul mate as idealistic as
you and who lives in the abstract. But you often fall for the
smooth charmer who carries you to sexual nirvana then
drops you back in the pumpkin patch the next morning.

Male Pisces Mars

You are one smooth operator. Assertive yet sensitive, you be-
guile potential lovers with your sexual chemistry. Think of
Aquarius Burt Reynolds, Cancer Tom Hanks. You can be so
easily distracted by love, that you frequently screw your way
in and out of divorce court with startling regularity. Your
ideal fantasy just stepped out of a 1950s black-and-white love
story where you are the hero, and he or she, the mysterious
stranger with a past, a pistol, and the police in hot pursuit.
Your real-life lover is more likely to need a nursemaid, or a
therapist.

Venus Is a Nympho

*I don't know if I'm going to burst out in tears and run off the
stage. Now that you're in the vulnerable position of having your
heart broken, some of these songs just rip me apart.*

ROD STEWART (JANUARY 10)
PISCES VENUS/CAPRICORN SUN

In Pisces, Venus becomes a siren, a mysterious lover who se-
duces with a look and who is addicted to falling in love. Pisces
Venus natives are sentimental and physically demonstrative.
As with all Pisces placements, these creatures have the unfor-
tunate habit of wasting themselves on loser/abusers who will

suck these poor Fish dry and pick their teeth with the bones. Pisces Venus' powerful inner strength often lies untapped because of a hesitant, acquiescing nature. Pisces Venus natives are moody and fickle and desire to be swept away by an all-consuming passion. When the tempest subsides, these Fish swim downstream, looking for another whirlpool of emotion.

Female Pisces Venus

Romance and money slip through your fingers faster than your last scheming lover left town. You are so illogical when choosing a partner that you often go against your keen intuition just so you can feel those waves of new love wash over you. You can be vulnerable and self-destructive, as was Aries Billie Holliday, or both seductress and seduced, like Aquarius Colette. Your imaginary lover is a combination Dudley Do-Right, Mr. Clean, and Casanova. But you usually end up with a blend of the flimflam man, Jabba-the-Hut, and Clyde Barrow.

Male Pisces Venus

Your charm lies in your vulnerability and gentlemanly good manners. Think Aquarius Tom Selleck, Gemini Andy Griffith. You have both an inexplicable talent for intuiting another's desire and the inspired ability to make his or her dream come true. In love, you are seldom without willing partners, however you long for another empathetic soul who is both ethereal and earthy. A Manhattan mermaid would suit you just fine.

Fatal Attractions

Pisces/Aries—Self-deluded dreamer with unrealistic expectations seeks self-serving romantic militant to validate my confused-in-love card. If you play nice, I'll stop drinking.

Pisces/Taurus—Weepy prisoner of love who's been locked in the tower of self-pity too long seeks big daddy with practical plan and thinking cap large enough for two. I'll bring chocolate. You bring a real life.

Pisces/Gemini—Introverted mystic with penchant for wrong choices and taste for light beer seeks extroverted gadabout with undersize conscience and church key for one steamy night that evaporates into thin air before dawn.

Pisces/Cancer—Sexually sublime romance savant who needs up-close-and-personal attention seeks winsome caretaker with loony sense of humor and double locks on the door. Nothing's perfect. This is close.

Pisces/Leo—Sweet-but-annoying private dancer with fishy character and unhealthy need to be needed seeks center-stage wild animal with hot body and temper to match for instant sexual attraction but no-future romance.

Pisces/Virgo—Permanently confused procrastinator who thrives on emotional chaos, beer, and peanuts seeks terminally enlightened, granola-eating organizer who lives by the Boy Scout oath and loves a challenge. Opposites attract. Could be sweet.

Pisces/Libra—Hopeless head case with irritated liver and wild sexual imagination seeks irritating nitpicker who has no imagination (and doesn't want one) and vicious mouth for the passive-aggressive duel to the death.

Pisces/Scorpio—Disillusioned, substance-abusing enabler, living in dream world, seeks selfish sex addict for sadomasochistic head games and true love.

Pisces/Sagittarius—Unstable-but-loving human doormat on permanent head trip seeks well-traveled bed pilot with dirty boots, for wine, swan songs, and one hot-sex-and-philosophy discussion.

Pisces/Capricorn—Underestimated underachiever with hand-me-down wardrobe and heart to match seeks politically correct, socially acceptable fraud for back-alley romance that could lead to up-front love.

Pisces/Aquarius—Self-educated drug tester and holistic healer with hands-on romantic style seeks romantically disconnected revolutionary who tells fantastic tales and loves to read for storybook romance. Doctor Strangelove meets Nurse Ratchet.

Pisces/Pisces—Myopic visionary with recipe for magic mushroom soup seeks self-made pharmacist and wine slob for reality-challenged love, heady sex, and fuzzy mornings after. The Ouija board sent me.

Scoring

Best Bets—Taurus, Cancer, Scorpio, Capricorn
Just Good Friends—Aries, Gemini, Pisces
Please Shoot Yourself Now—Libra, Sagittarius, Aquarius
The Dark Horse—Leo, Virgo

Passionate and Pithy Pisces

Mario Andretti
Drew Barrymore
Harry Belafonte
Kurt Cobain

Benicio Del Toro
Fabio
George Harrison
Tommy Lee
Sharon Stone
Elizabeth Taylor

Chapter Fourteen

Moon, Mars, and Venus Tables, 1940–2010

1940

JAN	FEB	MAR	APR	MAY	JUNE	JULY	AUG	SEPT	OCT	NOV	DEC
1LIB	1SAG	2CAP	1AQU	3ARI	2TAU	2GEM	2LEO	1VIR	2SCO	1SAG	2AQU
3SCO	4CAP	4AQU	3PIS	5TAU	4GEM	4CAN	4VIR	3LIB	4SAG	3CAP	5PIS
5SAG	6AQU	7PIS	6ARI	8GEM	6CAN	6LEO	6LIB	5SCO	6CAP	5AQU	7ARI
7CAP	9PIS	9ARI	8TAU	10CAN	9LEO	8VIR	9SCO	7SAG	9AQU	7PIS	10TAU
10AQU	11ARI	12TAU	11GEM	12LEO	11VIR	10LIB	11SAG	9CAP	11PIS	10ARI	12GEM
12PIS	14TAU	14GEM	13CAN	15VIR	13LIB	12SCO	13CAP	11AQU	14ARI	13TAU	15CAN
15ARI	16GEM	17CAN	15LEO	17LIB	15SCO	14SAG	15AQU	14PIS	16TAU	15GEM	17LEO
17TAU	18CAN	19LEO	17VIR	20SCO	17SAG	17CAP	18PIS	16ARI	19GEM	17CAN	19VIR
20GEM	20LEO	21VIR	19LIB	21SAG	19CAP	19AQU	20ARI	19TAU	21CAN	20LEO	21LIB
22CAN	22VIR	23LIB	21SCO	23CAP	22AQU	21PIS	23TAU	21GEM	23LEO	22VIR	23SCO
24LEO	24LIB	25SCO	23SAG	25AQU	24PIS	24ARI	25GEM	24CAN	26VIR	24LIB	26SAG
26VIR	26SCO	27SAG	26CAP	28PIS	27ARI	26TAU	28CAN	26LEO	28LIB	26SCO	28CAP
28LIB	29SAG	29CAP	28AQU	30ARI	29TAU	29GEM	30LEO	28VIR	30SCO	28SAG	30AQU
30SCO			30PIS			31CAN		30LIB		30CAP	

1941

JAN	FEB	MAR	APR	MAY	JUNE	JULY	AUG	SEPT	OCT	NOV	DEC
1PIS	2TAU	2TAU	1GEM	3LEO	1VIR	1LIB	1SAG	2AQU	1PIS	2TAU	2GEM
4ARI	5GEM	4GEM	3CAN	5VIR	4LIB	3SCO	3CAP	4PIS	4ARI	5GEM	5CAN
6TAU	7CAN	7CAN	5LEO	7LIB	6SCO	5SAG	5AQU	6ARI	6TAU	7CAN	7LEO
9GEM	10LEO	9LEO	8VIR	9SCO	8SAG	7CAP	8PIS	9TAU	9GEM	10LEO	10VIR
11CAN	12VIR	11VIR	10LIB	11SAG	10CAP	9AQU	10ARI	11GEM	11CAN	12VIR	12LIB
13LEO	14LIB	13LIB	12SCO	13CAP	12AQU	11PIS	13TAU	14CAN	14LEO	15LIB	14SCO
15VIR	16SCO	15SCO	14SAG	15AQU	14PIS	14ARI	15GEM	16LEO	16VIR	17SCO	16SAG
18LIB	18SAG	17SAG	16CAP	18PIS	16ARI	16TAU	18CAN	19VIR	18LIB	19SAG	18CAP
20SCO	20CAP	19CAP	18AQU	20ARI	19TAU	19GEM	20LEO	21LIB	20SCO	21CAP	20AQU
22SAG	23AQU	22AQU	20PIS	23TAU	21GEM	21CAN	22VIR	23SCO	22SAG	23AQU	22PIS
24CAP	25PIS	24PIS	23ARI	25GEM	24CAN	24LEO	24LIB	25SAG	24CAP	25PIS	24ARI
26AQU	27ARI	27ARI	25TAU	28CAN	26LEO	26VIR	26SCO	27CAP	26AQU	27ARI	27TAU
29PIS		29TAU	28GEM	30LEO	29VIR	28LIB	28SAG	29AQU	29PIS	30TAU	29GEM
31ARI			30CAN			30SCO	31CAP		31ARI		

1942

JAN	FEB	MAR	APR	MAY	JUNE	JULY	AUG	SEPT	OCT	NOV	DEC
1CAN	2VIR	1VIR	2SCO	2SAG	2AQU	1PIS	2TAU	1GEM	1CAN	2VIR	2LIB
3LEO	4LIB	4LIB	4SAG	4CAP	4PIS	4ARI	5GEM	4CAN	4LEO	5LIB	4SCO
6VIR	7SCO	6SCO	6CAP	6AQU	6ARI	6TAU	7CAN	6LEO	6VIR	7SCO	6SAG
8LIB	9SAG	8SAG	8AQU	8PIS	9TAU	9GEM	10LEO	9VIR	8LIB	9SAG	8CAP
10SCO	11CAP	10CAP	11PIS	10ARI	11GEM	11CAN	12VIR	11LIB	10SCO	11CAP	10AQU
12SAG	13AQU	12AQU	13ARI	13TAU	14CAN	14LEO	15LIB	13SCO	13SAG	13AQU	12PIS
14CAP	15PIS	14PIS	15TAU	15GEM	16LEO	16VIR	17SCO	15SAG	15CAP	15PIS	15ARI
16AQU	17ARI	17ARI	18GEM	18CAN	19VIR	18LIB	19SAG	17CAP	17AQU	17ARI	17TAU
19PIS	20TAU	19TAU	20CAN	20LEO	21LIB	21SCO	21CAP	20AQU	19PIS	20TAU	19GEM
21ARI	22GEM	21GEM	23LEO	23VIR	23SCO	23SAG	23AQU	22PIS	21ARI	22GEM	22CAN
23TAU	25CAN	24CAN	25VIR	25LIB	25SAG	25CAP	25PIS	24ARI	23TAU	25CAN	24LEO
26GEM	27LEO	26LEO	27LIB	27SCO	27CAP	27AQU	27ARI	26TAU	26GEM	27LEO	27VIR
28CAN		29VIR	30SCO	29SAG	29AQU	29PIS	30TAU	29GEM	28CAN	30VIR	29LIB
31LEO		31LIB		31CAP		31ARI			31LEO		

1943

JAN	FEB	MAR	APR	MAY	JUNE	JULY	AUG	SEPT	OCT	NOV	DEC
1SCO	1CAP	1CAP	1PIS	3TAU	1GEM	1CAN	2VIR	1LIB	1SCO	1CAP	1AQU
3SAG	3AQU	3AQU	3ARI	5GEM	4CAN	4LEO	5LIB	3SCO	3SAG	4AQU	3PIS
5CAP	5PIS	5PIS	5TAU	7CAN	6LEO	6VIR	7SCO	6SAG	5CAP	6PIS	5ARI
7AQU	7ARI	7ARI	8GEM	10LEO	9VIR	9LIB	10SAG	8CAP	7AQU	8ARI	7TAU
9PIS	10TAU	9TAU	10CAN	12VIR	11LIB	11SCO	12CAP	10AQU	9PIS	10TAU	10GEM
11ARI	12GEM	11GEM	13LEO	15LIB	14SCO	13SAG	14AQU	12PIS	12ARI	12GEM	12CAN
13TAU	14CAN	14CAN	15VIR	17SCO	16SAG	15CAP	16PIS	14ARI	14TAU	15CAN	14LEO
16GEM	17LEO	16LEO	18LIB	19SAG	18CAP	17AQU	18ARI	16TAU	16GEM	17LEO	17VIR
18CAN	19VIR	19VIR	20SCO	21CAP	20AQU	19PIS	20TAU	18GEM	18CAN	20VIR	19LIB
21LEO	22LIB	21LIB	22SAG	23AQU	22PIS	21ARI	22GEM	21CAN	21LEO	22LIB	22SCO
23VIR	24SCO	23SCO	24CAP	26PIS	24ARI	23TAU	25CAN	23LEO	23VIR	24SCO	24SAG
26LIB	26SAG	26SAG	26AQU	28ARI	26TAU	26GEM	27LEO	26VIR	26LIB	27SAG	26CAP
28SCO		28CAP	28PIS	30TAU	29GEM	28CAN	30VIR.	28LIB	28SCO	29CAP	28AQU
30SAG		30AQU	30ARI			31LEO			30SAG		30PIS

1944

JAN	FEB	MAR	APR	MAY	JUNE	JULY	AUG	SEPT	OCT	NOV	DEC
1ARI	2GEM	3CAN	1LEO	1VIR	3SCO	2SAG	1CAP	1PIS	1ARI	1GEM	1CAN
3TAU	4CAN	5LEO	4VIR	4LIB	5SAG	4CAP	3AQU	3ARI	3TAU	4CAN	3LEO
6GEM	7LEO	8VIR	6LIB	6SCO	7CAP	7AQU	5PIS	5TAU	5GEM	6LEO	6VIR
8CAN	9VIR	10LIB	9SCO	9SAG	9AQU	9PIS	7ARI	8GEM	7CAN	8VIR	8LIB
11LEO	12LIB	13SCO	11SAG	11CAP	11PIS	11ARI	9TAU	10CAN	10LEO	11LIB	11SCO
13VIR	14SCO	15SAG	14CAP	13AQU	13ARI	13TAU	11GEM	12LEO	12VIR	13SCO	13SAG
16LIB	17SAG	17CAP	16AQU	15PIS	16TAU	15GEM	14CAN	15VIR	15LIB	16SAG	15CAP
18SCO	19CAP	19AQU	18PIS	17ARI	18GEM	17CAN	16LEO	17LIB	17SCO	18CAP	18AQU
20SAG	21AQU	22PIS	20ARI	19TAU	20CAN	20LEO	18VIR	20SCO	19SAG	20AQU	20PIS
23CAP	23PIS	24ARI	22TAU	21GEM	22LEO	22VIR	21LIB	22SAG	22CAP	23PIS	22ARI
25AQU	25ARI	26TAU	24GEM	24CAN	25VIR	25LIB	24SCO	25CAP	24AQU	25ARI	24TAU
27PIS	27TAU	28GEM	26CAN	26LEO	27LIB	27SCO	26SAG	27AQU	26PIS	27TAU	26GEM
29ARI	29GEM	30CAN	29LEO	29VIR	30SCO	30SAG	28CAP	29PIS	28ARI	29GEM	28CAN
31TAU				31LIB			30AQU		30TAU		31LEO

1945

JAN	FEB	MAR	APR	MAY	JUNE	JULY	AUG	SEPT	OCT	NOV	DEC
2VIR	1LIB	3SCO	1SAG	1CAP	2PIS	1ARI	2GEM	2LEO	2VIR	1LIB	3SAG
4LIB	3SCO	5SAG	4CAP	3AQU	4ARI	3TAU	4CAN	5VIR	4LIB	3SCO	6CAP
7SCO	6SAG	8CAP	6AQU	6PIS	6TAU	6GEM	6LEO	7LIB	7SCO	6SAG	8AQU
9SAG	8CAP	10AQU	8PIS	8ARI	8GEM	8CAN	8VIR	10SCO	10SAG	8CAP	10PIS
12CAP	10AQU	12PIS	10ARI	10TAU	10CAN	10LEO	11LIB	12SAG	12CAP	11AQU	12ARI
14AQU	12PIS	14ARI	12TAU	12GEM	12LEO	12VIR	13SCO	15CAP	14AQU	13PIS	15TAU
16PIS	14ARI	16TAU	14GEM	14CAN	15VIR	15LIB	16SAG	17AQU	17PIS	15ARI	17GEM
18ARI	17TAU	18GEM	16CAN	16LEO	17LIB	17SCO	18CAP	19PIS	19ARI	17TAU	19CAN
20TAU	19GEM	20CAN	19LEO	18VIR	20SCO	20SAG	21AQU	21ARI	21TAU	19GEM	21LEO
22GEM	21CAN	22LEO	21VIR	21LIB	22SAG	22CAP	23PIS	23TAU	23GEM	21CAN	23VIR
25CAN	23LEO	25VIR	24LIB	23SCO	25CAP	24AQU	25ARI	25GEM	25CAN	23LEO	25LIB
27LEO	26VIR	27LIB	26SCO	26SAG	27AQU	26PIS	27TAU	27CAN	27LEO	26VIR	28SCO
29VIR	28LIB	30SCO	29SAG	28CAP	29PIS	29ARI	29GEM	30LEO	29VIR	28LIB	30SAG
				31AQU		31TAU	31CAN			30SCO	

1946

JAN	FEB	MAR	APR	MAY	JUNE	JULY	AUG	SEPT	OCT	NOV	DEC
2CAP	1AQU	2PIS	1ARI	2GEM	1CAN	2VIR	1LIB	2SAG	2CAP	1AQU	3ARI
4AQU	3PIS	4ARI	3TAU	4CAN	3LEO	4LIB	3SCO	5CAP	4AQU	3PIS	5TAU
6PIS	5ARI	6TAU	5GEM	6LEO	5VIR	7SCO	6SAG	7AQU	7PIS	5ARI	7GEM
9ARI	7TAU	8GEM	7CAN	8VIR	7LIB	9SAG	8CAP	9PIS	9ARI	7TAU	9CAN
11TAU	9GEM	11CAN	9LEO	11LIB	10SCO	12CAP	11AQU	12ARI	11TAU	10GEM	11LEO
13GEM	11CAN	13LEO	11VIR	13SCO	12SAG	14AQU	13PIS	14TAU	13GEM	12CAN	13VIR
15CAN	13LEO	15VIR	14LIB	16SAG	15CAP	17PIS	15ARI	16GEM	15CAN	14LEO	15LIB
17LEO	16VIR	17LIB	16SCO	18CAP	17AQU	19ARI	17TAU	18CAN	17LEO	16VIR	18SCO
19VIR	18LIB	20SCO	19SAG	21AQU	20PIS	21TAU	20GEM	20LEO	20VIR	18LIB	20SAG
22LIB	20SCO	22SAG	21CAP	23PIS	22ARI	23GEM	22CAN	22VIR	22LIB	20SCO	23CAP
24SCO	23SAG	25CAP	24AQU	26ARI	24TAU	25CAN	24LEO	25LIB	24SCO	23SAG	25AQU
27SAG	26CAP	27AQU	26PIS	28TAU	26GEM	27LEO	26VIR	27SCO	27SAG	25CAP	28PIS
29CAP	28AQU	30PIS	28ARI	30GEM	28CAN	30VIR	28LIB	29SAG	29CAP	28AQU	30ARI
			30TAU		30LEO		31SCO			30PIS	

1947

JAN	FEB	MAR	APR	MAY	JUNE	JULY	AUG	SEPT	OCT	NOV	DEC
1TAU	2CAN	1CAN	2VIR	1LIB	2SAG	2CAP	1AQU	2ARI	1TAU	2CAN	1LEO
3GEM	4LEO	3LEO	4LIB	3SCO	5CAP	4AQU	3PIS	4TAU	4GEM	4LEO	3VIR
5CAN	6VIR	5VIR	6SCO	6SAG	7AQU	7PIS	6ARI	6GEM	6CAN	6VIR	6LIB
7LEO	8LIB	7LIB	8SAG	8CAP	10PIS	9ARI	8TAU	9CAN	8LEO	8LIB	8SCO
9VIR	10SCO	10SCO	11CAP	11AQU	12ARI	12TAU	10GEM	11LEO	10VIR	11SCO	10SAG
12LIB	13SAG	12SAG	13AQU	13PIS	14TAU	14GEM	12CAN	13VIR	12LIB	13SAG	13CAP
14SCO	15CAP	15CAP	16PIS	16ARI	16GEM	16CAN	14LEO	15LIB	14SCO	15CAP	15AQU
16SAG	18AQU	17AQU	18ARI	18TAU	18CAN	18LEO	16VIR	17SCO	17SAG	18AQU	18PIS
19CAP	20PIS	20PIS	20TAU	20GEM	20LEO	20VIR	18LIB	19SAG	19CAP	20PIS	20ARI
22AQU	23ARI	22ARI	23GEM	22CAN	22VIR	22LIB	20SCO	22CAP	22AQU	23ARI	23TAU
24PIS	25TAU	24TAU	25CAN	24LEO	25LIB	24SCO	23SAG	24AQU	24PIS	25TAU	25GEM
26ARI	27GEM	26GEM	27LEO	26VIR	27SCO	27SAG	25CAP	27PIS	26ARI	27GEM	27CAN
29TAU		28CAN	29VIR	28LIB	29SAG	29CAP	28AQU	29ARI	29TAU	29CAN	29LEO
31GEM		31LEO		31SCO			30PIS		31GEM		31VIR

1948

JAN	FEB	MAR	APR	MAY	JUNE	JULY	AUG	SEPT	OCT	NOV	DEC
2LIB	3SAG	1SAG	2AQU	2PIS	1ARI	1TAU	2CAN	2VIR	1LIB	2SAG	2CAP
4SCO	5CAP	3CAP	5PIS	5ARI	3TAU	3GEM	4LEO	4LIB	3SCO	4CAP	4AQU
6SAG	8AQU	6AQU	7ARI	7TAU	6GEM	5CAN	6VIR	6SCO	6SAG	7AQU	6PIS
9CAP	10PIS	8PIS	10TAU	9GEM	8CAN	7LEO	8LIB	8SAG	8CAP	9PIS	9ARI
11AQU	13ARI	11ARI	12GEM	11CAN	10LEO	9VIR	10SCO	11CAP	10AQU	12ARI	12TAU
14PIS	15TAU	13TAU	14CAN	14LEO	12VIR	11LIB	12SAG	13AQU	13PIS	14TAU	14GEM
16ARI	17GEM	16GEM	16LEO	16VIR	14LIB	13SCO	14CAP	16PIS	15ARI	17GEM	16CAN
19TAU	20CAN	18CAN	18VIR	18LIB	16SCO	16SAG	17AQU	18ARI	18TAU	19CAN	18LEO
21GEM	22LEO	20LEO	21LIB	20SCO	18SAG	18CAP	19PIS	21TAU	20GEM	21LEO	20VIR
23CAN	24VIR	22VIR	23SCO	22SAG	21CAP	21AQU	22ARI	23GEM	23CAN	23VIR	22LIB
25LEO	26LIB	24LIB	25SAG	25CAP	23AQU	23PIS	24TAU	25CAN	25LEO	25LIB	25SCO
27VIR	28SCO	26SCO	27CAP	27AQU	26PIS	26ARI	27GEM	27LEO	27VIR	27SCO	27SAG
29LIB		28SAG	30AQU	29PIS	28ARI	28TAU	29CAN	29VIR	29LIB	29SAG	29CAP
31SCO		31CAP				30GEM	31LEO		31SCO		31AQU

1949

JAN	FEB	MAR	APR	MAY	JUNE	JULY	AUG	SEPT	OCT	NOV	DEC
3PIS	2ARI	1ARI	2GEM	2CAN	2VIR	2LIB	2SAG	1CAP	3PIS	2ARI	1TAU
5ARI	4TAU	3TAU	5CAN	4LEO	5LIB	4SCO	5CAP	3AQU	5ARI	4TAU	4GEM
8TAU	7GEM	6GEM	7LEO	6VIR	7SCO	6SAG	7AQU	6PIS	8TAU	7GEM	6CAN
10GEM	9CAN	8CAN	9VIR	8LIB	9SAG	8CAP	9PIS	8ARI	10GEM	9CAN	9LEO
12CAN	11LEO	10LEO	11LIB	10SCO	11CAP	11AQU	12ARI	11TAU	13CAN	11LEO	11VIR
15LEO	13VIR	13VIR	13SCO	12SAG	13AQU	13PIS	14TAU	13GEM	15LEO	14VIR	13LIB
17VIR	15LIB	15LIB	15SAG	15CAP	16PIS	15ARI	17GEM	15CAN	17VIR	16LIB	15SCO
19LIB	17SCO	17SCO	17CAP	17AQU	18ARI	18TAU	19CAN	18LEO	19LIB	18SCO	17SAG
21SCO	19SAG	19SAG	19AQU	19PIS	21TAU	20GEM	21LEO	20VIR	21SCO	20SAG	19CAP
23SAG	22CAP	21CAP	22PIS	22ARI	23GEM	23CAN	23VIR	22LIB	23SAG	22CAP	21AQU
25CAP	24AQU	23AQU	24ARI	24TAU	25CAN	25LEO	25LIB	24SCO	25CAP	24AQU	24PIS
28AQU	26PIS	26PIS	27TAU	27GEM	28LEO	27VIR	27SCO	26SAG	28AQU	26PIS	26ARI
30PIS		28ARI	29GEM	29CAN	30VIR	29LIB	30SAG	28CAP	30PIS	29ARI	29TAU
		31TAU		31LEO		31SCO		30AQU			31GEM

1950

JAN	FEB	MAR	APR	MAY	JUNE	JULY	AUG	SEPT	OCT	NOV	DEC
3CAN	1LEO	1LEO	1LIB	1SCO	1CAP	1AQU	2ARI	3GEM	3CAN	2LEO	1VIR
5LEO	3VIR	3VIR	3SCO	3SAG	3AQU	3PIS	4TAU	5CAN	5LEO	4VIR	3LIB
7VIR	6LIB	5LIB	5SAG	5CAP	5PIS	5ARI	7GEM	8LEO	7VIR	6LIB	6SCO
9LIB	8SCO	7SCO	7CAP	7AQU	8ARI	8TAU	9CAN	10VIR	10LIB	8SCO	8SAG
11SCO	10SAG	9SAG	10AQU	9PIS	10TAU	10GEM	11LEO	12LIB	12SCO	10SAG	10CAP
14SAG	12CAP	11CAP	12PIS	12ARI	13GEM	13CAN	14VIR	14SCO	14SAG	12CAP	12AQU
16CAP	14AQU	13AQU	14ARI	14TAU	15CAN	15LEO	16LIB	16SAG	16CAP	14AQU	14PIS
18AQU	16PIS	16PIS	17TAU	17GEM	18LEO	17VIR	18SCO	18CAP	18AQU	16PIS	16ARI
20PIS	19ARI	18ARI	19GEM	19CAN	20VIR	20LIB	20SAG	21AQU	20PIS	19ARI	19TAU
22ARI	21TAU	21TAU	22CAN	22LEO	22LIB	22SCO	22CAP	23PIS	23ARI	21TAU	21GEM
25TAU	24GEM	23GEM	24LEO	24VIR	25SCO	24SAG	24AQU	25ARI	25TAU	24GEM	24CAN
28GEM	26CAN	26CAN	27VIR	26LIB	27SAG	26CAP	27PIS	28TAU	28GEM	26CAN	26LEO
30CAN		28LEO	29LIB	28SCO	29CAP	28AQU	29ARI	30GEM	30CAN	29LEO	28VIR
		30VIR		30SAG		30PIS	31TAU				31LIB

1951

JAN	FEB	MAR	APR	MAY	JUNE	JULY	AUG	SEPT	OCT	NOV	DEC
2SCO	2CAP	2CAP	2PIS	2ARI	3GEM	3CAN	1LEO	3LIB	2SCO	1SAG	2AQU
4SAG	4AQU	4AQU	5ARI	4TAU	5CAN	5LEO	4VIR	5SCO	4SAG	3CAP	4PIS
6CAP	7PIS	6PIS	7TAU	7GEM	8LEO	8VIR	6LIB	7SAG	6CAP	5AQU	6ARI
8AQU	9ARI	8ARI	9GEM	9CAN	10VIR	10LIB	9SCO	9CAP	8AQU	7PIS	9TAU
10PIS	11TAU	11TAU	12CAN	12LEO	13LIB	12SCO	11SAG	11AQU	11PIS	9ARI	11GEM
12ARI	14GEM	13GEM	14LEO	14VIR	15SCO	14SAG	13CAP	13PIS	13ARI	11TAU	13CAN
15TAU	16CAN	16CAN	17VIR	16LIB	17SAG	16CAP	15AQU	15ARI	15TAU	14GEM	16LEO
17GEM	19LEO	18LEO	19LIB	19SCO	19CAP	18AQU	17PIS	18TAU	17GEM	16CAN	19VIR
20CAN	21VIR	20VIR	21SCO	21SAG	21AQU	20PIS	19ARI	20GEM	20CAN	19LEO	21LIB
22LEO	23LIB	23LIB	23SAG	23CAP	23PIS	23ARI	21TAU	23CAN	22LEO	21VIR	23SCO
25VIR	25SCO	25SCO	25CAP	25AQU	25ARI	25TAU	24GEM	25LEO	25VIR	24LIB	25SAG
27LIB	28SAG	27SAG	27AQU	27PIS	28TAU	27GEM	26CAN	28VIR	27LIB	26SCO	27CAP
29SCO		29CAP	29PIS	29ARI	30GEM	30CAN	29LEO	30LIB	29SCO	28SAG	29AQU
31SAG		31AQU		31TAU		31VIR				30CAP	31PIS

1952

JAN	FEB	MAR	APR	MAY	JUNE	JULY	AUG	SEPT	OCT	NOV	DEC
3ARI	1TAU	2GEM	1CAN	3VIR	2LIB	2SCO	2CAP	1AQU	2ARI	1TAU	2CAN
5TAU	3GEM	4CAN	3LEO	5LIB	4SCO	4SAG	4AQU	3PIS	4TAU	3GEM	5LEO
7GEM	6CAN	7LEO	6VIR	8SCO	6SAG	6CAP	6PIS	5ARI	6GEM	5CAN	7VIR
10CAN	9LEO	9VIR	8LIB	10SAG	8CAP	8AQU	8ARI	7TAU	9CAN	7LEO	10LIB
12LEO	11VIR	12LIB	10SCO	12CAP	10AQU	10PIS	10TAU	9GEM	11LEO	10VIR	12SCO
15VIR	14LIB	14SCO	13SAG	14AQU	12PIS	12ARI	13GEM	11CAN	14VIR	13LIB	15SAG
17LIB	16SCO	16SAG	15CAP	16PIS	15ARI	14TAU	15CAN	14LEO	16LIB	15SCO	17CAP
20SCO	18SAG	19CAP	17AQU	18ARI	17TAU	16GEM	18LEO	16VIR	19SCO	17SAG	19AQU
22SAG	20CAP	21AQU	19PIS	21TAU	19GEM	19CAN	20VIR	19LIB	21SAG	19CAP	21PIS
24CAP	22AQU	23PIS	21ARI	23GEM	22CAN	21LEO	23LIB	21SCO	23CAP	21AQU	23ARI
26AQU	24PIS	25ARI	23TAU	25CAN	24LEO	24VIR	25SCO	24SAG	25AQU	24PIS	25TAU
28PIS	26ARI	27TAU	26GEM	28LEO	27VIR	26LIB	27SAG	26CAP	27PIS	26ARI	27GEM
30ARI	29TAU	29GEM	28CAN	30VIR	29LIB	29SCO	30CAP	28AQU	29ARI	28TAU	30CAN
			30LEO			31SAG		30PIS		30GEM	

1953

JAN	FEB	MAR	APR	MAY	JUNE	JULY	AUG	SEPT	OCT	NOV	DEC
1LEO	3LIB	2LIB	1SCO	2CAP	1AQU	2ARI	1TAU	1CAN	1LEO	2LIB	2SCO
4VIR	5SCO	4SCO	3SAG	5AQU	3PIS	5TAU	3GEM	4LEO	4VIR	5SCO	5SAG
6LIB	7SAG	7SAG	5CAP	7PIS	5ARI	7GEM	5CAN	6VIR	6LIB	7SAG	7CAP
9SCO	10CAP	9CAP	7AQU	9ARI	7TAU	9CAN	8LEO	9LIB	9SCO	10CAP	9AQU
11SAG	12AQU	11AQU	10PIS	11TAU	9GEM	11LEO	10VIR	11SCO	11SAG	12AQU	11PIS
13CAP	14PIS	13PIS	12ARI	13GEM	12CAN	14VIR	13LIB	14SAG	13CAP	14PIS	14ARI
15AQU	16ARI	15ARI	14TAU	15CAN	14LEO	16LIB	15SCO	16CAP	16AQU	16ARI	16TAU
17PIS	18TAU	17TAU	16GEM	18LEO	16VIR	19SCO	18SAG	18AQU	18PIS	18TAU	18GEM
19ARI	20GEM	19GEM	18CAN	20VIR	19LIB	21SAG	20CAP	21PIS	20ARI	20GEM	20CAN
21TAU	22CAN	22CAN	20LEO	23LIB	21SCO	23CAP	22AQU	23ARI	22TAU	22CAN	22LEO
24GEM	25LEO	24LEO	23VIR	25SCO	24SAG	26AQU	24PIS	25TAU	24GEM	25LEO	25VIR
26CAN	27VIR	27VIR	25LIB	27SAG	26CAP	28PIS	26ARI	27GEM	26CAN	27VIR	27LIB
28LEO		29LIB	28SCO	30CAP	28AQU	30ARI	28TAU	29CAN	28LEO	30LIB	30SCO
31VIR			30SAG		30PIS		30GEM		31VIR		

1954

JAN	FEB	MAR	APR	MAY	JUNE	JULY	AUG	SEPT	OCT	NOV	DEC
1SAG	2AQU	1AQU	2ARI	1TAU	2CAN	1LEO	2LIB	1SCO	1SAG	1AQU	2PIS
3CAP	4PIS	3PIS	4TAU	3GEM	4LEO	4VIR	5SCO	4SAG	4CAP	5PIS	4ARI
6AQU	6ARI	5ARI	6GEM	5CAN	6VIR	6LIB	7SAG	6CAP	6AQU	7ARI	6TAU
8PIS	8TAU	7TAU	8CAN	8LEO	9LIB	9SCO	10CAP	9AQU	8PIS	9TAU	8GEM
10ARI	10GEM	10GEM	10LEO	10VIR	11SCO	11SAG	12AQU	11PIS	10ARI	11GEM	10CAN
12TAU	13CAN	12CAN	13VIR	12LIB	14SAG	14CAP	14PIS	13ARI	12TAU	13CAN	12LEO
14GEM	15LEO	14LEO	15LIB	15SCO	16CAP	16AQU	16ARI	15TAU	14GEM	15LEO	14VIR
16CAN	17VIR	16VIR	18SCO	17SAG	19AQU	18PIS	19TAU	17GEM	16CAN	17VIR	17LIB
19LEO	20LIB	19LIB	20SAG	20CAP	21PIS	20ARI	21GEM	19CAN	19LEO	20LIB	19SCO
21VIR	22SCO	21SCO	23CAP	22AQU	23ARI	22TAU	23CAN	21LEO	21VIR	22SCO	22SAG
23LIB	25SAG	24SAG	25AQU	25PIS	25TAU	24GEM	25LEO	24VIR	23LIB	25SAG	24CAP
26SCO	27CAP	26CAP	27PIS	27ARI	27GEM	27CAN	27VIR	26LIB	26SCO	27CAP	27AQU
28SAG		29AQU	29ARI	29TAU	29CAN	29LEO	30LIB	29SCO	28SAG	30AQU	29PIS
31CAP		31PIS		31GEM		31VIR			31CAP		31ARI

1955

JAN	FEB	MAR	APR	MAY	JUNE	JULY	AUG	SEPT	OCT	NOV	DEC
3TAU	1GEM	2CAN	1LEO	2LIB	1SCO	1SAG	2AQU	1PIS	1ARI	1GEM	1CAN
5GEM	3CAN	4LEO	3VIR	5SCO	4SAG	3CAP	5PIS	3ARI	3TAU	3CAN	3LEO
7CAN	5LEO	7VIR	5LIB	7SAG	6CAP	6AQU	7ARI	5TAU	5GEM	5LEO	5VIR
9LEO	7VIR	9LIB	8SCO	10CAP	9AQU	8PIS	9TAU	8GEM	7CAN	7VIR	7LIB
11VIR	10LIB	11SCO	10SAG	12AQU	11PIS	11ARI	11GEM	10CAN	9LEO	10LIB	9SCO
13LIB	12SCO	14SAG	13CAP	15PIS	13ARI	13TAU	13CAN	12LEO	11VIR	12SCO	12SAG
16SCO	15SAG	16CAP	15AQU	17ARI	16TAU	15GEM	15LEO	14VIR	13LIB	15SAG	14CAP
18SAG	17CAP	19AQU	18PIS	19TAU	18GEM	17CAN	18VIR	16LIB	16SCO	17CAP	17AQU
21CAP	19AQU	21PIS	20ARI	21GEM	20CAN	19LEO	20LIB	18SCO	18SAG	20AQU	19PIS
23AQU	22PIS	23ARI	22TAU	23CAN	22LEO	21VIR	22SCO	20SAG	21CAP	22PIS	22ARI
25PIS	24ARI	25TAU	24GEM	25LEO	24VIR	23LIB	25SAG	23CAP	23AQU	24ARI	24TAU
28ARI	26TAU	27GEM	26CAN	27VIR	26LIB	26SCO	27CAP	26AQU	26PIS	27TAU	26GEM
30TAU	28GEM	29CAN	28LEO	30LIB	28SCO	28SAG	30AQU	28PIS	28ARI	29GEM	28CAN
			30VIR			31CAP			30TAU		30LEO

1956

JAN	FEB	MAR	APR	MAY	JUNE	JULY	AUG	SEPT	OCT	NOV	DEC
1VIR	2SCO	3SAG	1CAP	1AQU	3ARI	2TAU	1GEM	1LEO	1VIR	1SCO	1SAG
3LIB	4SAG	5CAP	4AQU	4PIS	5TAU	4GEM	3CAN	3VIR	3LIB	3SAG	3CAP
6SCO	7CAP	8AQU	6PIS	6ARI	7GEM	6CAN	5LEO	5LIB	5SCO	6CAP	6AQU
8SAG	9AQU	10PIS	9ARI	8TAU	9CAN	8LEO	7VIR	7SCO	7SAG	8AQU	8PIS
11CAP	12PIS	12ARI	11TAU	11GEM	11LEO	10VIR	9LIB	10SAG	10CAP	11PIS	11ARI
13AQU	14ARI	15TAU	13GEM	13CAN	13VIR	12LIB	11SCO	12CAP	12AQU	13ARI	13TAU
16PIS	16TAU	17GEM	15CAN	15LEO	15LIB	15SCO	13SAG	15AQU	15PIS	16TAU	15GEM
18ARI	19GEM	19CAN	17LEO	17VIR	18SCO	17SAG	16CAP	17PIS	17ARI	18GEM	17CAN
20TAU	21CAN	21LEO	20VIR	19LIB	20SAG	20CAP	18AQU	20ARI	19TAU	20CAN	19LEO
22GEM	23LEO	23VIR	22LIB	21SCO	22CAP	22AQU	21PIS	22TAU	22GEM	22LEO	21VIR
24CAN	25VIR	25LIB	24SCO	24SAG	25AQU	25PIS	23ARI	24GEM	24CAN	24VIR	24LIB
26LEO	27LIB	28SCO	26SAG	26CAP	27PIS	27ARI	26TAU	26CAN	26LEO	26LIB	26SCO
28VIR	29SCO	30SAG	29CAP	29AQU	30ARI	20TAU	28GEM	29LEO	28VIR	29SCO	28SAG
31LIB				31PIS			30CAN		30LIB		31CAP

1957

JAN	FEB	MAR	APR	MAY	JUNE	JULY	AUG	SEPT	OCT	NOV	DEC
2AQU	1PIS	3ARI	1TAU	1GEM	1LEO	1VIR	1SCO	2CAP	2AQU	1PIS	1ARI
5PIS	3ARI	5TAU	4GEM	3CAN	4VIR	3LIB	4SAG	5AQU	4PIS	3ARI	3TAU
7ARI	6TAU	7GEM	6CAN	5LEO	6LIB	5SCO	6CAP	7PIS	7ARI	6TAU	5GEM
9TAU	8GEM	10CAN	8LEO	7VIR	8SCO	7SAG	8AQU	10ARI	9TAU	8GEM	8CAN
12GEM	10CAN	12LEO	10VIR	9LIB	10SAG	10CAP	11PIS	12TAU	12GEM	10CAN	10LEO
14CAN	12LEO	14VIR	12LIB	12SCO	12CAP	12AQU	13ARI	15GEM	14CAN	13LEO	12VIR
16LEO	14VIR	16LIB	14SCO	14SAG	15AQU	15PIS	16TAU	17CAN	16LEO	15VIR	14LIB
18VIR	16LIB	18SCO	16SAG	16CAP	17PIS	17ARI	18GEM	19LEO	18VIR	17LIB	16SCO
20LIB	18SCO	20SAG	19CAP	18AQU	20ARI	20TAU	21CAN	21VIR	21LIB	19SCO	18SAG
22SCO	21SAG	22CAP	21AQU	21PIS	22TAU	22GEM	23LEO	23LIB	23SCO	21SAG	21CAP
24SAG	23CAP	25AQU	24PIS	23ARI	25GEM	24CAN	25VIR	25SCO	25SAG	23CAP	23AQU
27CAP	26AQU	27PIS	26ARI	26TAU	27CAN	26LEO	27LIB	27SAG	27CAP	26AQU	25PIS
29AQU	28PIS	30ARI	29TAU	28GEM	29LEO	28VIR	29SCO	29CAP	29AQU	28PIS	28ARI
				30CAN		30LIB	31SAG				30TAU

1958

JAN	FEB	MAR	APR	MAY	JUNE	JULY	AUG	SEPT	OCT	NOV	DEC
2GEM	3LEO	2LEO	1VIR	2SCO	3CAP	2AQU	1PIS	2TAU	2GEM	1CAN	3VIR
4CAN	5VIR	4VIR	3LIB	4SAG	5AQU	4PIS	3ARI	5GEM	4CAN	3LEO	5LIB
6LEO	7LIB	6LIB	5SCO	6CAP	7PIS	7ARI	6TAU	7CAN	7LEO	5VIR	7SCO
8VIR	9SCO	8SCO	7SAG	8AQU	10ARI	9TAU	8GEM	9LEO	9VIR	7LIB	9SAG
10LIB	11SAG	10SAG	9CAP	11PIS	12TAU	12GEM	11CAN	11VIR	11LIB	9SCO	11CAP
12SCO	13CAP	12CAP	11AQU	13ARI	15GEM	14CAN	13LEO	13LIB	13SCO	11SAG	13AQU
15SAG	16AQU	15AQU	13PIS	16TAU	17CAN	17LEO	15VIR	15SCO	15SAG	13CAP	15PIS
17CAP	18PIS	17PIS	16ARI	18GEM	19LEO	19VIR	17LIB	18SAG	17CAP	16AQU	18ARI
19AQU	21ARI	20ARI	19TAU	21CAN	21VIR	21LIB	19SCO	20CAP	19AQU	18PIS	20TAU
22PIS	23TAU	22TAU	21GEM	23LEO	24LIB	23SCO	21SAG	22AQU	22PIS	20ARI	23GEM
24ARI	26GEM	25GEM	23CAN	25VIR	26SCO	25SAG	23CAP	24PIS	24ARI	23TAU	25CAN
27TAU	28CAN	27CAN	26LEO	27LIB	28SAG	27CAP	26AQU	27ARI	27TAU	25GEM	27LEO
29GEM		29LEO	28VIR	29SCO	30CAP	29AQU	28PIS	29TAU	29GEM	28CAN	30VIR
31CAN			30LIB	31SAG			31ARI			30LEO	

1959

JAN	FEB	MAR	APR	MAY	JUNE	JULY	AUG	SEPT	OCT	NOV	DEC
1LIB	1SAG	1SAG	1AQU	1PIS	2TAU	2GEM	1CAN	2VIR	1LIB	2SAG	1CAP
3SCO	4CAP	3CAP	4PIS	3ARI	5GEM	4CAN	3LEO	4LIB	3SCO	4CAP	3AQU
5SAG	6AQU	5AQU	6ARI	6TAU	7CAN	7LEO	5VIR	6SCO	5SAG	6AQU	5PIS
7CAP	8PIS	7PIS	8TAU	8GEM	9LEO	9VIR	8LIB	8SAG	7CAP	8PIS	8ARI
9AQU	10ARI	10ARI	11GEM	11CAN	12VIR	11LIB	10SCO	10CAP	10AQU	10ARI	10TAU
12PIS	13TAU	12TAU	14CAN	13LEO	14LIB	13SCO	12SAG	12AQU	12PIS	13TAU	13GEM
14ARI	15GEM	15GEM	16LEO	16VIR	16SCO	16SAG	14CAP	15PIS	14ARI	15GEM	15CAN
17TAU	18CAN	17CAN	18VIR	18LIB	18SAG	18CAP	16AQU	17ARI	17TAU	18CAN	18LEO
19GEM	20LEO	20LEO	20LIB	20SCO	20CAP	20AQU	18PIS	19TAU	19GEM	20LEO	20VIR
21CAN	22VIR	22VIR	22SCO	22SAG	22AQU	22PIS	20ARI	22GEM	22CAN	23VIR	22LIB
24LEO	24LIB	24LIB	24SAG	24CAP	24PIS	24ARI	22TAU	24CAN	24LEO	25LIB	25SCO
26VIR	27SCO	26SCO	26CAP	26AQU	27ARI	27TAU	25GEM	27LEO	26VIR	27SCO	27SAG
28LIB		28SAG	28AQU	28PIS	29TAU	29GEM	28CAN	29VIR	29LIB	29SAG	29CAP
30SCO		30CAP		30ARI			30LEO		31SCO		31AQU

1960

JAN	FEB	MAR	APR	MAY	JUNE	JULY	AUG	SEPT	OCT	NOV	DEC
2PIS	3TAU	1TAU	2CAN	2LEO	1VIR	1LIB	1SAG	2AQU	1PIS	2TAU	2GEM
4ARI	5GEM	4GEM	5LEO	5VIR	3LIB	3SCO	3CAP	4PIS	3ARI	4GEM	4CAN
6TAU	8CAN	6CAN	7VIR	7LIB	6SCO	5SAG	5AQU	6ARI	6TAU	7CAN	7LEO
9GEM	10LEO	9LEO	10LIB	9SCO	8SAG	7CAP	7PIS	8TAU	8GEM	9LEO	9VIR
11CAN	13VIR	11VIR	12SCO	11SAG	10CAP	9AQU	10ARI	11GEM	10CAN	12VIR	12LIB
14LEO	15LIB	13LIB	14SAG	13CAP	12AQU	11PIS	12TAU	13CAN	13LEO	14LIB	14SCO
16VIR	17SCO	15SCO	16CAP	15AQU	14PIS	13ARI	14GEM	16LEO	15VIR	16SCO	16SAG
19LIB	19SAG	17SAG	18AQU	17PIS	16ARI	15TAU	17CAN	18VIR	18LIB	19SAG	18CAP
21SCO	21CAP	20CAP	20PIS	20ARI	18TAU	18GEM	19LEO	20LIB	20SCO	21CAP	20AQU
23SAG	23AQU	22AQU	22ARI	22TAU	21GEM	20CAN	22VIR	23SCO	22SAG	23AQU	22PIS
25CAP	26PIS	24PIS	25TAU	24GEM	23CAN	23LEO	24LIB	25SAG	24CAP	25PIS	24ARI
27AQU	28ARI	26ARI	27GEM	27CAN	26LEO	25VIR	26SCO	27CAP	26AQU	27ARI	26TAU
29PIS		28TAU	30CAN	29LEO	28VIR	28LIB	29SAG	29AQU	28PIS	29TAU	29GEM
31ARI		31GEM				30SCO	31CAP		31ARI		31CAN

1961

JAN	FEB	MAR	APR	MAY	JUNE	JULY	AUG	SEPT	OCT	NOV	DEC
3LEO	2VIR	1VIR	2SCO	2SAG	2AQU	1PIS	2TAU	1GEM	3LEO	2VIR	1LIB
5VIR	4LIB	3LIB	4SAG	4CAP	4PIS	4ARI	4GEM	3CAN	5VIR	4LIB	2SCO
8LIB	6SCO	6SCO	6CAP	6AQU	6ARI	6TAU	7CAN	5LEO	8LIB	6SCO	6SAG
10SCO	9SAG	8SAG	9AQU	8PIS	8TAU	8GEM	9LEO	8VIR	10SCO	9SAG	8CAP
12SAG	11CAP	10CAP	11PIS	10ARI	10GEM	10CAN	12VIR	10LIB	13SAG	11CAP	10AQU
14CAP	13AQU	12AQU	13ARI	12TAU	13CAN	13LEO	14LIB	13SCO	15CAP	13AQU	13PIS
16AQU	15PIS	14PIS	15TAU	14GEM	16LEO	15VIR	17SCO	15SAG	17AQU	15PIS	15ARI
18PIS	17ARI	16ARI	17GEM	17CAN	18VIR	18LIB	19SAG	18CAP	19PIS	17ARI	17TAU
20ARI	19TAU	18TAU	19CAN	19LEO	21LIB	20SCO	21CAP	20AQU	21ARI	20TAU	19GEM
23TAU	21GEM	21GEM	22LEO	22VIR	23SCO	23SAG	23AQU	22PIS	23TAU	22GEM	21CAN
25GEM	24CAN	23CAN	25VIR	24LIB	25SAG	25CAP	25PIS	24ARI	25GEM	24CAN	24LEO
28CAN	26LEO	26LEO	27LIB	27SCO	27CAP	27AQU	27ARI	26TAU	28CAN	26LEO	26VIR
30LEO		28VIR	29SCO	29SAG	29AQU	29PIS	29TAU	28GEM	30LEO	29VIR	29LIB
		31LIB		31CAP		31ARI		30CAN			31SCO

1962

JAN	FEB	MAR	APR	MAY	JUNE	JULY	AUG	SEPT	OCT	NOV	DEC
3SAG	1CAP	1CAP	1PIS	1ARI	1GEM	1CAN	2VIR	3SCO	3SAG	1CAP	1AQU
5CAP	3AQU	3AQU	3ARI	3TAU	3CAN	3LEO	4LIB	5SAG	5CAP	4AQU	3PIS
7AQU	5PIS	5PIS	5TAU	5GEM	6LEO	5VIR	7SCO	8CAP	7AQU	6PIS	5ARI
9PIS	7ARI	7ARI	7GEM	7CAN	8VIR	8LIB	9SAG	10AQU	10PIS	8ARI	7TAU
11ARI	9TAU	9TAU	9CAN	9LEO	10LIB	10SCO	11CAP	12PIS	12ARI	10TAU	9GEM
13TAU	12GEM	11GEM	12LEO	12VIR	13SCO	13SAG	14AQU	14ARI	14TAU	12GEM	11CAN
15GEM	14CAN	13CAN	14VIR	14LIB	15SAG	15CAP	16PIS	16TAU	16GEM	14CAN	14LEO
18CAN	16LEO	16LEO	17LIB	17SCO	18CAP	17AQU	18ARI	18GEM	18CAN	16LEO	16VIR
20LEO	19VIR	18VIR	19SCO	19SAG	20AQU	19PIS	20TAU	20CAN	20LEO	19VIR	19LIB
23VIR	21LIB	21LIB	22SAG	21CAP	22PIS	21ARI	22GEM	23LEO	22VIR	21LIB	21SCO
25LIB	24SCO	23SCO	24CAP	24AQU	24ARI	23TAU	24CAN	25VIR	25LIB	24SCO	24SAG
28SCO	26SAG	26SAG	26AQU	26PIS	26TAU	26GEM	26LEO	28LIB	27SCO	26SAG	26CAP
30SAG		28CAP	28PIS	28ARI	28GEM	28CAN	29VIR	30SCO	30SAG	29CAP	28AQU
		30AQU		30TAU		30LEO	31LIB				30PIS

1963

JAN	FEB	MAR	APR	MAY	JUNE	JULY	AUG	SEPT	OCT	NOV	DEC
1ARI	2GEM	1GEM	2LEO	2VIR	3SCO	3SAG	1CAP	2PIS	2ARI	2GEM	2CAN
4TAU	4CAN	3CAN	4VIR	4LIB	5SAG	5CAP	4AQU	4ARI	4TAU	4CAN	4LEO
6GEM	6LEO	6LEO	7LIB	7SCO	8CAP	7AQU	6PIS	7TAU	6GEM	6LEO	6VIR
8CAN	9VIR	8VIR	9SCO	9SAG	10AQU	10PIS	8ARI	9GEM	8CAN	9VIR	8LIB
10LEO	11LIB	11LIB	12SAG	12CAP	12PIS	12ARI	10TAU	11CAN	10LEO	11LIB	11SCO
12VIR	14SCO	13SCO	14CAP	14AQU	15ARI	14TAU	12GEM	13LEO	12VIR	14SCO	13SAG
15LIB	16SAG	16SAG	17AQU	16PIS	17TAU	16GEM	14CAN	15VIR	15LIB	16SAG	16CAP
17SCO	19CAP	18CAP	19PIS	18ARI	19GEM	18CAN	17LEO	18LIB	17SCO	19CAP	18AQU
20SAG	21AQU	20AQU	21ARI	20TAU	21CAN	20LEO	19VIR	20SCO	20SAG	21AQU	21PIS
22CAP	23PIS	23PIS	23TAU	22GEM	23LEO	23VIR	21LIB	23SAG	22CAP	24PIS	23ARI
25AQU	25ARI	25ARI	25GEM	24CAN	25VIR	25LIB	24SCO	25CAP	25AQU	26ARI	25TAU
27PIS	27TAU	27TAU	27CAN	27LEO	28LIB	27SCO	26SAG	28AQU	27PIS	28TAU	27GEM
29ARI		29GEM	29LEO	29VIR	30SCO	30SAG	29CAP	30PIS	29ARI	30GEM	29CAN
31TAU		31CAN		31LIB			31AQU		31TAU		31LEO

1964

JAN	FEB	MAR	APR	MAY	JUNE	JULY	AUG	SEPT	OCT	NOV	DEC
2VIR	1LIB	2SCO	1SAG	1CAP	2PIS	1ARI	2GEM	2LEO	2VIR	2SCO	2SAG
5LIB	4SCO	4SAG	3CAP	3AQU	4ARI	4TAU	4CAN	5VIR	4LIB	5SAG	5CAP
7SCO	6SAG	7CAP	6AQU	5PIS	6TAU	6GEM	6LEO	7LIB	6SCO	8CAP	7AQU
10SAG	9CAP	9AQU	8PIS	8ARI	8GEM	8CAN	8VIR	9SCO	9SAG	10AQU	10PIS
12CAP	11AQU	12PIS	10ARI	10TAU	10CAN	10LEO	10LIB	11SAG	11CAP	13PIS	12ARI
15AQU	13PIS	14ARI	12TAU	12GEM	12LEO	12VIR	13SCO	14CAP	14AQU	15ARI	15TAU
17PIS	16ARI	16TAU	14GEM	14CAN	14VIR	14LIB	15SAG	16AQU	16PIS	17TAU	17GEM
19ARI	18TAU	18GEM	16CAN	16LEO	17LIB	16SCO	18CAP	19PIS	19ARI	19GEM	19CAN
21TAU	20GEM	20CAN	19LEO	18VIR	19SCO	19SAG	20AQU	21ARI	21TAU	21CAN	21LEO
24GEM	22CAN	22LEO	21VIR	20LIB	22SAG	21CAP	23PIS	23TAU	23GEM	23LEO	23VIR
26CAN	24LEO	25VIR	23LIB	23SCO	24CAP	24AQU	25ARI	25GEM	25CAN	25VIR	25LIB
28LEO	26VIR	27LIB	26SCO	25SAG	27AQU	26PIS	27TAU	28CAN	27LEO	28LIB	27SCO
30VIR	28LIB	29SCO	28SAG	28CAP	29PIS	29ARI	29GEM	30LEO	29VIR	30SCO	30SAG
				30AQU		31TAU	31CAN		31LIB		

1965

JAN	FEB	MAR	APR	MAY	JUNE	JULY	AUG	SEPT	OCT	NOV	DEC
1CAP	2PIS	2PIS	3TAU	2GEM	1CAN	2VIR	3SCO	1SAG	1CAP	2PIS	2ARI
4AQU	5ARI	4ARI	5GEM	4CAN	3LEO	4LIB	5SAG	4CAP	4AQU	5ARI	5TAU
6PIS	7TAU	6TAU	7CAP	6LEO	5VIR	6SCO	7CAP	6AQU	6PIS	7TAU	7GEM
9ARI	9GEM	9GEM	9LEO	8VIR	7LIB	9SAG	10AQU	9PIS	9ARI	9GEM	9CAN
11TAU	11CAN	11CAN	11VIR	11LIB	9SCO	11CAP	13PIS	11ARI	11TAU	12CAN	11LEO
13GEM	13LEO	13LEO	13LIB	13SCO	12SAG	14AQU	15ARI	14TAU	13GEM	14LEO	13VIR
15CAN	16VIR	15VIR	16SCO	15SAG	14CAP	16PIS	17TAU	16GEM	15CAN	16VIR	15LIB
17LEO	18LIB	17LIB	18SAG	18CAP	16AQU	19ARI	20GEM	18CAN	17LEO	18LIB	17SCO
19VIR	20SCO	19SCO	20CAP	20AQU	19PIS	21TAU	22CAN	20LEO	20VIR	20SCO	20SAG
21LIB	22SAG	22SAG	23AQU	23PIS	21ARI	23GEM	24LEO	22VIR	22LIB	22SAG	22CAP
23SCO	25CAP	24CAP	25PIS	25ARI	24TAU	25CAN	26VIR	24LIB	24SCO	25CAP	25AQU
26SAG	27AQU	27AQU	28ARI	27TAU	26GEM	27LEO	28LIB	26SCO	26SAG	27AQU	27PIS
28CAP		29PIS	30TAU	30GEM	28CAN	29VIR	30SCO	29SAG	28CAP	30PIS	30ARI
31AQU		31ARI			30LEO	31LIB			31AQU		

1966

JAN	FEB	MAR	APR	MAY	JUNE	JULY	AUG	SEPT	OCT	NOV	DEC
1TAU	2CAN	1CAN	2VIR	1LIB	2SAG	1CAP	2PIS	1ARI	1TAU	2CAN	2LEO
3GEM	4LEO	3LEO	4LIB	3SCO	4CAP	4AQU	5ARI	4TAU	3GEM	4LEO	4VIR
5CAN	6VIR	5VIR	6SCO	5SAG	6AQU	6PIS	7TAU	6GEM	6CAN	6VIR	6LIB
7LEO	8LIB	7LIB	8SAG	8CAP	9PIS	9ARI	10GEM	9CAN	8LEO	8LIB	8SCO
9VIR	10SCO	9SCO	10CAP	10AQU	11ARI	11TAU	12CAN	11LEO	10VIR	11SCO	10SAG
11LIB	12SAG	12SAG	13AQU	12PIS	14TAU	14GEM	14LEO	13VIR	12LIB	13SAG	12CAP
14SCO	15CAP	14CAP	15PIS	15ARI	16GEM	16CAN	16VIR	15LIB	14SCO	15CAP	14AQU
16SAG	17AQU	16AQU	18ARI	17TAU	18CAN	18LEO	18LIB	17SCO	16SAG	17AQU	17PIS
18CAP	20PIS	19PIS	20TAU	20GEM	20LEO	20VIR	20SCO	19SAG	18CAP	20PIS	19ARI
21AQU	22ARI	21ARI	22GEM	22CAN	23VIR	22LIB	22SAG	21CAP	21AQU	22ARI	22TAU
23PIS	25TAU	24TAU	25CAN	24LEO	25LIB	24SCO	25CAP	23AQU	23PIS	25TAU	24GEM
26ARI	27GEM	26GEM	27LEO	26VIR	27SCO	26SAG	27AQU	26PIS	26ARI	27GEM	27CAN
28TAU		29CAN	29VIR	28LIB	29SAG	29CAP	30PIS	28ARI	28TAU	29CAN	29LEO
31GEM		31LEO		31SCO		31AQU			31GEM		31VIR

1967

JAN	FEB	MAR	APR	MAY	JUNE	JULY	AUG	SEPT	OCT	NOV	DEC
2LIB	3SAG	2SAG	3AQU	2PIS	1ARI	1TAU	2CAN	1LEO	2LIB	1SCO	2CAP
4SCO	5CAP	4CAP	5PIS	5ARI	4TAU	3GEM	4LEO	3VIR	4SCO	3SAG	4AQU
6SAG	7AQU	6AQU	8ARI	7TAU	6GEM	6CAN	7VIR	5LIB	6SAG	5CAP	7PIS
9CAP	10PIS	9PIS	10TAU	10GEM	9CAN	8LEO	9LIB	7SCO	9CAP	7AQU	9ARI
11AQU	12ARI	11ARI	13GEM	12CAN	11LEO	10VIR	11SCO	9SAG	11AQU	9PIS	12TAU
13PIS	15TAU	14TAU	15CAN	15LEO	13VIR	12LIB	13SAG	11CAP	13PIS	12ARI	14GEM
16ARI	17GEM	16GEM	17LEO	17VIR	15LIB	15SCO	15CAP	14AQU	16ARI	14TAU	17CAN
18TAU	19CAN	19CAN	20VIR	19LIB	17SCO	17SAG	17AQU	16PIS	18TAU	17GEM	19LEO
21GEM	22LEO	21LEO	22LIB	21SCO	19SAG	19CAP	20PIS	18ARI	21GEM	19CAN	21VIR
23CAN	24VIR	23VIR	24SCO	23SAG	21CAP	21AQU	22ARI	21TAU	23CAN	22LEO	24LIB
25LEO	26LIB	25LIB	26SAG	25CAP	24AQU	23PIS	25TAU	23GEM	26LEO	24VIR	26SCO
27VIR	28SCO	27SCO	28CAP	27AQU	26PIS	26ARI	27GEM	26CAN	28VIR	26LIB	28SAG
29LIB		29SAG	30AQU	30PIS	28ARI	28TAU	30CAN	28LEO	30LIB	28SCO	30CAP
31SCO		31CAP				31GEM		30VIR		30SAG	

1968

	JAN	FEB	MAR	APR	MAY	JUNE	JULY	AUG	SEPT	OCT	NOV	DEC
	1AQU	2ARI	3TAU	2GEM	1CAN	2VIR	2LIB	3SAG	1CAP	2PIS	1ARI	1TAU
	3PIS	4TAU	5GEM	4CAN	4LEO	5LIB	4SCO	5CAP	3AQU	5ARI	3TAU	3GEM
	6ARI	7GEM	8CAN	7LEO	6VIR	7SCO	6SAG	7AQU	5PIS	7TAU	6GEM	6CAN
	8TAU	9CAN	10LEO	9VIR	8LIB	9SAG	8CAP	9PIS	7ARI	10GEM	8CAN	8LEO
	11GEM	12LEO	12VIR	11LIB	10SCO	11CAP	10AQU	11ARI	10TAU	12CAN	11LEO	11VIR
	13CAN	14VIR	14LIB	13SCO	12SAG	13AQU	12PIS	13TAU	12GEM	15LEO	13VIR	13LIB
	15LEO	16LIB	17SCO	15SAG	14CAP	15PIS	15ARI	16GEM	15CAN	17VIR	16LIB	15SCO
	18VIR	18SCO	19SAG	17CAP	16AQU	17ARI	17TAU	18CAN	17LEO	19LIB	18SCO	17SAG
	20LIB	20SAG	21CAP	19AQU	19PIS	20TAU	20GEM	21LEO	20VIR	21SCO	20SAG	19CAP
	22SCO	22CAP	23AQU	21PIS	21ARI	22GEM	22CAN	23VIR	22LIB	23SAG	22CAP	21AQU
	24SAG	25AQU	25PIS	24ARI	24TAU	25CAN	25LEO	25LIB	24SCO	25CAP	24AQU	23PIS
	26CAP	27PIS	28ARI	26TAU	26GEM	27LEO	27VIR	28SCO	26SAG	27AQU	26PIS	26ARI
	28AQU	29ARI	30TAU	29GEM	29CAN	30VIR	29LIB	30SAG	28CAP	30PIS	28ARI	28TAU
	31PIS				31LEO				30AQU			30GEM

1969

	JAN	FEB	MAR	APR	MAY	JUNE	JULY	AUG	SEPT	OCT	NOV	DEC
	2CAN	1LEO	2VIR	1LIB	1SCO	1CAP	1AQU	1ARI	2GEM	2CAN	1LEO	1VIR
	4LEO	3VIR	5LIB	3SCO	3SAG	3AQU	3PIS	3TAU	5CAN	4LEO	3VIR	3LIB
	7VIR	6LIB	7SCO	5SAG	5CAP	5PIS	5ARI	6GEM	7LEO	7VIR	6LIB	5SCO
	9LIB	8SCO	9SAG	8CAP	7AQU	7ARI	7TAU	8CAN	10VIR	9LIB	8SCO	8SAG
	12SCO	10SAG	11CAP	10AQU	9PIS	10TAU	10GEM	11LEO	12LIB	12SCO	10SAG	10CAP
	14SAG	12CAP	13AQU	12PIS	11ARI	12GEM	12CAN	13VIR	14SCO	14SAG	12CAP	12AQU
	16CAP	14AQU	16PIS	14ARI	14TAU	15CAN	15LEO	16LIB	17SAG	16CAP	14AQU	14PIS
	18AQU	16PIS	18ARI	16TAU	16GEM	17LEO	17VIR	18SCO	19CAP	18AQU	16PIS	16ARI
	20PIS	18ARI	20TAU	19GEM	19CAN	20VIR	20LIB	20SAG	21AQU	20PIS	19ARI	18TAU
	22ARI	21TAU	22GEM	21CAN	21LEO	22LIB	22SCO	22CAP	23PIS	22ARI	21TAU	20GEM
	24TAU	23GEM	25CAN	24LEO	24VIR	25SCO	24SAG	24AQU	25ARI	25TAU	23GEM	23CAN
	27GEM	26CAN	27LEO	26VIR	26LIB	27SAG	26CAP	26PIS	27TAU	27GEM	26CAN	25LEO
	29CAN	28LEO	30VIR	29LIB	28SCO	29CAP	28AQU	29ARI	29GEM	29CAN	28LEO	28VIR
					30SAG		30PIS	31TAU				30LIB

1970

JAN	FEB	MAR	APR	MAY	JUNE	JULY	AUG	SEPT	OCT	NOV	DEC
2SCO	2CAP	2CAP	2PIS	2ARI	2GEM	2CAN	1LEO	2LIB	2SCO	3CAP	2AQU
4SAG	4AQU	4AQU	4ARI	4TAU	5CAN	4LEO	3VIR	5SCO	4SAG	5AQU	4PIS
6CAP	6PIS	6PIS	6TAU	6GEM	7LEO	7VIR	6LIB	7SAG	6CAP	7PIS	6ARI
8AQU	8ARI	8ARI	9GEM	8CAN	10VIR	10LIB	8SCO	9CAP	9AQU	9ARI	8TAU
10PIS	11TAU	10TAU	11CAN	11LEO	12LIB	12SCO	11SAG	11AQU	11PIS	11TAU	11GEM
12ARI	13GEM	12GEM	14LEO	13VIR	15SCO	14SAG	13CAP	13PIS	13ARI	13GEM	13CAN
14TAU	15CAN	15CAN	16VIR	16LIB	17SAG	16CAP	15AQU	15ARI	15TAU	16CAN	15LEO
17GEM	18LEO	17LEO	19LIB	18SCO	19CAP	18AQU	17PIS	17TAU	17GEM	18LEO	18VIR
19CAN	20VIR	20VIR	21SCO	20SAG	21AQU	20PIS	19ARI	19GEM	19CAN	20VIR	20LIB
22LEO	23LIB	22LIB	23SAG	23CAP	23PIS	22ARI	21TAU	22CAN	22LEO	23LIB	23SCO
24VIR	25SCO	25SCO	25CAP	25AQU	25ARI	25TAU	23GEM	24LEO	24VIR	25SCO	25SAG
27LIB	28SAG	27SAG	27AQU	27PIS	27TAU	27GEM	26CAN	27VIR	27LIB	28SAG	27CAP
29SCO		29CAP	30PIS	29ARI	30GEM	29CAN	28LEO	29LIB	29SCO	30CAP	29AQU
31SAG		31AQU		31TAU			31VIR		31SAG		31PIS

1971

JAN	FEB	MAR	APR	MAY	JUNE	JULY	AUG	SEPT	OCT	NOV	DEC
3ARI	1TAU	2GEM	1CAN	1LEO	2LIB	2SCO	1SAG	2AQU	1PIS	2TAU	1GEM
5TAU	3GEM	5CAN	3LEO	3VIR	5SCO	4SAG	3CAP	4PIS	3ARI	4GEM	3CAN
7GEM	5CAN	7LEO	6VIR	6LIB	7SAG	7CAP	5AQU	6ARI	5TAU	6CAN	5LEO
9CAN	8LEO	10VIR	8LIB	8SCO	9CAP	9AQU	7PIS	8TAU	7GEM	8LEO	8VIR
12LEO	10VIR	12LIB	11SCO	11SAG	11AQU	11PIS	9ARI	10GEM	9CAN	10VIR	10LIB
14VIR	13LIB	15SCO	13SAG	13CAP	14PIS	13ARI	11TAU	12CAN	12LEO	13LIB	13SCO
17LIB	15SCO	17SAG	16CAP	15AQU	16ARI	15TAU	13GEM	14LEO	14VIR	15SCO	15SAG
19SCO	18SAG	19CAP	18AQU	17PIS	18TAU	17GEM	16CAN	17VIR	16LIB	18SAG	17CAP
22SAG	20CAP	22AQU	20PIS	20ARI	20GEM	19CAN	18LEO	19LIB	19SCO	20CAP	20AQU
24CAP	22AQU	24PIS	22ARI	22TAU	22CAN	22LEO	20VIR	22SCO	22SAG	23AQU	22PIS
26AQU	24PIS	26ARI	24TAU	24GEM	24LEO	24VIR	23LIB	24SAG	24CAP	25PIS	24ARI
28PIS	26ARI	28TAU	26GEM	26CAN	27VIR	27LIB	26SCO	27CAP	26AQU	27ARI	26TAU
30ARI	28TAU	30GEM	28CAN	28LEO	29LIB	29SCO	28SAG	29AQU	29PIS	29TAU	28GEM
				30VIR			30CAP		31ARI		30CAN

1972

JAN	FEB	MAR	APR	MAY	JUNE	JULY	AUG	SEPT	OCT	NOV	DEC
2LEO	3LIB	1LIB	2SAG	2CAP	1AQU	3ARI	1TAU	1CAN	1LEO	2LIB	1SCO
4VIR	5SCO	4SCO	5CAP	5AQU	3PIS	5TAU	3GEM	4LEO	3VIR	4SCO	4SAG
6LIB	8SAG	6SAG	7AQU	7PIS	5ARI	7GEM	5CAN	6VIR	5LIB	7SAG	7CAP
9SCO	10CAP	9CAP	10PIS	9ARI	7TAU	9CAN	7LEO	8LIB	8SCO	9CAP	9AQU
11SAG	12AQU	11AQU	12ARI	11TAU	9GEM	11LEO	10VIR	11SCO	10SAG	12AQU	11PIS
14CAP	15PIS	13PIS	14TAU	13GEM	11CAN	13VIR	12LIB	13SAG	13CAP	14PIS	14ARI
16AQU	17ARI	15ARI	16GEM	15CAN	14LEO	15LIB	14SCO	16CAP	15AQU	16ARI	16TAU
18PIS	19TAU	17TAU	18CAN	17LEO	16VIR	18SCO	17SAG	18AQU	18PIS	18TAU	18GEM
20ARI	21GEM	19GEM	20LEO	19VIR	18LIB	20SAG	19CAP	20PIS	20ARI	20GEM	20CAN
23TAU	23CAN	21CAN	22VIR	22LIB	21SCO	23CAP	22AQU	22ARI	22TAU	22CAN	22LEO
25GEM	25LEO	24LEO	25LIB	24SCO	23SAG	25AQU	24PIS	24TAU	24GEM	24LEO	24VIR
27CAN	28VIR	26VIR	27SCO	27SAG	26CAP	28PIS	26ARI	27GEM	26CAN	27VIR	26LIB
29LEO		28LIB	30SAG	29CAP	28AQU	30ARI	28TAU	29CAN	28LEO	29LIB	29SCO
31VIR		31SCO			30PIS		30GEM		30VIR		31SAG

1973

JAN	FEB	MAR	APR	MAY	JUNE	JULY	AUG	SEPT	OCT	NOV	DEC
3CAP	2AQU	1AQU	2ARI	1TAU	2CAN	1LEO	2LIB	1SCO	3CAP	2AQU	1PIS
5AQU	4PIS	3PIS	4TAU	3GEM	4LEO	3VIR	4SCO	3SAG	5AQU	4PIS	4ARI
8PIS	6ARI	5ARI	6GEM	5CAN	6VIR	5LIB	7SAG	5CAP	8PIS	6ARI	6TAU
10AIR	8TAU	8TAU	8CAN	7LEO	8LIB	8SCO	9CAP	8AQU	10ARI	9TAU	8GEM
12TAU	10GEM	10GEM	10LEO	10VIR	11SCO	10SAG	12AQU	10PIS	12TAU	11GEM	10CAN
14GEM	13CAN	12CAN	12VIR	12LIB	13SAG	13CAP	14PIS	13ARI	14GEM	13CAN	12LEO
16CAN	15LEO	14LEO	15LIB	14SCO	16CAP	15AQU	16ARI	15TAU	16CAN	15LEO	14VIR
18LEO	17VIR	16VIR	17SCO	17SAG	18AQU	18PIS	19TAU	17GEM	19LEO	17VIR	16LIB
20VIR	19LIB	18LIB	20SAG	19CAP	21PIS	20ARI	21GEM	19CAN	21VIR	19LIB	19SCO
23LIB	21SCO	21SCO	22CAP	22AQU	23ARI	22TAU	23CAN	21LEO	23LIB	22SCO	21SAG
25SCO	24SAG	23SAG	25AQU	24PIS	25TAU	25GEM	25LEO	23VIR	25SCO	24SAG	24CAP
28SAG	26CAP	26CAP	27PIS	27ARI	27GEM	27CAN	27VIR	26LIB	28SAG	26CAP	26AQU
30CAP		28AQU	29ARI	29TAU	29CAN	29LEO	29LIB	28SCO	30CAP	29AQU	29PIS
		31PIS		31GEM		31VIR		30SAG			31ARI

1974

JAN	FEB	MAR	APR	MAY	JUNE	JULY	AUG	SEPT	OCT	NOV	DEC
2TAU	1GEM	2CAN	1LEO	2LIB	1SCO	3CAP	2AQU	3ARI	2TAU	1GEM	1CAN
5GEM	3CAN	4LEO	3VIR	4SCO	3SAG	5AQU	4PIS	5TAU	5GEM	3CAN	3LEO
7CAN	5LEO	7VIR	5LIB	7SAG	6CAP	8PIS	7ARI	8GEM	7CAN	5LEO	5VIR
9LEO	7VIR	9LIB	7SCO	9CAP	8AQU	10ARI	9TAU	10CAN	9LEO	8VIR	7LIB
11VIR	9LIB	11SCO	9SAG	12AQU	11PIS	13TAU	11GEM	12LEO	11VIR	10LIB	9SCO
13LIB	11SCO	13SAG	12CAP	14PIS	13ARI	15GEM	13CAN	14VIR	13LIB	12SCO	11SAG
15SCO	14SAG	16CAP	14AQU	17ARI	15TAU	17CAN	15LEO	16LIB	15SCO	14SAG	14CAP
17SAG	16CAP	18AQU	17PIS	19TAU	18GEM	19LEO	17VIR	18SCO	18SAG	16CAP	16AQU
20CAP	19AQU	21PIS	19ARI	21GEM	20CAN	21VIR	19LIB	20SAG	20CAP	19AQU	19PIS
22AQU	21PIS	23ARI	22TAU	23CAN	22LEO	23LIB	22SCO	23CAP	22AQU	21PIS	21ARI
25PIS	24ARI	25TAU	24GEM	25LEO	24VIR	25SCO	24SAG	25AQU	25PIS	24ARI	24TAU
27ARI	26TAU	27GEM	26CAN	27VIR	26LIB	28SAG	26CAP	28PIS	27ARI	26TAU	26GEM
30TAU	28GEM	30CAN	28LEO	30LIB	28SCO	30CAP	29AQU	30ARI	30TAU	28GEM	28CAN
			30VIR		30SAG		31PIS				30LEO

1975

JAN	FEB	MAR	APR	MAY	JUNE	JULY	AUG	SEPT	OCT	NOV	DEC
1VIR	2SCO	1SCO	2CAP	2AQU	3ARI	3TAU	1GEM	2LEO	2VIR	2SCO	2SAG
3LIB	4SAG	3SAG	4AQU	4PIS	5TAU	5GEM	4CAN	4VIR	4LIB	4SAG	4CAP
5SCO	6CAP	5CAP	7PIS	7ARI	8GEM	7CAN	6LEO	6LIB	6SCO	6CAP	6AQU
8SAG	9AQU	8AQU	9ARI	9TAU	10CAN	9LEO	8VIR	8SCO	8SAG	9AQU	8PIS
10CAP	11PIS	10PIS	12TAU	11GEM	12LEO	11VIR	10LIB	10SAG	10CAP	11PIS	11ARI
12AQU	14ARI	13ARI	14GEM	14CAN	14VIR	14LIB	12SCO	13CAP	12AQU	14ARI	13TAU
15PIS	16TAU	15TAU	15CAN	16LEO	16LIB	16SCO	14SAG	15AQU	15PIS	16TAU	16GEM
17ARI	19GEM	18GEM	19LEO	18VIR	18SCO	18SAG	16CAP	18PIS	17ARI	19GEM	18CAN
20TAU	21CAN	20CAN	21VIR	20LIB	21SAG	20CAP	19AQU	20ARI	20TAU	21CAN	20LEO
22GEM	23LEO	22LEO	23LIB	22SCO	23CAP	23AQU	21PIS	23TAU	22GEM	23LEO	23VIR
24CAN	25VIR	24VIR	25SCO	24SAG	25AQU	25PIS	24ARI	25GEM	25CAN	25VIR	25LIB
26LEO	27LIB	26LIB	27SAG	27CAP	28PIS	28ARI	26TAU	27CAN	27LEO	27LIB	27SCO
28VIR		28SCO	29CAP	29AQU	30ARI	30TAU	29GEM	30LEO	29VIR	30SCO	29SAG
30LIB		30SAG		31PIS			31CAN		31LIB		31CAP

1976

JAN	FEB	MAR	APR	MAY	JUNE	JULY	AUG	SEPT	OCT	NOV	DEC
2AQU	1PIS	2ARI	1TAU	3CAN	1LEO	1VIR	1SCO	2CAP	1AQU	2ARI	2TAU
5PIS	4ARI	4TAU	3GEM	5LEO	4VIR	3LIB	4SAG	4AQU	4PIS	5TAU	5GEM
7ARI	6TAU	7GEM	6CAN	7VIR	6LIB	5SCO	6CAP	7PIS	6ARI	8GEM	7CAN
10TAU	9GEM	9CAN	8LEO	10LIB	8SCO	7SAG	8AQU	9ARI	9TAU	10CAN	10LEO
12GEM	11CAN	12LEO	10VIR	12SCO	10SAG	9CAP	10PIS	11TAU	11GEM	12LEO	12VIR
15CAN	13LEO	14VIR	12LIB	14SAG	12CAP	12AQU	13ARI	14GEM	14CAN	15VIR	14LIB
17LEO	15VIR	16LIB	14SCO	16CAP	14AQU	14PIS	15TAU	17CAN	16LEO	17LIB	16SCO
19VIR	17LIB	18SCO	16SAG	18AQU	17PIS	16ARI	18GEM	19LEO	18VIR	19SCO	18SAG
21LIB	19SCO	20SAG	18CAP	20PIS	19ARI	19TAU	20CAN	21VIR	21LIB	21SAG	20CAP
23SCO	21SAG	22CAP	20AQU	23ARI	22TAU	21GEM	22LEO	23LIB	23SCO	23CAP	22AQU
25SAG	24CAP	24AQU	23PIS	25TAU	24GEM	24CAN	25VIR	25SCO	25SAG	25AQU	25PIS
27CAP	26AQU	27PIS	25ARI	28GEM	26CAN	26LEO	27LIB	27SAG	27CAP	27PIS	27ARI
30AQU	28PIS	29ARI	28TAU	30CAN	29LEO	28VIR	29SCO	29CAP	29AQU	30ARI	30TAU
			30GEM			30LIB	31SAG		31PIS		

1977

JAN	FEB	MAR	APR	MAY	JUNE	JULY	AUG	SEPT	OCT	NOV	DEC
1GEM	2LEO	2LEO	2LIB	2SCO	2CAP	2AQU	3ARI	1TAU	1GEM	3LEO	2VIR
4CAN	5VIR	4VIR	5SCO	4SAG	4AQU	4PIS	5TAU	4GEM	4CAN	5VIR	5LIB
6LEO	7LIB	6LIB	7SAG	6CAP	7PIS	6ARI	7GEM	6CAN	6LEO	7LIB	7SCO
8VIR	9SCO	8SCO	9CAP	8AQU	9ARI	9TAU	10CAN	9LEO	9VIR	9SCO	9SAG
10LIB	11SAG	10SAG	11AQU	10PIS	11TAU	11GEM	12LEO	11VIR	11LIB	11SAG	11CAP
13SCO	13CAP	12CAP	13PIS	13ARI	14GEM	14CAN	15VIR	13LIB	13SCO	13CAP	13AQU
15SAG	15AQU	15AQU	15ARI	15TAU	16CAN	16LEO	17LIB	16SCO	15SAG	15AQU	15PIS
17CAP	17PIS	17PIS	18TAU	18GEM	19LEO	19VIR	19SCO	18SAG	17CAP	18PIS	17ARI
19AQU	20ARI	19ARI	20GEM	20CAN	21VIR	21LIB	21SAG	20CAP	19AQU	20ARI	19TAU
21PIS	22TAU	22TAU	23CAN	23LEO	24LIB	23SCO	24CAP	22AQU	21PIS	22TAU	22GEM
23ARI	25GEM	24GEM	25LEO	25VIR	26SCO	25SAG	26AQU	24PIS	24ARI	25GEM	25CAN
26TAU	27CAN	27CAN	28VIR	27LIB	28SAG	27CAP	28PIS	26ARI	26TAU	27CAN	27LEO
28GEM		29LEO	30LIB	29SCO	30CAP	29AQU	30ARI	29TAU	28GEM	30LEO	30VIR
31CAN		31VIR		31SAG		31PIS			31CAN		

1978

JAN	FEB	MAR	APR	MAY	JUNE	JULY	AUG	SEPT	OCT	NOV	DEC
1LIB	2SAG	1SAG	1AQU	1PIS	1TAU	1GEM	2LEO	1VIR	1LIB	2SAG	1CAP
3SCO	4CAP	3CAP	3PIS	3ARI	4GEM	4CAN	5VIR	4LIB	3SCO	4CAP	3AQU
5SAG	6AQU	5AQU	6ARI	5TAU	6CAN	6LEO	7LIB	6SCO	5SAG	6AQU	5PIS
7CAP	8PIS	7PIS	8TAU	8GEM	9LEO	9VIR	10SCO	8SAG	8CAP	8PIS	7ARI
9AQU	10ARI	9ARI	10GEM	10CAN	11VIR	11LIB	12SAG	10CAP	10AQU	10ARI	10TAU
11PIS	12TAU	12TAU	13CAN	13LEO	14LIB	13SCO	14CAP	12AQU	12PIS	12TAU	12GEM
13ARI	15GEM	14GEM	15LEO	15VIR	16SCO	16SAG	16AQU	14PIS	14ARI	15GEM	14CAN
16TAU	17CAN	16CAN	18VIR	17LIB	18SAG	18CAP	18PIS	17ARI	16TAU	17CAN	17LEO
18GEM	20LEO	19LEO	20LIB	20SCO	20CAP	20AQU	20ARI	19TAU	18GEM	20LEO	19VIR
21CAN	22VIR	21VIR	22SCO	22SAG	22AQU	22PIS	22TAU	21GEM	21CAN	22VIR	22LIB
23LEO	24LIB	24LIB	24SAG	24CAP	24PIS	24ARI	25GEM	23CAN	23LEO	25LIB	24SCO
26VIR	27SCO	26SCO	26CAP	26AQU	26ARI	26TAU	27CAN	26LEO	26VIR	27SCO	27SAG
28LIB		28SAG	29AQU	28PIS	29TAU	28GEM	30LEO	28VIR	28LIB	29SAG	29CAP
30SCO		30CAP		30ARI		31CAN			31SCO		31AQU

1979

JAN	FEB	MAR	APR	MAY	JUNE	JULY	AUG	SEPT	OCT	NOV	DEC
2PIS	2TAU	2TAU	3CAN	2LEO	1VIR	1LIB	2SAG	1CAP	2PIS	1ARI	2GEM
4ARI	5GEM	4GEM	5LEO	5VIR	4LIB	4SCO	4CAP	3AQU	4ARI	3TAU	4CAN
6TAU	7CAN	6CAN	8VIR	7LIB	6SCO	6SAG	6AQU	5PIS	6TAU	5GEM	7LEO
8GEM	9LEO	9LEO	10LIB	10SCO	8SAG	8CAP	8PIS	7ARI	8GEM	7CAN	9VIR
11CAN	12VIR	11VIR	12SCO	12SAG	11CAP	10AQU	10ARI	9TAU	11CAN	9LEO	12LIB
13LEO	15LIB	14LIB	15SAG	14CAP	13AQU	12PIS	13TAU	11GEM	13LEO	12VIR	14SCO
16VIR	17SCO	16SCO	17CAP	16AQU	15PIS	14ARI	15GEM	13CAN	16VIR	14LIB	17SAG
18LIB	19SAG	19SAG	19AQU	18PIS	17ARI	16TAU	17CAN	16LEO	18LIB	17SCO	19CAP
21SCO	21CAP	21CAP	21PIS	21ARI	19TAU	19GEM	20LEO	18VIR	21SCO	19SAG	21AQU
23SAG	24AQU	23AQU	23ARI	23TAU	21GEM	21CAN	22VIR	21LIB	23SAG	22CAP	23PIS
25CAP	26PIS	25PIS	25TAU	25GEM	24CAN	23LEO	25LIB	23SCO	25CAP	24AQU	25ARI
27AQU	28ARI	27ARI	28GEM	27CAN	26LEO	26VIR	27SCO	26SAG	28AQU	26PIS	27TAU
29PIS		29TAU	30CAN	30LEO	29VIR	28LIB	30SAG	28CAP	30PIS	28ARI	30GEM
31ARI		31GEM				31SCO		30AQU		30TAU	

1980

JAN	FEB	MAR	APR	MAY	JUN	JULY	AUG	SEPT	OCT	NOV	DEC
1CAN	2VIR	3LIB	2SCO	1SAG	2AQU	2PIS	2TAU	3CAN	2LEO	1VIR	1LIB
3LEO	4LIB	5SCO	4SAG	4CAP	4PIS	4ARI	4GEM	5LEO	5VIR	3LIB	3SCO
6VIR	7SCO	8SAG	6CAP	6AQU	6ARI	6TAU	6CAN	7VIR	7LIB	6SCO	6SAG
8LIB	9SAG	10CAP	9AQU	8PIS	9TAU	8GEM	9LEO	10LIB	10SCO	8SAG	8CAP
11SCO	12CAP	12AQU	11PIS	10ARI	11GEM	10CAN	11VIR	12SCO	12SAG	11CAP	10AQU
13SAG	14AQU	14PIS	13ARI	12TAU	13CAN	12LEO	14LIB	15SAG	15CAP	13AQU	13PIS
15CAP	16PIS	16ARI	15TAU	14GEM	15LEO	15VIR	16SCO	17CAP	17AQU	15PIS	15ARI
17AQU	18ARI	18TAU	17GEM	16CAN	17VIR	17LIB	19SAG	20AQU	19PIS	18ARI	17TAU
19PIS	20TAU	20GEM	19CAN	19LEO	20LIB	20SCO	21CAP	22PIS	21ARI	20TAU	19GEM
21ARI	22GEM	23CAN	21LEO	21VIR	22SCO	22SAG	23AQU	24ARI	23TAU	22GEM	21CAN
24TAU	24CAN	25LEO	24VIR	24LIB	25SAG	25CAP	25PIS	26TAU	25GEM	24CAN	23LEO
26GEM	27LEO	27VIR	26LIB	26SCO	27CAP	27AQU	27ARI	28GEM	27CAN	26LEO	25VIR
28CAN	29VIR	30LIB	29SCO	29SAG	29AQU	29PIS	29TAU	30CAN	29LEO	28VIR	28LIB
30LEO				31CAP		31ARI	31GEM				30SCO

1981

JAN	FEB	MAR	APR	MAY	JUNE	JULY	AUG	SEPT	OCT	NOV	DEC
2SAG	1CAP	2AQU	1PIS	1ARI	1GEM	2LEO	1VIR	2SCO	2SAG	1CAP	1AQU
4CAP	3AQU	5PIS	3ARI	3TAU	3CAN	5VIR	3LIB	5SAG	5CAP	3AQU	3PIS
7AQU	5PIS	7ARI	5TAU	5GEM	5LEO	7LIB	6SCO	7CAP	7AQU	6PIS	5ARI
9PIS	7ARI	9TAU	7GEM	7CAN	7VIR	10SCO	8SAG	10AQU	9PIS	8ARI	7TAU
11ARI	9TAU	11GEM	9CAN	9LEO	10LIB	12SAG	11CAP	12PIS	11ARI	10TAU	9GEM
13TAU	12GEM	13CAN	11LEO	11VIR	12SCO	15CAP	13AQU	14ARI	13TAU	12GEM	11CAN
15GEM	14CAN	15LEO	14VIR	13LIB	15SAG	17AQU	16PIS	16TAU	15GEM	14CAN	13LEO
17CAN	16LEO	18VIR	16LIB	16SCO	17CAP	19PIS	18ARI	18GEM	18CAN	16LEO	16VIR
20LEO	18VIR	20LIB	19SCO	18SAG	20AQU	21ARI	20TAU	20CAN	20LEO	18VIR	18LIB
22VIR	21LIB	22SCO	21SAG	21CAP	22PIS	24TAU	22GEM	22LEO	22VIR	21LIB	20SCO
24LIB	23SCO	25SAG	24CAP	23AQU	24ARI	26GEM	24CAN	25VIR	24LIB	23SCO	23SAG
27SCO	26SAG	27CAP	26AQU	26PIS	26TAU	28CAN	26LEO	27LIB	27SCO	26SAG	25CAP
29SAG	28CAP	30AQU	28PIS	28ARI	28GEM	30LEO	28VIR	29SCO	29SAG	28CAP	28AQU
				30TAU	30CAN		31LIB				30PIS

1982

JAN	FEB	MAR	APR	MAY	JUNE	JULY	AUG	SEPT	OCT	NOV	DEC
2ARI	2GEM	1GEM	2LEO	1VIR	2SCO	2SAG	1CAP	2PIS	2ARI	2GEM	2CAN
4TAU	4CAN	3CAN	4VIR	4LIB	5SAG	4CAP	3AQU	4ARI	4TAU	4CAN	4LEO
6GEM	6LEO	6LEO	6LIB	6SCO	7CAP	7AQU	6PIS	7TAU	6GEM	6LEO	6VIR
8CAN	8VIR	8VIR	9SCO	8SAG	10AQU	9PIS	8ARI	9GEM	8CAN	9VIR	8LIB
10LEO	11LIB	10LIB	11SAG	11CAP	12PIS	12ARI	10TAU	11CAN	10LEO	11LIB	10SCO
12VIR	13SCO	12SCO	14CAP	13AQU	15ARI	14TAU	13GEM	13LEO	12VIR	13SCO	13SAG
14LIB	15SAG	15SAG	16AQU	16PIS	17TAU	16GEM	15CAN	15VIR	15LIB	15SAG	15CAP
17SCO	18CAP	17CAP	19PIS	18ARI	19GEM	18CAN	17LEO	17LIB	17SCO	18CAP	18AQU
19SAG	20AQU	20AQU	21ARI	20TAU	21CAN	20LEO	19VIR	19SCO	19SAG	21AQU	20PIS
22CAP	23PIS	22PIS	23TAU	22GEM	23LEO	22VIR	21LIB	22SAG	22CAP	23PIS	23ARI
24AQU	25ARI	24ARI	25GEM	24CAN	25VIR	24LIB	23SCO	24CAP	24AQU	25ARI	25TAU
26PIS	27TAU	27TAU	27CAN	26LEO	27LIB	27SCO	25SAG	27AQU	27PIS	28TAU	27GEM
29ARI		29GEM	29LEO	29VIR	29SCO	29SAG	28CAP	29PIS	29ARI	30GEM	29CAN
31TAU		31CAN		31LIB			31AQU		31TAU		31LEO

1983

JAN	FEB	MAR	APR	MAY	JUNE	JULY	AUG	SEPT	OCT	NOV	DEC
2VIR	1LIB	2SCO	1SAG	1CAP	2PIS	2ARI	1TAU	1CAN	1LEO	1LIB	1SCO
4LIB	3SCO	5SAG	3CAP	3AQU	5ARI	4TAU	3GEM	3LEO	3VIR	3SCO	3SAG
7SCO	5SAG	7CAP	6AQU	6PIS	7TAU	7GEM	5CAN	5VIR	5LIB	6SAG	5CAP
9SAG	8CAP	10AQU	8PIS	8ARI	9GEM	9CAN	7LEO	7LIB	7SCO	8CAP	8AQU
12CAP	10AQU	12PIS	11ARI	11TAU	11CAN	11LEO	9VIR	10SCO	9SAG	10AQU	10PIS
14AQU	13PIS	15ARI	13TAU	13GEM	13LEO	13VIR	11LIB	12SAG	11CAP	13PIS	13ARI
17PIS	15ARI	17TAU	15GEM	15CAN	15VIR	15LIB	13SCO	14CAP	14AQU	15ARI	15TAU
19ARI	18TAU	19GEM	18CAN	17LEO	17LIB	17SCO	15SAG	17AQU	16PIS	18TAU	17GEM
21TAU	20GEM	21CAN	20LEO	19VIR	20SCO	19SAG	18CAP	19PIS	19ARI	20GEM	20CAN
24GEM	22CAN	23LEO	22VIR	21LIB	22SAG	22CAP	20AQU	22TAU	21TAU	22CAN	22LEO
26CAN	24LEO	26VIR	24LIB	23SCO	24CAP	24AQU	23PIS	24ARI	24GEM	24LEO	24VIR
28LEO	26VIR	28LIB	26SCO	26SAG	27AQU	27PIS	25ARI	26GEM	26CAN	26VIR	26LIB
30VIR	28LIB	30SCO	28SAG	28CAP	29PIS	29ARI	28TAU	29CAN	28LEO	29LIB	28SCO
				31AQU			30GEM		30VIR		30SAG

1984

JAN	FEB	MAR	APR	MAY	JUNE	JULY	AUG	SEPT	OCT	NOV	DEC
2CAP	3PIS	1PIS	2TAU	2GEM	1CAN	2VIR	2SCO	1SAG	1CAP	2PIS	1ARI
4AQU	5ARI	4ARI	5GEM	4CAN	3LEO	4LIB	5SAG	3CAP	3AQU	4ARI	4TAU
6PIS	8TAU	6TAU	7CAN	6LEO	5VIR	6SCO	7CAP	6AQU	5PIS	7TAU	6GEM
9ARI	10GEM	8GEM	9LEO	9VIR	7LIB	9SAG	9AQU	8PIS	8ARI	9GEM	9CAN
11TAU	12CAN	11CAN	11VIR	11LIB	9SCO	11CAP	12PIS	11ARI	10TAU	12CAN	11LEO
14GEM	15LEO	13LEO	13LIB	13SCO	11SAG	13AQU	14ARI	13TAU	13GEM	14LEO	13VIR
16CAN	17VIR	15VIR	15SCO	16SAG	13CAP	16PIS	17TAU	16GEM	15CAN	16VIR	15LIB
18LEO	19LIB	17LIB	17SAG	17CAP	16AQU	18ARI	19GEM	18CAN	18LEO	18LIB	17SCO
20VIR	21SCO	19SCO	20CAP	19AQU	18PIS	21TAU	22CAN	20LEO	20VIR	20SCO	20SAG
22LIB	23SAG	21SAG	22AQU	22PIS	21ARI	23GEM	24LEO	22VIR	22LIB	22SAG	22CAP
24SCO	25CAP	23CAP	25PIS	24ARI	23TAU	25CAN	26VIR	24LIB	24SCO	24CAP	24AQU
26SAG	28AQU	26AQU	27ARI	27TAU	26GEM	27LEO	28LIB	26SCO	26SAG	27AQU	26PIS
29CAP		28PIS	30TAU	29GEM	28CAN	29VIR	30SCO	28SAG	28CAP	29PIS	29ARI
31AQU		31ARI			30LEO	31LIB			30AQU		31TAU

1985

JAN	FEB	MAR	APR	MAY	JUNE	JULY	AUG	SEPT	OCT	NOV	DEC
3GEM	2CAN	1CAN	2VIR	1LIB	2SAG	1CAP	2PIS	1ARI	3GEM	2CAN	1LEO
5CAN	4LEO	3LEO	4LIB	3SCO	4CAP	3AQU	4ARI	3TAU	5CAN	4LEO	4VIR
7LEO	6VIR	5VIR	6SCO	5SAG	6AQU	5PIS	7TAU	6GEM	8LEO	6VIR	6LIB
9VIR	8LIB	7LIB	8SAG	7CAP	8PIS	9ARI	9GEM	8CAN	10VIR	9LIB	8SCO
12LIB	10SCO	9SCO	10CAP	9AQU	11ARI	10TAU	12CAN	10LEO	12LIB	11SCO	10SAG
14SCO	12SAG	11SAG	12AQU	12PIS	13TAU	13GEM	14LEO	13VIR	14SCO	13SAG	12CAP
16SAG	14CAP	14CAP	14PIS	14ARI	16GEM	15CAN	16VIR	15LIB	16SAG	15CAP	14AQU
18CAP	17AQU	16AQU	17ARI	17TAU	18CAN	18LEO	18LIB	17SCO	18CAP	17AQU	16PIS
20AQU	19PIS	18PIS	20TAU	19GEM	20LEO	20VIR	20SCO	19SAG	20AQU	19PIS	19ARI
23PIS	21ARI	21ARI	22GEM	22CAN	23VIR	22LIB	22SAG	21CAP	23PIS	21ARI	21TAU
25ARI	24TAU	23TAU	25CAN	24LEO	25LIB	24SCO	25CAP	23ARI	25ARI	24TAU	24GEM
28TAU	27GEM	26GEM	27LEO	26VIR	27SCO	26SAG	27AQU	25PIS	28TAU	26GEM	26CAN
30GEM		38CAN	29VIR	29LIB	29SAG	28CAP	29PIS	28ARI	30GEM	29CAN	29LEO
		31LEO		31SCO		31AQU		30TAU			31VIR

1986

JAN	FEB	MAR	APR	MAY	JUNE	JULY	AUG	SEPT	OCT	NOV	DEC
2LIB	1SCO	2SAG	2AQU	2PIS	3TAU	3GEM	2CAN	3VIR	2LIB	1SCO	2CAP
4SCO	3SAG	4CAP	5PIS	4ARI	5GEM	5CAN	4LEO	5LIB	4SCO	3SAG	4AQU
6SAG	5CAP	6AQU	7ARI	7TAU	8CAN	8LEO	6VIR	7SCO	7SAG	5CAP	6PIS
8CAP	7AQU	8PIS	9TAU	9GEM	11LEO	10VIR	9LIB	9SAG	9CAP	7AQU	9ARI
11AQU	9PIS	11ARI	12GEM	12CAN	13VIR	12LIB	11SCO	11CAP	11AQU	9PIS	11TAU
13PIS	11ARI	13TAU	14CAN	14LEO	15LIB	15SCO	13SAG	14AQU	13PIS	11ARI	14GEM
15ARI	14TAU	16GEM	17LEO	17VIR	17SCO	17SAG	15CAP	16PIS	15ARI	14TAU	16CAN
17TAU	16GEM	18CAN	19VIR	19LIB	19SAG	19CAP	17AQU	18ARI	18TAU	16GEM	19LEO
20GEM	19CAN	21LEO	21LIB	21SCO	21CAP	21AQU	19PIS	20TAU	20GEM	19CAN	21VIR
22CAN	21LEO	23VIR	24SCO	23SAG	23AQU	23PIS	22ARI	23GEM	23CAN	21LEO	24LIB
25LEO	24VIR	25LIB	26SAG	25CAP	26PIS	25ARI	24TAU	25CAN	25LEO	24VIR	26SCO
27VIR	26LIB	27SCO	28CAP	27AQU	28ARI	28TAU	26GEM	28LEO	27VIR	26LIB	28SAG
29LIB	28SCO	29SAG	30AQU	29PIS	30TAU	30GEM	29CAN	30VIR	30LIB	28SCO	30CAP
		31CAP		31ARI			31LEO			30SAG	

1987

JAN	FEB	MAR	APR	MAY	JUNE	JULY	AUG	SEPT	OCT	NOV	DEC
1AQU	1ARI	1ARI	2GEM	2CAN	3VIR	3LIB	1SCO	2CAP	1AQU	2ARI	1TAU
3PIS	4TAU	3TAU	4CAN	4LEO	5LIB	5SCO	4SAG	4AQU	3PIS	4TAU	4GEM
5ARI	6GEM	5GEM	7LEO	7VIR	8SCO	7SAG	6CAP	6PIS	6ARI	6GEM	6CAN
7TAU	9CAN	8CAN	9VIR	9LIB	10SAG	9CAP	8AQU	8ARI	8TAU	9CAN	8LEO
10GEM	11LEO	10LEO	12LIB	11SCO	12CAP	11AQU	10PIS	10TAU	10GEM	11LEO	11VIR
12CAN	14VIR	13VIR	14SCO	13SAG	14AQU	13PIS	12ARI	13GEM	12CAN	14VIR	14LIB
15LEO	16LIB	15LIB	16SAG	15CAP	16PIS	15ARI	14TAU	15CAN	15LEO	16LIB	16SCO
17VIR	18SCO	18SCO	18CAP	17AQU	18ARI	18TAU	16GEM	17LEO	17VIR	18SCO	18SAG
20LIB	21SAG	20SAG	20AQU	20PIS	20TAU	20GEM	19CAN	20VIR	20LIB	21SAG	20CAP
22SCO	23CAP	22CAP	22PIS	22ARI	23GEM	22CAN	21LEO	22LIB	22SCO	23CAP	22AQU
24SAG	25AQU	24AQU	25ARI	24TAU	25CAN	25LEO	24VIR	25SCO	24SAG	25AQU	24PIS
26CAP	27PIS	26PIS	27TAU	26GEM	28LEO	27VIR	26LIB	27SAG	26CAP	27PIS	26ARI
28AQU		28ARI	29GEM	29CAN	30VIR	30LIB	29SCO	29CAP	29AQU	29ARI	29TAU
30PIS		30TAU		31LEO			31SAG		31PIS		31GEM

1988

JAN	FEB	MAR	APR	MAY	JUNE	JULY	AUG	SEPT	OCT	NOV	DEC
2CAN	1LEO	2VIR	1LIB	3SAG	1CAP	1AQU	1ARI	2GEM	1CAN	2VIR	2LIB
5LEO	4VIR	4LIB	3SCO	5CAP	3AQU	3PIS	3TAU	4CAN	4LEO	5LIB	5SCO
7VIR	6LIB	7SCO	5SAG	7AQU	5PIS	5ARI	5GEM	6LEO	6VIR	7SCO	7SAG
10LIB	9SCO	9SAG	8CAP	9PIS	8ARI	7TAU	8CAN	9VIR	9LIB	10SAG	9CAP
12SCO	11SAG	11CAP	10AQU	11ARI	10TAU	9GEM	10LEO	11LIB	11SCO	12CAP	12AQU
15SAG	13CAP	14AQU	12PIS	13TAU	12GEM	11CAN	13VIR	14SCO	14SAG	14AQU	14PIS
17CAP	15AQU	16PIS	14ARI	16GEM	14CAN	14LEO	15LIB	16SAG	16CAP	17PIS	16ARI
19AQU	17PIS	18ARI	16TAU	18CAN	17LEO	16VIR	18SCO	19CAP	18AQU	19ARI	18TAU
21PIS	19ARI	20TAU	18GEM	20LEO	19VIR	19LIB	20SAG	21AQU	20PIS	21TAU	20GEM
23ARI	21TAU	22GEM	20CAN	23VIR	22LIB	21SCO	22CAP	23PIS	22ARI	23GEM	22CAN
25TAU	23GEM	24CAN	23LEO	25LIB	24SCO	24SAG	24AQU	25ARI	24TAU	25CAN	25LEO
27GEM	26CAN	27LEO	25VIR	28SCO	26SAG	26CAP	26PIS	27TAU	26GEM	27LEO	27VIR
30CAN	28LEO	29VIR	29LIB	30SAG	29CAP	28AQU	28ARI	29GEM	29CAN	30VIR	30LIB
			30SCO			30PIS	30TAU		31LEO		

1989

JAN	FEB	MAR	APR	MAY	JUNE	JULY	AUG	SEPT	OCT	NOV	DEC
1SCO	2CAP	2CAP	2PIS	2ARI	2GEM	2CAN	3VIR	1LIB	1SCO	2CAP	2AQU
4SAG	4AQU	4AQU	4ARI	4TAU	4CAN	4LEO	5LIB	4SCO	4SAG	5AQU	4PIS
6CAP	6PIS	6PIS	6TAU	6GEM	7LEO	6VIR	8SCO	6SAG	6CAP	7PIS	7ARI
8AQU	8ARI	8ARI	8GEM	8CAN	9VIR	9LIB	10SAG	9CAP	9AQU	9ARI	9TAU
10PIS	11TAU	10TAU	11CAN	10LEO	11LIB	11SCO	12CAP	11AQU	11PIS	11TAU	11GEM
12ARI	13GEM	12GEM	13LEO	13VIR	14SCO	14SAG	15AQU	13PIS	13ARI	13GEM	13CAN
14TAU	15CAN	14CAN	15VIR	15LIB	16SAG	16CAP	17PIS	15ARI	15TAU	15CAN	15LEO
16GEM	17LEO	17LEO	18LIB	18SCO	19CAP	18AQU	19ARI	17TAU	17GEM	17LEO	17VIR
19CAN	20VIR	19VIR	20SCO	20SAG	21AQU	20PIS	21TAU	19GEM	19CAN	20VIR	19LIB
21LEO	22LIB	22LIB	23SAG	22CAP	23PIS	23ARI	23GEM	21CAN	21LEO	22LIB	22SCO
23VIR	25SCO	24SCO	25CAP	25AQU	25ARI	25TAU	25CAN	24LEO	23VIR	25SCO	24SAG
26LIB	27SAG	27SAG	28AQU	27PIS	27TAU	27GEM	28LEO	26VIR	26LIB	27SAG	27CAP
29SCO		29CAP	30PIS	29ARI	30GEM	29CAN	30VIR	29LIB	28SCO	30CAP	29AQU
31SAG		31AQU		31TAU		31LEO			31SAG		

1990

	JAN	FEB	MAR	APR	MAY	JUNE	JULY	AUG	SEPT	OCT	NOV	DEC
	1PIS	1TAU	2GEM	1CAN	3VIR	1LIB	1SCO	2CAP	1AQU	1PIS	2TAU	1GEM
	3ARI	3GEM	5CAN	3LEO	5LIB	4SCO	4SAG	5AQU	3PIS	3ARI	4GEM	3CAN
	5TAU	5CAN	7LEO	5VIR	8SCO	6SAG	6CAP	7PIS	6ARI	5TAU	6CAN	5LEO
	7GEM	8LEO	9VIR	8LIB	10SAG	9CAP	9AQU	9ARI	8TAU	7GEM	8LEO	7VIR
	9CAN	10VIR	12LIB	10SCO	13CAP	11AQU	11PIS	12TAU	10GEM	9CAN	10VIR	9LIB
	11LEO	12LIB	14SCO	13SAG	15AQU	14PIS	13ARI	14GEM	12CAN	11LEO	12LIB	12SCO
	13VIR	15SCO	16SAG	15CAP	17PIS	16ARI	15TAU	16CAN	14LEO	14VIR	15SCO	14SAG
	16LIB	17SAG	19CAP	18AQU	20ARI	18TAU	17GEM	18LEO	16VIR	16LIB	17SAG	17CAP
	18SCO	20CAP	21AQU	20PIS	22TAU	20GEM	19CAN	20VIR	19LIB	18SCO	20CAP	19AQU
	21SAG	22AQU	24PIS	22ARI	24GEM	22CAN	21LEO	22LIB	21SCO	21SAG	22AQU	22PIS
	23CAP	24PIS	26ARI	24TAU	26CAN	24LEO	24VIR	25SCO	24SAG	23CAP	25PIS	24ARI
	26AQU	26ARI	28TAU	26GEM	28LEO	26VIR	26LIB	27SAG	26CAP	26AQU	27ARI	26TAU
	28PIS	28TAU	30GEM	28CAN	30VIR	29LIB	28SCO	30CAP	29AQU	28PIS	29TAU	28GEM
	30ARI			30LEO			31SAG			30ARI		30CAN

1991

	JAN	FEB	MAR	APR	MAY	JUNE	JULY	AUG	SEPT	OCT	NOV	DEC
	1LEO	2LIB	2LIB	3SAG	2CAP	1AQU	1PIS	2TAU	3CAN	2LEO	2LIB	2SCO
	4VIR	4SCO	4SCO	5CAP	4AQU	4PIS	3ARI	4GEM	5LEO	4VIR	5SCO	4SAG
	6LIB	7SAG	6SAG	8AQU	7PIS	6ARI	6TAU	6CAN	7VIR	6LIB	7SAG	7CAP
	8SCO	9CAP	9CAP	10PIS	10ARI	8TAU	8GEM	8LEO	9LIB	8SCO	10CAP	9AQU
	11SAG	12AQU	11AQU	12ARI	12TAU	10GEM	10CAN	10VIR	11SCO	11SAG	12AQU	12PIS
	13CAP	14PIS	14PIS	15TAU	14GEM	12CAN	12LEO	12LIB	13SAG	13CAP	15PIS	14ARI
	16AQU	17ARI	16ARI	17GEM	16CAN	14LEO	14VIR	15SCO	16CAP	16AQU	17ARI	17TAU
	18PIS	19TAU	18TAU	19CAN	18LEO	16VIR	16LIB	17SAG	18AQU	18PIS	19TAU	19GEM
	20ARI	21GEM	20GEM	21LEO	20VIR	19LIB	18SCO	20CAP	21PIS	21ARI	21GEM	21CAN
	23TAU	23CAN	22CAN	23VIR	22LIB	21SCO	21SAG	22AQU	23ARI	23TAU	23CAN	23LEO
	25GEM	25LEO	25LEO	25LIB	25SCO	23SAG	23CAP	25PIS	25TAU	25GEM	25LEO	25VIR
	27CAN	27VIR	27VIR	28SCO	27SAG	26CAP	26AQU	27ARI	28GEM	27CAN	28VIR	27LIB
	29LEO		29LIB	30SAG	30CAP	29AQU	28PIS	29TAU	30CAN	29LEO	20LIB	29SCO
	31VIR		31SCO				31ARI	31GEM		31VIR	

1992

JAN	FEB	MAR	APR	MAY	JUNE	JULY	AUG	SEPT	OCT	NOV	DEC
1SAG	2AQU	3PIS	1ARI	1TAU	2CAN	1LEO	2LIB	2SAG	2CAP	1AQU	1PIS
3CAP	4PIS	5ARI	4TAU	3GEM	4LEO	3VIR	4SCO	5CAP	5AQU	3PIS	3ARI
6AQU	7ARI	8TAU	6GEM	5CAN	6VIR	5LIB	6SAG	7AQU	7PIS	6ARI	6TAU
8PIS	9TAU	10GEM	8CAN	8LEO	8LIB	7SCO	8CAP	10PIS	10ARI	8TAU	8GEM
11ARI	12GEM	12CAN	10LEO	10VIR	10SCO	10SAG	11AQU	12ARI	12TAU	11GEM	10CAN
13TAU	14CAN	14LEO	12VIR	12LIB	13SAG	12CAP	13PIS	15TAU	14GEM	13CAN	12LEO
15GEM	16LEO	16VIR	15LIB	14SCO	15CAP	15AQU	16ARI	17GEM	17CAN	15LEO	14VIR
17CAN	18VIR	18LIB	17SCO	16SAG	17AQU	17PIS	18TAU	19CAN	19LEO	17VIR	16LIB
19LEO	20LIB	20SCO	19SAG	19CAP	20PIS	20ARI	21GEM	21LEO	21VIR	19LIB	19SCO
21VIR	22SCO	23SAG	21CAP	21AQU	22ARI	22TAU	23CAN	24VIR	23LIB	21SCO	21SAG
23LIB	24SAG	25CAP	24AQU	24PIS	25TAU	24GEM	25LEO	26LIB	25SCO	24SAG	23CAP
25SCO	27CAP	27AQU	26PIS	26ARI	27GEM	27CAN	27VIR	28SCO	27SAG	26CAP	26AQU
28SAG	29AQU	30PIS	29ARI	28TAU	29CAN	29LEO	29LIB	30SAG	29CAP	28AQU	28PIS
30CAP				31GEM		31VIR	31SCO				31ARI

1993

JAN	FEB	MAR	APR	MAY	JUNE	JULY	AUG	SEPT	OCT	NOV	DEC
2TAU	1GEM	2CAN	1LEO	2LIB	1SCO	2CAP	1AQU	2ARI	2TAU	1GEM	3LEO
4GEM	3CAN	5LEO	3VIR	4SCO	3SAG	5AQU	3PIS	5TAU	4GEM	3CAN	5VIR
7CAN	5LEO	7VIR	5LIB	6SAG	5CAP	7PIS	6ARI	7GEM	7CAN	5LEO	7LIB
9LEO	7VIR	9LIB	7SCO	9CAP	7AQU	10ARI	9TAU	10CAN	9LEO	8VIR	9SCO
11VIR	9LIB	11SCO	9SAG	11AQU	10PIS	12TAU	11GEM	12LEO	11VIR	10LIB	11SAG
13LIB	11SCO	13SAG	11CAP	13PIS	12ARI	15GEM	13CAN	14VIR	13LIB	12SCO	13CAP
15SCO	13SAG	15CAP	14AQU	16ARI	15TAU	17CAN	15LEO	16LIB	15SCO	14SAG	15AQU
17SAG	16CAP	17AQU	16PIS	18TAU	17GEM	19LEO	17VIR	18SCO	17SAG	16CAP	18PIS
19CAP	18AQU	20PIS	19ARI	21GEM	19CAN	21VIR	19LIB	20SAG	19CAP	18AQU	20ARI
22AQU	21PIS	22ARI	21TAU	23CAN	22LEO	23LIB	21SCO	22CAP	22AQU	20PIS	23TAU
24PIS	23ARI	25TAU	24GEM	25LEO	24VIR	25SCO	24SAG	24AQU	24PIS	23ARI	25GEM
27ARI	26TAU	27GEM	26CAN	28VIR	26LIB	27SAG	26CAP	27PIS	27ARI	26TAU	28CAN
29TAU	28GEM	30CAN	28LEO	30LIB	28SCO	30CAP	28AQU	29ARI	29TAU	28GEM	30LEO
			30VIR		30SAG		31PIS			30CAN	

1994	JAN	FEB	MAR	APR	MAY	JUNE	JULY	AUG	SEPT	OCT	NOV	DEC
	1VIR	2SCO	1SCO	1CAP	1AQU	2ARI	2TAU	1GEM	2LEO	2VIR	2SCO	2SAG
	3LIB	4SAG	3SAG	4AQU	3PIS	5TAU	4GEM	3CAN	4VIR	4LIB	4SAG	4CAP
	5SCO	6CAP	5CAP	6PIS	6ARI	7GEM	7CAN	6LEO	6LIB	6SCO	6CAP	6AQU
	8SAG	8AQU	7AQU	9ARI	8TAU	10CAN	9LEO	8VIR	8SCO	8SAG	8AQU	8PIS
	10CAP	11PIS	10PIS	11TAU	11GEM	12LEO	11VIR	10LIB	10SAG	10CAP	11PIS	10ARI
	12AQU	13ARI	12ARI	14GEM	13CAN	14VIR	14LIB	12SCO	13CAP	12AQU	13ARI	13TAU
	14PIS	16TAU	15TAU	16CAN	16LEO	16LIB	16SCO	14SAG	15AQU	14PIS	15TAU	15GEM
	17ARI	18GEM	17GEM	18LEO	18VIR	19SCO	18SAG	16CAP	17PIS	17ARI	18GEM	18CAN
	19TAU	20CAN	20CAN	21VIR	20LIB	21SAG	20CAP	18AQU	19ARI	19TAU	20CAN	20LEO
	22GEM	23LEO	22LEO	23LIB	22SCO	23CAP	22AQU	21PIS	22TAU	22GEM	23LEO	23VIR
	24CAN	25VIR	24VIR	25SCO	24SAG	25AQU	24PIS	23ARI	24GEM	24CAN	25VIR	25LIB
	26LEO	27LIB	26LIB	27SAG	26CAP	27PIS	27ARI	26TAU	27CAN	27LEO	28LIB	27SCO
	28VIR		28SCO	29CAP	28AQU	29ARI	29TAU	28GEM	29LEO	29VIR	30SCO	29SAG
	31LIB		30SAG		31PIS			31CAN		31LIB		31CAP

1995	JAN	FEB	MAR	APR	MAY	JUNE	JULY	AUG	SEPT	OCT	NOV	DEC
	2AQU	1PIS	2ARI	1TAU	1GEM	2LEO	2VIR	3SCO	1SAG	2AQU	1PIS	3TAU
	4PIS	3ARI	5TAU	3GEM	3CAN	5VIR	4LIB	5SAG	3CAP	5PIS	3ARI	5GEM
	7ARI	5TAU	7GEM	6CAN	6LEO	7LIB	6SCO	7CAP	5AQU	7ARI	5TAU	8CAN
	9TAU	8GEM	10CAN	9LEO	8VIR	9SCO	8SAG	9AQU	7PIS	9TAU	8GEM	10LEO
	12GEM	10CAN	12LEO	11VIR	10LIB	11SAG	10CAP	11PIS	9ARI	12GEM	10CAN	13VIR
	14CAN	13LEO	14VIR	13LIB	13SCO	13CAP	12AQU	13ARI	12TAU	14CAN	13LEO	15LIB
	16LEO	15VIR	17LIB	15SCO	15SAG	15AQU	14PIS	15TAU	14GEM	17LEO	15VIR	17SCO
	19VIR	17LIB	19SCO	17SAG	17CAP	17PIS	17ARI	18GEM	17CAN	19VIR	18LIB	19SAG
	21LIB	19SCO	21SAG	19CAP	19AQU	19ARI	19TAU	20CAN	19LEO	21LIB	20SCO	21CAP
	23SCO	22SAG	23CAP	21AQU	21PIS	22TAU	22GEM	23LEO	22VIR	23SCO	22SAG	23AQU
	25SAG	24CAP	25AQU	24PIS	23ARI	24GEM	24CAN	25VIR	24LIB	26SAG	24CAP	25PIS
	27CAP	26AQU	27PIS	26ARI	26TAU	27CAN	27LEO	28LIB	26SCO	28CAP	26AQU	28ARI
	30AQU	28PIS	30ARI	28TAU	28GEM	29LEO	29VIR	30SCO	28SAG	30AQU	28PIS	30TAU
					31CAN		31LIB		30CAP		30ARI	

1996

JAN	FEB	MAR	APR	MAY	JUNE	JULY	AUG	SEPT	OCT	NOV	DEC
1GEM	3LEO	1LEO	2LIB	2SCO	2CAP	2AQU	2ARI	1TAU	3CAN	2LEO	2VIR
4CAN	5VIR	3VIR	4SCO	4SAG	4AQU	4PIS	4TAU	3GEM	5LEO	4VIR	4LIB
6LEO	8LIB	6LIB	7SAG	6CAP	6PIS	6ARI	7GEM	6CAN	8VIR	7LIB	6SCO
9VIR	10SCO	8SCO	9CAP	8AQU	9ARI	8TAU	9CAN	8LEO	10LIB	9SCO	9SAG
11LIB	12SAG	10SAG	11AQU	10PIS	11TAU	11GEM	12LEO	11VIR	13SCO	11SAG	11CAP
14SCO	14CAP	13CAP	13PIS	12ARI	13GEM	13CAN	14VIR	13LIB	15SAG	13CAP	13AQU
16SAG	16AQU	15AQU	15ARI	15TAU	16CAN	16LEO	17LIB	15SCO	17CAP	16AQU	15PIS
18CAP	18PIS	17PIS	17TAU	17GEM	18LEO	18VIR	19SCO	18SAG	19AQU	18PIS	17ARI
20AQU	20ARI	19ARI	20GEM	19CAN	21VIR	21LIB	21SAG	20CAP	21PIS	20ARI	19TAU
22PIS	23TAU	21TAU	22CAN	22LEO	23LIB	23SCO	24CAP	22AQU	23ARI	22TAU	22GEM
24ARI	25GEM	23GEM	25LEO	25VIR	26SCO	25SAG	26AQU	24PIS	26TAU	24GEM	24CAN
26TAU	27CAN	26CAN	27VIR	27LIB	28SAG	27CAP	28PIS	26ARI	28GEM	27CAN	26LEO
29GEM		28LEO	30LIB	29SCO	30CAP	29AQU	30ARI	28TAU	30CAN	29LEO	29VIR
31CAN		31VIR		31SAG		31PIS		30GEM			31LIB

1997

JAN	FEB	MAR	APR	MAY	JUNE	JULY	AUG	SEPT	OCT	NOV	DEC
3SCO	1SAG	1SAG	1AQU	1PIS	1TAU	1GEM	2LEO	3LIB	2SCO	1SAG	1CAP
5SAG	4CAP	3CAP	4PIS	3ARI	4GEM	3CAN	4VIR	6SCO	5SAG	4CAP	3AQU
7CAP	6AQU	5AQU	6ARI	5TAU	6CAN	5LEO	7LIB	8SAG	8CAP	6AQU	5PIS
9AQU	8PIS	7PIS	8TAU	7GEM	8LEO	8VIR	9SCO	10CAP	10AQU	8PIS	8ARI
11PIS	10ARI	9ARI	10GEM	9CAN	11VIR	10LIB	12SAG	12AQU	12PIS	10ARI	10TAU
13ARI	12TAU	11TAU	12CAN	12LEO	13LIB	13SCO	14CAP	15PIS	14ARI	12TAU	12GEM
15TAU	14GEM	13GEM	14LEO	14VIR	16SCO	15SAG	16AQU	17ARI	16TAU	14GEM	14CAN
18GEM	16CAN	16CAN	17VIR	17LIB	18SAG	18CAP	18PIS	19TAU	18GEM	17CAN	16LEO
20CAN	19LEO	18LEO	19LIB	19SCO	20CAP	20AQU	20ARI	21GEM	20CAN	19LEO	19VIR
23LEO	21VIR	21VIR	22SCO	22SAG	22AQU	22PIS	22TAU	23CAN	23LEO	21VIR	21LIB
25VIR	24LIB	23LIB	24SAG	24CAP	24PIS	24ARI	24GEM	25LEO	25VIR	24LIB	24SCO
29LIB	26SCO	26SCO	27CAP	26AQU	26ARI	26TAU	27CAN	28VIR	28LIB	26SCO	26SAG
30SCO		28SAG	29AQU	28PIS	29TAU	28GEM	29LEO	30LIB	30SCO	29SAG	28CAP
		30CAP		30ARI		30CAN	31VIR				31AQU

1998

	JAN	FEB	MAR	APR	MAY	JUNE	JULY	AUG	SEPT	OCT	NOV	DEC
	2PIS	2TAU	2TAU	2CAN	2LEO	3LIB	3SCO	2SAG	3AQU	2PIS	1ARI	2GEM
	4ARI	4GEM	4GEM	4LEO	4VIR	5SCO	5SAG	4CAP	5PIS	4ARI	3TAU	4CAN
	6TAU	7CAN	6CAN	7VIR	7LIB	8SAG	8CAP	6AQU	7ARI	6TAU	5GEM	6LEO
	8GEM	9LEO	8LEO	9LIB	9SCO	10CAP	10AQU	8PIS	9TAU	8GEM	7CAN	9VIR
	10CAN	11VIR	11VIR	12SCO	12SAG	13AQU	12PIS	11ARI	11GEM	10CAN	9LEO	11LIB
	13LEO	14LIB	13LIB	14SAG	14CAP	15PIS	14ARI	13TAU	13CAN	13LEO	11VIR	14SCO
	15VIR	16SCO	16SCO	17CAP	16AQU	17ARI	16TAU	15GEM	15LEO	15VIR	14LIB	16SAG
	18LIB	19SAG	18SAG	19AQU	19PIS	19TAU	18GEM	17CAN	18VIR	17LIB	16SCO	19CAP
	20SCO	21CAP	21CAP	21PIS	21ARI	21GEM	21CAN	19LEO	20LIB	20SCO	19SAG	21AQU
	23SAG	23AQU	23AQU	23ARI	23TAU	23CAN	23LEO	21VIR	23SCO	23SAG	21CAP	23PIS
	25CAP	25PIS	25PIS	25TAU	25GEM	25LEO	25VIR	24LIB	25SAG	25CAP	24AQU	25ARI
	27AQU	27ARI	27ARI	27GEM	27CAN	28VIR	28LIB	26SCO	28CAP	27AQU	26PIS	28TAU
	29PIS		29TAU	29CAN	29LEO	30LIB	30SCO	29SAG	30AQU	30PIS	28ARI	30GEM
	31ARI		31GEM		31VIR			31CAP			30TAU	

1999

	JAN	FEB	MAR	APR	MAY	JUNE	JULY	AUG	SEPT	OCT	NOV	DEC
	1CAN	1VIR	1VIR	2SCO	2SAG	3AQU	2PIS	1ARI	2GEM	1CAN	1VIR	1LIB
	3LEO	4LIB	3LIB	4SAG	4CAP	5PIS	5ARI	3TAU	4CAN	3LEO	4LIB	3SCO
	5VIR	6SCO	6SCO	7CAP	7AQU	8ARI	7TAU	5GEM	6LEO	5VIR	6SCO	6SAG
	7LIB	9SAG	8SAG	9AQU	9PIS	10TAU	9GEM	7CAN	8VIR	8LIB	9SAG	8CAP
	10SCO	11CAP	11CAP	12PIS	11ARI	12GEM	11CAN	9LEO	10LIB	10SCO	11CAP	11AQU
	12SAG	14AQU	13AQU	14ARI	13TAU	14CAN	13LEO	12VIR	13SCO	12SAG	14AQU	13PIS
	15CAP	16PIS	15PIS	16TAU	15GEM	16LEO	15VIR	14LIB	15SAG	15CAP	16PIS	16ARI
	17AQU	18ARI	17ARI	18GEM	17CAN	18VIR	17LIB	16SCO	18CAP	17AQU	18ARI	18TAU
	19PIS	20TAU	19TAU	20CAN	19LEO	20LIB	20SCO	19SAG	20AQU	20PIS	21TAU	20GEM
	22ARI	22GEM	21GEM	22LEO	21VIR	23SCO	22SAG	21CAP	22PIS	22ARI	23GEM	22CAN
	24TAU	24CAN	23CAN	24VIR	24LIB	25SAG	25CAP	24AQU	25ARI	24TAU	25CAN	24LEO
	26GEM	26LEO	26LEO	27LIB	26SCO	28CAP	27AQU	26PIS	27TAU	26GEM	27LEO	26VIR
	28CAN		28VIR	29SCO	29SAG	30AQU	30PIS	28ARI	29GEM	28CAN	29VIR	28LIB
	30LEO		30LIB		31CAP			30TAU		30LEO		31SCO

2000

JAN	FEB	MAR	APR	MAY	JUNE	JULY	AUG	SEPT	OCT	NOV	DEC
3SAG	1CAP	2AQU	1PIS	3TAU	1GEM	2LEO	1VIR	2SCO	1SAG	3AQU	2PIS
5CAP	4AQU	4PIS	3ARI	5GEM	3CAN	4VIR	3LIB	4SAG	4CAP	5PIS	5ARI
7AQU	6PIS	7ARI	5TAU	7CAN	5LEO	7LIB	5SCO	6CAP	6AQU	8ARI	7TAU
10PIS	8ARI	9TAU	7GEM	9LEO	7VIR	9SCO	8SAG	9AQU	9PIS	10TAU	9GEM
12ARI	11TAU	11GEM	9CAN	11VIR	9LIB	11SAG	10CAP	11PIS	11ARI	12GEM	11CAN
14TAU	13GEM	13CAN	11LEO	13LIB	12SCO	14CAP	13AQU	14ARI	13TAU	14CAN	13LEO
16GEM	15CAN	15LEO	14VIR	15SCO	14SAG	16AQU	15PIS	16TAU	16GEM	16LEO	15VIR
18CAN	17LEO	17VIR	16LIB	18SAG	17CAP	19PIS	18ARI	18GEM	18CAN	18VIR	18LIB
20LEO	19VIR	20LIB	18SCO	20CAP	19AQU	21ARI	20TAU	20CAN	20LEO	20LIB	20SCO
23VIR	21LIB	22SCO	21SAG	23AQU	22PIS	24TAU	22GEM	23LEO	22VIR	23SCO	22SAG
25LIB	23SCO	24SAG	23CAP	25PIS	24ARI	26GEM	24CAN	25VIR	24LIB	25SAG	25CAP
27SCO	26SAG	27CAP	26AQU	28ARI	26TAU	28CAN	26LEO	27LIB	26SCO	27CAP	27AQU
29SAG	28CAP	29AQU	28PIS	30TAU	28GEM	30LEO	28VIR	29SCO	29SAG	30AQU	30PIS
			30ARI		30CAN		30LIB		31CAP		

2001

JAN	FEB	MAR	APR	MAY	JUNE	JULY	AUG	SEPT	OCT	NOV	DEC
1ARI	2GEM	1GEM	2LEO	1VIR	2SCO	1SAG	3AQU	1PIS	1ARI	2GEM	2CAN
4TAU	4CAN	4CAN	4VIR	3LIB	4SAG	4CAP	5PIS	4ARI	4TAU	4CAN	4LEO
6GEM	6LEO	6LEO	6LIB	6SCO	7CAP	6AQU	8ARI	6TAU	6GEM	7LEO	6VIR
8CAN	8VIR	8VIR	8SCO	8SAG	9AQU	9PIS	10TAU	9GEM	8CAN	9VIR	8LIB
10LEO	10LIB	10LIB	10SAG	10CAP	11PIS	11ARI	12GEM	11CAN	10LEO	11LIB	10SCO
12VIR	12SCO	12SCO	13CAP	13AQU	14ARI	14TAU	15CAN	13LEO	13VIR	13SCO	12SAG
14LIB	15SAG	14SAG	15AQU	15PIS	16TAU	16GEM	17LEO	15VIR	15LIB	15SAG	15CAP
16SCO	17CAP	16CAP	18PIS	18ARI	19GEM	18CAN	19VIR	17LIB	17SCO	17CAP	17AQU
18SAG	20AQU	19AQU	20ARI	20TAU	21CAN	20LEO	21LIB	19SCO	19SAG	20AQU	20PIS
21CAP	22PIS	22PIS	23TAU	22GEM	23LEO	22VIR	23SCO	21SAG	21CAP	22PIS	22ARI
23AQU	25ARI	24ARI	25GEM	24CAN	25VIR	24LIB	25SAG	24CAP	23AQU	25ARI	25TAU
26PIS	27TAU	26TAU	27CAN	27LEO	27LIB	26SCO	27CAP	26AQU	26PIS	27TAU	27GEM
28ARI		29GEM	29LEO	29VIR	29SCO	29SAG	20AQU	29PIS	28ARI	30GEM	29CAN
31TAU		31CAN		31LIB		31CAP			31TAU		31LEO

2002

	JAN	FEB	MAR	APR	MAY	JUNE	JULY	AUG	SEPT	OCT	NOV	DEC
	2VIR	1LIB	2SCO	1SAG	2AQU	1PIS	1ARI	2GEM	1CAN	1LEO	1LIB	1SCO
	4LIB	3SCO	4SAG	3CAP	5PIS	4ARI	4TAU	5CAN	3LEO	3VIR	3SCO	3SAG
	6SCO	5SAG	6CAP	5AQU	7ARI	6TAU	6GEM	7LEO	5VIR	5LIB	5SAG	5CAP
	9SAG	7CAP	9AQU	8PIS	10TAU	9GEM	8CAN	9VIR	7LIB	7SCO	7CAP	7AQU
	11CAP	10AQU	11PIS	10ARI	12GEM	11CAN	11LEO	11LIB	9SCO	9SAG	10AQU	9PIS
	13AQU	12PIS	14ARI	13TAU	15CAN	13LEO	13VIR	13SCO	12SAG	11CAP	12PIS	12ARI
	16PIS	15ARI	16TAU	15GEM	17LEO	15VIR	15LIB	15SAG	14CAP	13AQU	15ARI	14TAU
	18ARI	17TAU	19GEM	18CAN	19VIR	18LIB	17SCO	18CAP	16AQU	16PIS	17TAU	17GEM
	21TAU	20GEM	21CAN	20LEO	21LIB	20SCO	19SAG	20AQU	19PIS	18ARI	20GEM	19CAN
	23GEM	22CAN	24LEO	22VIR	23SCO	22SAG	21CAP	22PIS	21ARI	21TAU	22CAN	22LEO
	26CAN	24LEO	26VIR	24LIB	25SAG	24CAP	24AQU	25ARI	24TAU	23GEM	24LEO	24VIR
	28LEO	26VIR	28LIB	26SCO	28CAP	26AQU	26PIS	27TAU	26GEM	26CAN	27VIR	26LIB
	30VIR	28LIB	30SCO	28SAG	30AQU	29PIS	28ARI	30GEM	29CAN	28LEO	29LIB	28SCO
				30CAP			31TAU			30VIR		30SAG

2003

	JAN	FEB	MAR	APR	MAY	JUNE	JULY	AUG	SEPT	OCT	NOV	DEC
	1CAP	2PIS	1PIS	3TAU	2GEM	1CAN	1LEO	2LIB	2SAG	1CAP	2PIS	2ARI
	3AQU	5ARI	4ARI	5GEM	5CAN	4LEO	3VIR	4SCO	4CAP	4AQU	5ARI	4TAU
	6PIS	7TAU	6TAU	8CAN	7LEO	6VIR	5LIB	6SAG	6AQU	6PIS	7TAU	7GEM
	8ARI	10GEM	9GEM	10LEO	10VIR	8LIB	7SCO	8CAP	9PIS	8ARI	10GEM	9CAN
	11TAU	12CAN	11CAN	12VIR	12LIB	10SCO	10SAG	10AQU	11ARI	11TAU	12CAN	12LEO
	13GEM	14LEO	14LEO	14LIB	14SCO	12SAG	12CAP	12PIS	13TAU	13GEM	15LEO	14VIR
	16CAN	16VIR	16VIR	16SCO	16SAG	14CAP	14AQU	15ARI	16GEM	16CAN	17VIR	16LIB
	18LEO	18LIB	18LIB	18SAG	18CAP	16AQU	16PIS	17TAU	18CAN	18LEO	19LIB	19SCO
	20VIR	21SCO	20SCO	20CAP	20AQU	19PIS	18ARI	20GEM	21LEO	21VIR	21SCO	21SAG
	22LIB	23SAG	22SAG	23AQU	22PIS	21ARI	21TAU	22CAN	23VIR	23LIB	23SAG	23CAP
	24SCO	25CAP	24CAP	25PIS	25ARI	23TAU	23GEM	24LEO	25LIB	25SCO	25CAP	25AQU
	26SAG	27AQU	26AQU	27ARI	27TAU	26GEM	26CAN	27VIR	27SCO	27SAG	27AQU	27PIS
	29CAP		29PIS	30TAU	30GEM	28CAN	28LEO	29LIB	29SAG	29CAP	29PIS	29ARI
	31AQU		31ARI				30VIR	31SCO		31AQU		

2004

	JAN	FEB	MAR	APR	MAY	JUNE	JULY	AUG	SEPT	OCT	NOV	DEC
	1TAU	2CAN	3LEO	1VIR	1LIB	2SAG	1CAP	1PIS	2TAU	2GEM	1CAN	1LEO
	3GEM	4LEO	5VIR	4LIB	3SCO	4CAP	3AQU	4ARI	5GEM	5CAN	3LEO	3VIR
	6CAN	7VIR	7LIB	6SCO	5SAG	6AQU	5PIS	6TAU	7CAN	7LEO	6VIR	6LIB
	8LEO	9LIB	9SCO	8SAG	7CAP	8PIS	7ARI	8GEM	10LEO	10VIR	8LIB	8SCO
	10VIR	11SCO	12SAG	10CAP	9AQU	10ARI	10TAU	11CAN	12VIR	12LIB	10SCO	10SAG
	13LIB	13SAG	14CAP	12AQU	11PIS	12TAU	12GEM	13LEO	14LIB	14SCO	13SAG	12CAP
	15SCO	15CAP	16AQU	14PIS	14ARI	15GEM	15CAN	16VIR	17SCO	16SAG	15CAP	14AQU
	17SAG	17AQU	18PIS	16ARI	16TAU	17CAN	17LEO	18LIB	19SAG	18CAP	17AQU	16PIS
	19CAP	20PIS	20ARI	19TAU	19GEM	20LEO	20VIR	20SCO	21CAP	20AQU	19PIS	18ARI
	21AQU	22ARI	23TAU	21GEM	21CAN	22VIR	22LIB	23SAG	23AQU	23PIS	21ARI	21TAU
	23PIS	24TAU	25GEM	24CAN	24LEO	25LIB	24SCO	25CAP	25PIS	25ARI	23TAU	23GEM
	25ARI	27GEM	28CAN	26LEO	26VIR	27SCO	26SAG	27AQU	27ARI	27TAU	26GEM	25CAN
	28TAU	29CAN	30LEO	29VIR	28LIB	29SAG	28CAP	29PIS	30TAU	29GEM	28CAN	28LEO
	30GEM				31SCO		30AQU	31ARI				31VIR

2005

	JAN	FEB	MAR	APR	MAY	JUNE	JULY	AUG	SEPT	OCT	NOV	DEC
	2LIB	1SCO	2SAG	3AQU	2PIS	3TAU	2GEM	1CAN	2VIR	2LIB	1SCO	2CAP
	4SCO	3SAG	4CAP	5PIS	4ARI	5GEM	5CAN	3LEO	5LIB	4SCO	3SAG	4AQU
	6SAG	5CAP	6AQU	7ARI	6TAU	7CAN	7LEO	6VIR	7SCO	7SAG	5CAP	7PIS
	8CAP	7AQU	8PIS	9TAU	9GEM	10LEO	10VIR	8LIB	9SAG	9CAP	7AQU	9ARI
	10AQU	9PIS	10ARI	11GEM	11CAN	12VIR	12LIB	11SCO	12CAP	11AQU	9PIS	11TAU
	12PIS	11ARI	13TAU	14CAN	14LEO	15LIB	15SCO	13SAG	14AQU	13PIS	11ARI	13GEM
	15ARI	13TAU	15GEM	16LEO	16VIR	17SCO	17SAG	15CAP	16PIS	15ARI	14TAU	15CAN
	17TAU	16GEM	17CAN	19VIR	18LIB	19SAG	19CAP	17AQU	18ARI	17TAU	16GEM	18LEO
	19GEM	18CAN	20LEO	21LIB	21SCO	21CAP	21AQU	19PIS	20TAU	19GEM	18CAN	20VIR
	24LEO	23VIR	25LIB	26SAG	25CAP	23AQU	25ARI	23TAU	24CAN	24LEO	23VIR	25SCO
	27VIR	25LIB	27SCO	28CAP	27AQU	25PIS	27TAU	26GEM	27LEO	27VIR	26LIB	28SAG
	29LIB	28SCO	29SAG	30AQU	29PIS	28ARI	29GEM	28CAN	29VIR	29LIB	28SCO	30CAP
			31CAP		31ARI	30TAU		31LEO			30SAG	

2006

JAN	FEB	MAR	APR	MAY	JUNE	JULY	AUG	SEPT	OCT	NOV	DEC
1AQU	1ARI	1ARI	1GEM	1CAN	2VIR	2LIB	1SCO	2CAP	1AQU	2ARI	1TAU
3PIS	3TAU	3TAU	4CAN	3LEO	5LIB	5SCO	3SAG	4AQU	4PIS	4TAU	3GEM
5ARI	6GEM	5GEM	6LEO	6VIR	7SCO	7SAG	6CAP	6PIS	6ARI	6GEM	6CAN
7TAU	8LEO	7CAN	9VIR	8LIB	10SAG	9CAP	8AQU	8ARI	8TAU	8CAN	8LEO
9GEM	10LEO	10LEO	11LIB	11SCO	12CAP	11AQU	10PIS	10TAU	10GEM	10LEO	10VIR
12CAN	13VIR	12VIR	14SCO	13SAG	14AQU	13PIS	12ARI	12GEM	12CAN	13VIR	13LIB
14LEO	16LIB	15LIB	16SAG	15CAP	16PIS	15ARI	14TAU	14CAN	14LEO	15LIB	15SCO
17VIR	18SCO	17SCO	18CAP	18AQU	18ARI	17TAU	16GEM	17LEO	17VIR	18SCO	18SAG
19LIB	20SAG	20SAG	20AQU	20PIS	20TAU	20GEM	18CAN	19VIR	19LIB	20SAG	20CAP
22SCO	23CAP	22CAP	22PIS	22ARI	22GEM	22CAN	21LEO	22LIB	22SCO	23CAP	22AQU
24SAG	25AQU	25AQU	25ARI	24TAU	25CAN	24LEO	23VIR	24SCO	24SAG	25AQU	24PIS
26CAP	27PIS	26PIS	27TAU	26GEM	27LEO	27VIR	26LIB	27SAG	26CAP	27PIS	27ARI
28AQU		28ARI	29GEM	28CAN	29VIR	29LIB	28SCO	29CAP	29AQU	29ARI	29TAU
30PIS		30TAU		31LEO			31SAG		31PIS		31GEM

2007

JAN	FEB	MAR	APR	MAY	JUNE	JULY	AUG	SEPT	OCT	NOV	DEC
2CAN	1LEO	2VIR	1LIB	1SCO	2CAP	2AQU	2ARI	1TAU	2CAN	3VIR	3LIB
4LEO	3VIR	5LIB	3SCO	3SAG	4AQU	4PIS	4TAU	3GEM	4LEO	5LIB	5SCO
7VIR	5LIB	7SCO	6SAG	6CAP	7PIS	6ARI	6GEM	5CAN	7VIR	8SCO	8SAG
9LIB	8SCO	10SAG	8CAP	8AQU	9ARI	8TAU	9CAN	7LEO	9LIB	10SAG	10CAP
12SCO	10SAG	12CAP	11AQU	10PIS	11TAU	10GEM	11LEO	9VIR	12SCO	13CAP	13AQU
14SAG	13CAP	14AQU	13PIS	12ARI	13GEM	12CAN	13VIR	12LIB	14SAG	15AQU	15PIS
16CAP	15AQU	17PIS	15ARI	14TAU	15CAN	14LEO	15LIB	14SCO	17CAP	18PIS	17ARI
19AQU	17PIS	19ARI	17TAU	16GEM	17LEO	17VIR	18SCO	17SAG	19AQU	20ARI	19TAU
21PIS	19ARI	21TAU	19GEM	18CAN	19VIR	19LIB	20SAG	19CAP	21PIS	22TAU	21GEM
23ARI	21TAU	23GEM	21CAN	21LEO	22LIB	22SCO	23CAP	22AQU	23ARI	24GEM	23CAN
25TAU	23GEM	25CAN	23LEO	23VIR	24SCO	24SAG	25AQU	24PIS	25TAU	26CAN	25LEO
27GEM	25CAN	27LEO	26VIR	25LIB	27SAG	27CAP	27PIS	26ARI	27GEM	28LEO	27VIR
29CAN	28LEO	29VIR	28LIB	28SCO	29CAP	29AQU	29ARI	28TAU	29CAN	30VIR	30LIB
				31SAG		31PIS		30GEM	31LEO		

2008

JAN	FEB	MAR	APR	MAY	JUNE	JULY	AUG	SEPT	OCT	NOV	DEC
1SCO	3CAP	1CAP	2PIS	2ARI	2GEM	2CAN	2VIR	1LIB	2SAG	2CAP	2AQU
4SAG	5AQU	3AQU	4ARI	4TAU	4CAN	4LEO	4LIB	3SCO	5CAP	4AQU	4PIS
6CAP	7PIS	6PIS	6TAU	6GEM	6LEO	6VIR	7SCO	6SAG	8AQU	7PIS	6ARI
9AQU	10ARI	8ARI	8GEM	8CAN	8VIR	8LIB	9SAG	8CAP	10PIS	9ARI	9TAU
11PIS	12TAU	10TAU	10CAN	10LEO	11LIB	10SCO	12CAP	11AQU	13ARI	11TAU	11GEM
13ARI	14GEM	12GEM	13LEO	12VIR	13SCO	13SAG	14AQU	13PIS	15TAU	13GEM	13CAN
15TAU	16CAN	14CAN	15VIR	14LIB	16SAG	15CAP	17PIS	15ARI	17GEM	15CAN	15LEO
18GEM	18LEO	16LEO	17LIB	17SCO	18CAP	18AQU	19ARI	17TAU	19CAN	17LEO	17VIR
20CAN	20VIR	19VIR	20SCO	19SAG	21AQU	20PIS	21TAU	19GEM	21LEO	19VIR	19LIB
22LEO	23LIB	21LIB	22SAG	22CAP	23PIS	23ARI	23GEM	22CAN	23VIR	21LIB	21SCO
24VIR	25SCO	23SCO	25CAP	24AQU	25ARI	25TAU	25CAN	24LEO	25LIB	24SCO	24SAG
26LIB	28SAG	26SAG	27AQU	27PIS	28TAU	27GEM	27LEO	26VIR	28CSO	27SAG	26CAP
29SCO		28CAP	30PIS	29ARI	30GEM	29CAN	30VIR	28LIB	30SAG	29CAP	29AQU
31SAG		31AQU		31TAU		31LEO		30SCO			31PIS

2009

JAN	FEB	MAR	APR	MAY	JUNE	JULY	AUG	SEPT	OCT	NOV	DEC
3ARI	1TAU	3GEM	1CAN	2VIR	1LIB	3SAG	2CAP	3PIS	3ARI	1TAU	1GEM
5TAU	3GEM	5CAN	3LEO	5LIB	3SCO	5CAP	4AQU	5ARI	5TAU	4GEM	3CAN
7GEM	5CAN	7LEO	5VIR	7SCO	6SAG	8AQU	7PIS	8TAU	7GEM	6CAN	5LEO
9CAN	7LEO	9VIR	7LIB	9SAG	8CAP	10PIS	9ARI	10GEM	9CAN	8LEO	7VIR
11LEO	10VIR	11LIB	10SCO	12CAP	11AQU	13ARI	11TAU	12CAN	12LEO	10VIR	9LIB
13VIR	12LIB	13SCO	12SAG	14AQU	13PIS	15TAU	14GEM	14LEO	14VIR	12LIB	11SCO
15LIB	14SCO	16SAG	15CAP	17PIS	16ARI	17GEM	16CAN	16VIR	16LIB	14SCO	14SAG
18SCO	16SAG	18CAP	17AQU	19ARI	18TAU	19CAN	18LEO	18LIB	18SCO	17SAG	16CAP
20SAG	19CAP	21AQU	20PIS	21TAU	20GEM	21LEO	20VIR	20SCO	20SAG	19CAP	19AQU
23CAP	21AQU	23PIS	22ARI	24GEM	22CAN	23VIR	22LIB	23SAG	23CAP	21AQU	21PIS
25AQU	24PIS	26ARI	24TAU	26CAN	24LEO	26LIB	24SCO	25CAP	25AQU	24PIS	24ARI
28PIS	26ARI	28TAU	26GEM	28LEO	26VIR	28SCO	26SAG	28AQU	28PIS	26ARI	26TAU
30ARI	28TAU	30GEM	28CAN	30VIR	28LIB	30SAG	29CAP	30PIS	30ARI	28TAU	28GEM
			30LEO		30SCO		31AQU				30CAN

2010	JAN	FEB	MAR	APR	MAY	JUNE	JULY	AUG	SEPT	OCT	NOV	DEC
	1LEO	2LIB	1LIB	2SAG	2CAP	1AQU	3ARI	2TAU	3CAN	2LEO	3LIB	2SCO
	3VIR	4SCO	3SCO	4CAP	4AQU	3PIS	5TAU	4GEM	5LEO	4VIR	5SCO	4SAG
	6LIB	6SAG	6SAG	7AQU	7PIS	6ARI	8GEM	6CAN	7VIR	6LIB	7SAG	6CAP
	8SCO	9CAP	8CAP	9PIS	9ARI	8TAU	10CAN	8LEO	9LIB	8SCO	9CAP	9AQU
	10SAG	11AQU	11AQU	12ARI	12TAU	10GEM	12LEO	10VIR	11SCO	10SAG	11AQU	11PIS
	13CAP	14PIS	13PIS	14TAU	14GEM	12CAN	14VIR	12LIB	13SAG	12CAP	14PIS	14ARI
	15AQU	16ARI	16ARI	17GEM	16CAN	14LEO	16LIB	14SCO	15CAP	15AQU	16ARI	16TAU
	18PIS	19TAU	18TAU	19CAN	18LEO	17VIR	18SCO	17SAG	18AQU	17PIS	19TAU	18GEM
	20ARI	21GEM	20GEM	21LEO	20VIR	19LIB	20SAG	19CAP	20PIS	20ARI	21GEM	21CAN
	22TAU	23CAN	23CAN	23VIR	22LIB	21SCO	23CAP	21AQU	23ARI	22TAU	23CAN	23LEO
	25GEM	25LEO	25LEO	25LIB	25SCO	23SAG	25AQU	24PIS	25TAU	25GEM	26LEO	25VIR
	27CAN	27VIR	27VIR	27SCO	27SAG	25CAP	28PIS	26ARI	28GEM	27CAN	28VIR	27LIB
	29LEO		29LIB	29SAG	29CAP	28AQU	30ARI	29TAU	30CAN	29LEO	30LIB	29SCO
	31VIR		31SCO			30PIS		31GEM		31VIR		31SAG

	1940	1941	1942	1943	1944	1945	1946	1947	1948	1949
JAN	3ARI	4SAG	11TAU	26CAP	GEM	5CAP	CAN	25AQU	VIR	4AQU
FEB	16TAU	17CAP	TAU	CAP	GEM	14AQU	CAN	AQU	12LEO	11PIS
MAR	TAU	CAP	7GEM	8AQU	28CAN	24PIS	CAN	4PIS	LEO	21ARI
APR	1GEM	2AQU	26CAN	17PIS	CAN	PIS	22LEO	11ARI	LEO	29TAU
MAY	17CAN	16PIS	CAN	27ARI	22LEO	2ARI	LEO	20TAU	18VIR	TAU
JUN	CAN	PIS	13LEO	ARI	LEO	11TAU	20VIR	30GEM	VIR	9GEM
JUL	3LEO	2ARI	LEO	7TAU	11VIR	23GEM	VIR	GEM	17LIB	23CAN
AUG	19VIR	ARI	1VIR	23GEM	28LIB	GEM	9LIB	13CAN	LIB	CAN
SEP	VIR	ARI	17LIB	GEM	LIB	7CAN	24SCO	30LEO	3SCO	6LEO
OCT	5LIB	ARI	LIB	GEM	13SCO	CAN	SCO	LEO	17SAG	26VIR
NOV	20SCO	ARI	1SCO	GEM	25SAG	11LEO	6SAG	LEO	26CAP	VIR
DEC	SCO	ARI	15SAG	GEM	SAG	26CAN	17CAP	1VIR	CAP	26LIB

	1950	1951	1952	1953	1954	1955	1956	1957	1958	1959
JAN	LIB	22PIS	19SCO	PIS	SCO	15ARI	13SAG	28TAU	SAG	TAU
FEB	LIB	PIS	SCO	7ARI	9SAG	26TAU	28CAP	TAU	3CAP	10GEM
MAR	28VIR	1ARI	SCO	20TAU	SAG	TAU	CAP	17GEM	17AQU	GEM
APR	VIR	10TAU	SCO	TAU	12CAP	10GEM	14AQU	GEM	26PIS	10CAN
MAY	VIR	21GEM	SCO	1GEM	CAP	25CAN	AQU	4CAN	PIS	31LEO
JUN	11LIB	GEM	SCO	13CAN	CAP	CAN	3PIS	21LEO	7ARI	LEO
JUL	LIB	3CAN	SCO	29LEO	2SAG	11LEO	PIS	LEO	21TAU	20VIR
AUG	10SCO	18LEO	27SAG	LEO	24CAP	27VIR	PIS	8VIR	TAU	VIR
SEP	25SAG	LEO	SAG	14VIR	CAP	VIR	PIS	23LIB	20GEM	5LIB
OCT	SAG	4VIR	12CAP	VIR	21AQU	13LIB	PIS	LIB	28TAU	21SCO
NOV	6CAP	24LIB	21AQU	1LIB	AQU	28SCO	PIS	8SCO	TAU	SCO
DEC	15AQU	LIB	30PIS	20SCO	4PIS	SCO	6ARI	22SAG	TAU	3SAG

	1960	1961	1962	1963	1964	1965	1966	1967	1968	1969
JAN	13CAP	CAN	CAP	LEO	13AQU	VIR	30PIS	LIB	9PIS	SCO
FEB	22AQU	CAN	1AQU	LEO	20PIS	VIR	PIS	12SCO	16ARI	25SAG
MAR	AQU	CAN	12PIS	LEO	29ARI	VIR	9ARI	31LIB	27TAU	SAG
APR	2PIS	CAN	19ARI	LEO	ARI	VIR	17TAU	LIB	TAU	SAG
MAY	11ARI	5LEO	28TAU	LEO	7TAU	VIR	28GEM	LIB	8GEM	SAG
JUN	20TAU	28VIR	TAU	3VIR	17GEM	28LIB	GEM	LIB	20CAN	SAG
JUL	TAU	VIR	8GEM	26LIB	30CAN	LIB	10CAN	19SCO	CAN	SAG
AUG	1GEM	16LIB	22CAN	LIB	CAN	20SCO	25LEO	SCO	5LEO	SAG
SEP	20CAN	LIB	CAN	12SCO	14LEO	SCO	LEO	9SAG	21VIR	21CAP
OCT	CAN	1SCO	11LEO	25SAG	LEO	4SAG	12VIR	22CAP	VIR	CAP
NOV	CAN	13SAG	LEO	SAG	5VIR	14CAP	VIR	CAP	9LIB	4AQU
DEC	CAN	24CAP	LEO	5CAP	VIR	23AQU	3LIB	1AQU	29SCO	15PIS

	1970	1971	1972	1973	1974	1975	1976	1977	1978	1979
JAN	24ARI	22SAG	ARI	SAG	TAU	21CAP	GEM	CAP	25CAN	20AQU
FEB	ARI	SAG	10TAU	12CAP	27GEM	CAP	GEM	9AQU	CAN	27PIS
MAR	6TAU	12CAP	26GEM	26AQU	GEM	3AQU	18CAN	19PIS	CAN	PIS
APR	18GEM	CAP	GEM	AQU	20CAN	11PIS	CAN	27ARI	10LEO	6ARI
MAY	GEM	3AQU	12CAN	7PIS	CAN	21ARI	16LEO	ARI	LEO	15TAU
JUN	2CAN	AQU	28LEO	20ARI	8LEO	30TAU	LEO	5TAU	13VIR	25GEM
JUL	18LEO	AQU	LEO	ARI	27VIR	TAU	6VIR	17GEM	VIR	GEM
AUG	LEO	AQU	14VIR	12TAU	VIR	14GEM	24LIB	31CAN	4LIB	8CAN
SEP	2VIR	AQU	30LIB	TAU	12LIB	GEM	LIB	CAN	19SCO	24LEO
OCT	20LIB	AQU	LIB	29ARI	28SCO	17CAN	8SCO	26LEO	SCO	LEO
NOV	LIB	6PIS	15SCO	ARI	SCO	25GEM	20SAG	LEO	1SAG	19VIR
DEC	6SCO	26ARI	30SAG	24TAU	10SAG	GEM	31CAP	LEO	12CAP	VIR

	1980	1981	1982	1983	1984	1985	1986	1987	1988	1989
JAN	VIR	AQU	LIB	17PIS	10SCO	PIS	SCO	8ARI	8SAG	19TAU
FEB	VIR	6PIS	LIB	24ARI	SCO	2ARI	2SAG	20TAU	22CAP	TAU
MAR	11LEO	16ARI	LIB	ARI	SCO	14TAU	27CAP	TAU	CAP	11GEM
APR	LEO	25TAU	LIB	5TAU	SCO	26GEM	CAP	5GEM	6AQU	28CAN
MAY	3VIR	TAU	LIB	16GEM	SCO	GEM	CAP	20CAN	22PIS	CAN
JUN	VIR	5GEM	LIB	29CAN	SCO	9CAN	CAP	CAN	PIS	16LEO
JUL	10LIB	18CAN	LIB	CAN	SCO	24LEO	CAP	6LEO	13ARI	LEO
AUG	29SCO	CAN	3SCO	13LEO	17SAG	LEO	CAP	22VIR	ARI	3VIR
SEP	SCO	1LEO	19SAG	29VIR	SAG	9VIR	CAP	VIR	ARI	19LIB
OCT	12SAG	20VIR	31CAP	VIR	5CAP	27LIB	8AQU	8LIB	24PIS	LIB
NOV	21CAP	VIR	CAP	18LIB	15AQU	LIB	25PIS	23SCO	1ARI	3SCO
DEC	30AQU	15LIB	10AQU	LIB	25PIS	14SCO	PIS	SCO	ARI	17SAG

	1990	1991	1992	1993	1994	1995	1996	1997	1998	1999
JAN	29CAP	20GEM	9CAP	CAN	27AQU	22LEO	8AQU	3LIB	25PIS	26SCO
FEB	CAP	GEM	17AQU	CAN	AQU	LEO	15PIS	LIB	PIS	SCO
MAR	11AQU	GEM	27PIS	CAN	7PIS	LEO	24ARI	8VIR	4ARI	SCO
APR	20PIS	2CAN	PIS	27LEO	14ARI	LEO	ARI	VIR	12TAU	SCO
MAY	31ARI	26LEO	5ARI	LEO	23TAU	25VIR	2TAU	VIR	23GEM	5LIB
JUN	ARI	LEO	14TAU	23VIR	TAU	VIR	12GEM	19LIB	GEM	LIB
JUL	12TAU	15VIR	26GEM	VIR	3GEM	21LIB	25CAN	LIB	6CAN	4SCO
AUG	31GEM	VIR	GEM	11LIB	16CAN	LIB	CAN	14SCO	20LEO	SCO
SEP	GEM	1LIB	12CAN	26SCO	CAN	7SCO	9LEO	28SAG	LEO	2SAG
OCT	GEM	16SCO	CAN	SCO	4LEO	20SAG	30VIR	SAG	7VIR	16CAP
NOV	GEM	28SAG	CAN	9SAG	LEO	30CAP	VIR	9CAP	27LIB	26AQU
DEC	14TAU	SAG	CAN	19CAP	12VIR	CAP	VIR	18AQU	LIB	AQU

	2000	2001	2002	2003	2004	2005	2006	2007	2008	2009	2010
JAN	3PIS	SCO	18ARI	16SAG	ARI	SAG	TAU	16CAP	GEM	CAP	LEO
FEB	11ARI	14SAG	ARI	SAG	3TAU	6CAP	17GEM	25AQU	GEM	4AQU	LEO
MAR	22TAU	SAG	1TAU	4CAP	21GEM	20AQU	GEM	AQU	4CAN	14PIS	LEO
APR	TAU	SAG	13GEM	21AQU	GEM	30PIS	13CAN	6PIS	CAN	22ARI	LEO
MAY	3GEM	SAG	28CAN	AQU	7CAN	PIS	CAN	15ARI	9LEO	31TAU	LEO
JUN	16CAN	SAG	CAN	16PIS	23LEO	11ARI	3LEO	24TAU	LEO	TAU	7VIR
JUL	31LEO	SAG	13LEO	PIS	LEO	27TAU	22VIR	TAU	1VIR	11GEM	29LIB
AUG	LEO	SAG	29VIR	PIS	10VIR	TAU	VIR	7GEM	19LIB	25CAN	LIB
SEP	16VIR	8CAP	VIR	PIS	26LIB	TAU	7LIB	28CAN	LIB	CAN	14SCO
OCT	VIR	27AQU	15LIB	PIS	LIB	TAU	23SCO	CAN	3SCO	16LEO	28SAG
NOV	3LIB	AQU	LIB	PIS	10SCO	TAU	SCO	CAN	16SAG	LEO	SAG
DEC	23SCO	8PIS	1SCO	16ARI	25SAG	TAU	5SAG	31GEM	27CAP	LEO	7CAP

	1940	1941	1942	1943	1944	1945	1946	1947	1948	1949
JAN	18PIS	13CAP	AQU	8AQU	2SAG 27CAP	5PIS	22AQU	5SAG	17PIS	13CAP
FEB	12ARI	6AQU	AQU	1PIS 25ARI	21AQU	2ARI	15PIS	6CAP	11ARI	6AQU
MAR	8TAU	2PIS 26ARI	AQU	21TAU	16PIS	11TAU	11ARI	4AQU 30PIS	8TAU	2PIS 26ARI
APR	4GEM	20TAU	6PIS	15GEM	10ARI	7ARI	4TAU 29GEM	24ARI	4GEM	19TAU
MAY	6CAN	14GEM	5ARI	11CAN	4TAU 29GEM	ARI	23CAN	19TAU	7CAN	13GEM
JUN	CAN	7CAN	1TAU 27GEM	7LEO	22CAN	4TAU	17LEO	13GEM	29GEM	7CAN
JUL	5GEM 31CAN	2LEO 26VIR	23CAN	7VIR	16LEO	7GEM	13VIR	8CAN	GEM	1LEO 26VIR
AUG	CAN	20LIB	16LEO	VIR	10VIR	4CAN 30LEO	9LIB	1LEO 26VIR	2CAN	20LIB
SEP	8LEO	14SCO	10VIR	VIR	3LIB 28SCO	24VIR	6SCO	19LIB	8LEO	14SCO
OCT	6VIR	10SAG	4LIB 28SCO	VIR	22SAG	18LIB	16SAG	13SCO	6VIR	10SAG
NOV	1LIB 26SCO	6CAP	21SAG	9LIB	16CAP	12SCO	8SCO	6SAG 30CAP	1LIB 25SCO	5CAP
DEC	20SAG	5AQU	15CAP	8SCO	10AQU	6SAG 29CAP	SCO	24AQU	20SAG	6AQU

	1950	1951	1952	1953	1954	1955	1956	1957	1958	1959
JAN	AQU	7AQU 31PIS	2SAG 27CAP	5PIS	22AQU	6SAG	17PIS	12CAP	AQU	7AQU 31PIS
FEB	AQU	24ARI	20AQU	2ARI	15PIS	5CAP	11ARI	5AQU	AQU	24ARI
MAR	AQU	21TAU	16PIS	14TAU 31ARI	11ARI	4AQU 30PIS	7TAU	1PIS 25ARI	AQU	20TAU
APR	6PIS	15GEM	9ARI	ARI	4TAU 28GEM	24ARI	4GEM	18TAU	6PIS	14GEM
MAY	5ARI	10CAN	4TAU 28GEM	ARI	23CAN	19TAU	7CAN	13GEM	5ARI 31TAU	10CAN
JUN	1TAU 27GEM	7LEO	22CAN	5TAU	17LEO	13GEM	23GEM	6CAN	26GEM	6LEO
JUL	22CAN	7VIR	16LEO	7GEM	13VIR	7CAN	GEM	1LEO 25VIR	22CAN	8VIR
AUG	16LEO	VIR	9VIR	3CAN 29LEO	8LIB	1LEO 25VIR	4CAN	19LIB	15LEO	VIR
SEP	9VIR	VIR	3LIB 27SCO	23VIR	6SCO	18LIB	8LEO	14SCO	9VIR	19LEO 25VIR
OCT	4LIB 28SCO	VIR	21SAG	18LIB	23SAG 27SCO	12SCO	5VIR 31LIB	9SAG	3LIB 27SCO	VIR
NOV	20SAG	9LIB	15CAP	11SCO	SCO	5SAG 29CAP	25SCO	5CAP	20SAG	9LIB
DEC	14CAP	7SCO	10AQU	5SAG 29CAP	SCO	24AQU	19SAG	6AQU	14CAP	7SCO

	1960	1961	1962	1963	1964	1965	1966	1967	1968	1969
JAN	2SAG 26CAP	4PIS	21AQU	6SAG	16PIS	12CAP	AQU	6AQU 30PIS	1SAG 26CAP	4PIS
FEB	20AQU	1ARI	14PIS	5CAP	10ARI	5AQU	6CAP 25AQU	23ARI	19AQU	1ARI
MAR	15PIS	ARI	10ARI	4AQU 29PIS	7TAU	1PIS 25ARI	AQU	20TAU	15PIS	ARI
APR	9ARI	ARI	3TAU 28GEM	23ARI	3GEM	18TAU	6PIS	14GEM	8ARI	ARI
MAY	3TAU 28GEM	ARI	22CAN	18TAU	8CAN	12GEM	4ARI 31TAU	10CAN	3TAU 27GEM	ARI
JUN	21CAN	5TAU	17LEO	12GEM	17GEM	6CAN 30LEO	26GEM	6LEO	20CAN	5TAU
JUL	15LEO	6GEM	12VIR	7CAN 31LEO	GEM	25VIR	21CAN	8VIR	15LEO	6GEM
AUG	9VIR	3CAN 29LEO	8LIB	25VIR	5CAN	19LIB	15LEO	VIR	8VIR	3CAN 28LEO
SEP	2LIB 26SCO	23VIR	6SCO	18LIB	7LEO	13SCO	8VIR	9LEO	2LIB 26SCO	22VIR
OCT	21SAG	17LIB	SCO	12SCO	5VIR 31LIB	9SAG	2LIB 26SCO	1VIR	21SAG	17LIB
NOV	15CAP	11SCO	SCO	5SAG 29CAP	24SCO	5CAP	19SAG	9LIB	14CAP	10SCO
DEC	10AQU	4SAG 28CAP	SCO	23AQU	19SAG	6AQU	13CAP	7SCO	9AQU	4SAC 28CAP

	1970	1971	1972	1973	1974	1975	1976	1977	1978	1979
JAN	21AQU	6SAG	16PIS	11CAP	29CAP	6AQU 30PIS	1SAG 26CAP	4PIS	20AQU	7SAG
FEB	13PIS	5CAP	10ARI	4AQU 28PIS	28AQU	23ARI	19AQU	2ARI	13PIS	5CAP
MAR	10ARI	3AQU 29PIS	6TAU	24ARI	AQU	19TAU	14PIS	ARI	9ARI	3AQU 28PIS
APR	3TAU 27GEM	23ARI	3GEM	17TAU	6PIS	13GEM	8ARI	ARI	2TAU 27GEM	22ARI
MAY	22CAN	18TAU	10CAN	12GEM	4ARI 31TAU	9CAN	2TAU 26GEM	ARI	21CAN	17TAU
JUN	16LEO	12GEM	11GEM	5CAN 30LEO	25GEM	6LEO	20CAN	6TAU	16LEO	11GEM
JUL	12VIR	6CAN 31LEO	GEM	24VIR	20CAN	9VIR	14LEO	6GEM	11VIR	6CAN 30LEO
AUG	8LIB	24VIR	5CAN	18LIB	14LEO	VIR	8VIR	2CAN 28LEO	7LIB	23VIR
SEP	6SCO	17LIB	7LEO	13SCO	8VIR	2LEO	1LIB 25SCO	22VIR	7SCO	17LIB
OCT	SCO	11SCO	5VIR 30LIB	9SAG	2LIB 26SCO	4VIR	20SAG	16LIB	SCO	11SCO
NOV	SCO	4SAG 28CAP	24SCO	5CAP	19SAG	9LIB	14CAP	9SCO	SCO	4SAG 28CAP
DEC	SCO	23AQU	18SAG	7AQU	13CAP	6SCO	9AQU	3SAG 27CAP	SCO	22AQU

	1980	1981	1982	1983	1984	1985	1986	1987	1988	1989
JAN	15PIS	11CAP	22CAP	5AQU 29PIS	25CAP	4PIS	20AQU	7SAG	15PIS	10CAP
FEB	9ARI	4AQU 28PIS	CAP	22ARI	18AQU	2ARI	12PIS	4CAP	9ARI	3AQU 27PIS
MAR	6TAU	23ARI	2AQU	19TAU	14PIS	ARI	8ARI	3AQU 28PIS	6TAU	23ARI
APR	3GEM	17TAU	6PIS	13GEM	7ARI	ARI	2TAU 26GEM	22ARI	3GEM	16TAU
MAY	12CAN	11GEM	4ARI 30TAU	9CAN	1TAU 26GEM	ARI	21CAN	17TAU	17CAN 27GEM	11GEM
JUN	5GEM	5CAN 29LEO	25GEM	6LEO	19CAN	6TAU	15LEO	11GEM	GEM	4CAN 29LEO
JUL	GEM	24VIR	20CAN	10VIR	14LEO	6GEM	11VIR	5CAN 30LEO	GEM	23VIR
AUG	6CAN	18LIB	14LEO	27LEO	7VIR 31LIB	2CAN 27LEO	7LIB	23VIR	6CAN	17LIB
SEP	7LEO	12SCO	7VIR	LEO	25SCO	21VIR	7SCO	16LIB	7LEO	12SCO
OCT	4VIR 30LIB	8SAG	1LIB 25SCO	5VIR	20SAG	16LIB	SCO	10SCO	4VIR 29LIB	8SAG
NOV	23SCO	5CAP	18SAG	9LIB	13CAP	9SCO	SCO	3SAG 27CAP	23SCO	5CAP
DEC	18SAG	8AQU	12CAP	6SCO 31SAG	8AQU	3SAG 27CAP	SCO	22AQU	17SAG	9AQU

	1990	1991	1992	1993	1994	1995	1996	1997	1998	1999
JAN	16CAP	4AQU 28PIS	25CAP	3PIS	19AQU	7SAG	14PIS	10CAP	9CAP	4AQU 28PIS
FEB	CAP	22ARI	18AQU	2ARI	12PIS	4CAP	8ARI	2AQU 26PIS	CAP	21ARI
MAR	3AQU	18TAU	13PIS	ARI	8ARI	2AQU 28PIS	5TAU	23ARI	4AQU	18TAU
APR	6PIS	12GEM	7ARI	ARI	1TAU 26GEM	21ARI	3GEM	16TAU	6PIS	12GEM
MAY	3ARI 30TAU	8CAN	1TAU 25GEM	ARI	20CAN	16TAU	GEM	10GEM	3ARI 29TAU	8CAN
JUN	24GEM	5LEO	19CAN	6TAU	15LEO	10GEM	GEM	3CAN 28LEO	24GEM	5LEO
JUL	19CAN	11VIR	13LEO	5GEM	11VIR	5CAN 29LEO	GEM	23VIR	19CAN	12VIR
AUG	13LEO	21LEO	7VIR 31LIB	1CAN 27LEO	7LIB	22VIR	7CAN	17LIB	13LEO	15LEO
SEP	7VIR	LEO	24SCO	21VIR	7SCO	15LIB	6LEO	11SCO	6VIR 30LIB	LEO
OCT	1LIB 25SCO	6VIR	19SAG	15LIB	SCO	10SCO	3VIR 29LIB	8SAG	24SCO	7VIR
NOV	18SAG	9LIB	13CAP	8SCO	SCO	3SAG 27CAP	22 SCO	5CAP	17SAG	8LIB
DEC	12CAP	6SCO 31SAG	8AQU	2SAG 26CAP	SCO	21AQU	17SAG	11AQU	11CAP	5SCO 30SAG

	2000	2001	2002	2003	2004	2005	2006	2007	2008	2009	2010
JAN	24CAP	3PIS	18AQU	7SAG	14PIS	9CAP	1CAP	2AQU 27PIS	24CAP	3PIS	18AQU
FEB	17AQU	2ARI	11PIS	4CAP	8ARI	2AQU 26PIS	CAP	21ARI	17AQU	2ARI	11PIS
MAR	13PIS	ARI	7ARI	2AQU 27PIS	5TAU	22ARI	5AQU	17TAU	12PIS	ARI	7ARI 31TAU
APR	6ARI 30TAU	ARI	1TAU 25GEM	21ARI	3GEM	15TAU	5PIS	11GEM	6ARI 30TAU	11PIS 24ARI	24GEM
MAY	25GEM	ARI	20CAN	16TAU	GEM	9GEM	3ARI 29TAU	8CAN	24GEM	ARI	19CAN
JUN	18CAN	6TAU	14LEO	9GEM	GEM	3CAN 28LEO	23GEM	5LEO	18CAN	6TAU	14LEO
JUL	13LEO	5GEM	10VIR	4CAN 28LEO	GEM	22VIR	18CAN	14VIR	12LEO	5GEM 31CAN	10VIR
AUG	6VIR 30LIB	1CAN 26LEO	7LIB	22VIR	7CAN	16LIB	12LEO	8LEO	5VIR 30LIB	26LEO	6LIB
SEP	24SCO	20VIR	7SCO	15LIB	6LEO	11SCO	6VIR 30LIB	LEO	23SCO	20VIR	8SCO
OCT	19SAG	15LIB	SCO	9SCO	3VIR 28LIB	7SAG	24SCO	8VIR	18SAG	14LIB	SCO
NOV	12CAP	8SCO	SCO	2SAG 26CAP	22SCO	17SAG	17SAG	8LIB	12CAP	7SCO	7LIB 29SCO
DEC	8AQU	2SAG 26CAP	SCO	21AQU	16SAG	15AQU	11CAP	5SCO 30SAG	7AQU	1SAG 25CAP	SCO

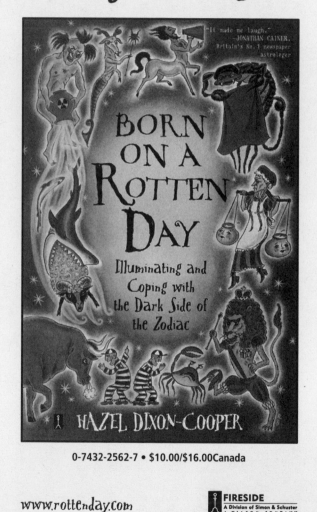